A Practical Guide to Reflective Supervision

Edited by Sherryl Scott Heller and Linda Gilkerson

ZERO
TO
THREE®

National Center for Infants,
Toddlers, and Families

Washington, DC

Published by

ZERO TO THREE
2000 M St., NW, Suite 200
Washington, DC 20036-3307
(202) 638-1144
Fax: (202) 638-0851
Toll-free orders (800) 899-4301
Web: http://www.zerotothree.org

The mission of the ZERO TO THREE Press is to publish authoritative research, practical resources, and new ideas for those who work with and care about infants, toddlers, and their families. Books are selected for publication by an independent Editorial Board. The views contained in this book are those of the authors and do not necessarily reflect those of ZERO TO THREE: National Center for Infants, Toddlers and Families, Inc.

These materials are intended for education and training to help promote a high standard of care by professionals. Use of these materials is voluntary and their use does not confer any professional credentials or qualification to take any registration, certification, board or licensure examination, and neither confers nor infers competency to perform any related professional functions.

The user of these materials is solely responsible for compliance with all local, state or federal rules, regulations or licensing requirements. Despite efforts to ensure that these materials are consistent with acceptable practices, they are not intended to be used as a compliance guide and are not intended to supplant or to be used as a substitute for or in contravention of any applicable local, state or federal rules, regulations or licensing requirements. ZERO TO THREE expressly disclaims any liability arising from use of these materials in contravention of such rules, regulations or licensing requirements.

The views expressed in these materials represent the opinions of the respective authors. Publication of these materials does not constitute an endorsement by ZERO TO THREE of any view expressed herein, and ZERO TO THREE expressly disclaims any liability arising from any inaccuracy or misstatement.

Cover and text design: Design Consultants

Library of Congress Cataloging-in-Publication Data

A practical guide to reflective supervision / edited by Sherryl Scott Heller and Linda Gilkerson.
    p. cm.
  ISBN 978-1-934019-36-8
 1. Social workers--Supervision of. 2. Child welfare workers--Supervision of. 3. Family services--Management. 4. Family social work.
I. Heller, Sherryl Scott. II. Gilkerson, Linda, 1947-
  HV40.54.P73 2009
  361.0068'3--dc22

                                                                                                    2009037092

For permission for academic photocopying (for course packets, study materials, etc.) by copy centers, educators, or university bookstores or libraries, of this and other ZERO TO THREE materials, please contact Copyright Clearance Center, 222 Rosewood Drive, Danvers, MA 01923; phone, (978) 750-8400; fax, (978) 750-4744; or visit its Web site at www.copyright.com.

10 9 8 7 6 5 4 3 2 1

ISBN 978-1-934019-36-8

Printed in the United States of America

Suggested citations:

Book citation: Scott Heller, S., & Gilkerson, L. (Eds.). (2009). *A practical guide to reflective supervision*. Washington, DC: ZERO TO THREE.

Chapter citation: Shahmoon-Shanok, R. (2009). What is reflective supervision? In S. Scott Heller & L. Gilkerson (Eds.), *A practical guide to reflective supervision* (pp. 7–23). Washington, DC: ZERO TO THREE.

DEDICATION

To Emily Fenichel, who mentored the infant–family field with brilliance and love.

TABLE OF CONTENTS

FOREWORD

This is indeed a timely book. The term *reflective supervision* is heard more and more frequently as a range of infant–family programs become interested in learning about what it is and what role it can play in enhancing the quality of services they provide. This book will surely promote a "growth spurt" as readers scour its pages for both conceptual understanding and practical guidance about incorporating reflective supervision into their day-to-day work.

The underlying assumption running throughout the chapters is that the ability to reflect is a capacity that can be built, strengthened, and nurtured. The editors and authors underscore how important it is for professionals who care for young children and families in any setting to pay attention to, and try to understand, their experiences and feelings—both for themselves and for children and families. Staff well-being and quality of services go hand in hand.

As the editors note, *A Practical Guide to Reflective Supervision* is written for both program administrators and professionals who want to learn to provide—or provide more effective—reflective supervision. They describe the book as a guidebook or map for bringing reflective supervision into a variety of programs that serve young children and their families. Chapter authors in turn describe a step-by-step process for introducing reflective supervision into a program and nurturing its development while keeping each program's unique makeup at the forefront of planning and implementation. They give voice through a series of rich vignettes to the questions and concerns that undertaking such a change will elicit—both at the individual and organizational levels. Questions that frequently arise about the "mechanics" of reflective supervision (e.g., type, frequency, length) are addressed and a range of possibilities explored. Challenges associated with one of the continuing dilemmas in our field—combining reflective and administrative supervision—are brought forward for examination, and a new paradigm is offered for the reader's consideration.

This book also provides a solid foundation for professionals seeking to learn about the nature and structure of the reflective supervision relationship itself—how it begins and builds over time as trust develops. Readers will benefit from thinking about the ways in which disharmony within this relationship can be addressed and, often, resolved.

What makes this book so useful is the obvious commitment of its editors and authors to keep it "real." There is no attempt to suggest that it is easy to bring reflective supervision into a program. It is hard work, and it takes time. This book, with its many illustrations, reflective questions, checklists, exercises, and other user-friendly tools, can serve as an invaluable guide for those willing to undertake and benefit from the effort.

Linda Eggbeer
Washington, DC

Acknowledgments

Born to a journalist of Irish descent, I am a storyteller at heart and want to acknowledge the story of how this book came to be. Hurricane Katrina struck the New Orleans area on August 28, 2005. While the majority of the city remained underwater for weeks, the entire population of New Orleans was spread across the country. The largest group of citizens, many of whom had extremely limited resources, ended up in Baton Rouge and the surrounding area. Less than a month after Hurricane Katrina, Hurricane Rita hit the coast, and Baton Rouge acquired another influx of people in need, nearly doubling its size. This placed an incredible burden on the city government, nonprofit organizations, churches, schools, and general population.

One Early Head Start (EHS) Program, YWCA EHS led by Charlotte Provenza, played a heroic role in convening community partners and seeking funding for a major program expansion to attempt to meet the compelling needs of traumatized children, families, and staff. Within 1 year, the EHS program grew from two sites serving about 70 families to six sites serving over 200 families and shifted from working with adolescent mothers to serving families displaced by Katrina and Rita. This expansion changed everything: the families served had different needs, new staff were hired who had less experience with EHS, new and old staff were struggling with displacement and trauma from the hurricanes, and the leadership hierarchy changed as new management positions were created and filled. Even daily activities were impacted, contributing to an already increased level of stress. For the next 3 months Neil Boris and I (who had been working in the center on an infant mental health research grant from Administration for Children and Families [ACF]) shifted our efforts from research to consultation so that we could support the EHS staff and families as they struggled with the chaos, instability, and change that had been thrust upon us all.

One thing that was clear to the administration was the importance of reflective supervision (RS) and mental health services for the staff and families. Neil and I along with Angela Keyes and Amy Cavanaugh (all of whom authored chapters in this book) and other colleagues worked to bring RS to this program as a lifeline for leadership and staff during this tumultuous time. It soon became apparent to me that there was no single publication that providers could use to learn about RS and how to provide it in the first year or two of its existence. One thing led to another and Neil Boris, Charley Zeanah, and Rachel Chazan Cohen all urged me to contact Linda Gilkerson about creating a resource on RS. Over the past months of numerous phone calls, e-mails, and writing, the form of this book took shape. And now here it is—hopefully one positive thing to come out of two terrible storms!

First, I would like to thank my co-editor, Linda Gilkerson. Her calm presence and wisdom were essential to the creation of this book. Collaborating with her on this book was an incredible experience. In addition, the chapter authors of this book managed to take a brief description of Linda's and my vision of their chapter and run with it. They created chapters full of insight and guidance that fit together as a whole yet also stand alone. I appreciate their dedication to and patience with this project.

I am fortunate to have had many people influence me and my efforts in editing this book; too many to name them all, although a few deserve special recognition. I would like to thank Claire Peebles, a friend and colleague who helped me to recognize how important RS was to me. And I also would like to thank the ACF Early Promotion and Intervention Research Consortium (EPIRC) led by Rachel Chazan Cohen and including Linda Beeber, Neil Boris, Brenda Jones Harden, Neena Malik, and Jane Squires. The group helped me to synthesize some of my thoughts and urged the writing of this book (two EPIRC members even contributed chapters!). And a special thanks to Neil Boris, who saw that this project was more than a journal article and urged me to turn it into a book.

I was very lucky in my early professional development to be mentored by two wonderful and committed individuals, Charley Zeanah and Julie Larrieu. Much of what I do today has its roots in the myriad of things I learned from them. There are numerous members of Tulane University's Infant Team—each member's (present and past) commitment to the mental health of all children and families continues to sustain my work. I also want to acknowledge my current professional family which has been very supportive of (and patient with) the writing and editing process: Allison Boothe, Angela Keyes, Mary Margaret Gleason, and Geoff Nagle. Their sense of teamwork and belief in the reflective process are inspiring.

And, most important, I wish to thank my own family. My remarkable husband, Vince, and three terrific children, Gus, Marigny, and Jack, continue to amaze me. They have supported my professional endeavors from day one—even when it meant sacrificing family time. And they continue to remind me daily of what life is really all about—love, laughter, and listening.

Sherryl Scott Heller

*   *   *   *   *

From my first position over 35 years ago to the present, my work has involved the supervision of others. This is the guide that I needed as a beginning supervisor and that I turn to now as a veteran to sustain reflection within my supervisory practice. My deepest thanks go to Sherryl Scott Heller for the rich, fun opportunity to collaborate on this valuable tool and for her tireless work to bring our book to completion, amid loving care for three children and tending a busy career. I thank Charley Zeanah for linking us up and gratefully acknowledge all the chapter authors, who have shared their earned wisdom so generously.

Like so many others, my education in RS came from ZERO TO THREE; from Emily Fenichel, whose memory in so many hearts guides the field today; from Linda Eggbeer, the champion of RS; and from Rebecca Shamoon Shanok, whose first paper on RS created the sustaining image of a partner on a journey. I thank my colleagues and dear friends for their mentorship along my journey: Mary Claire Heffron, Mary Morse, and Deborah Weatherston, and Erikson family, Fran Stott and Judy Bertacchi. I also wish to acknowledge my collaborator, Heidelise Als, PhD, who immediately grasped the relevance and encouraged me to define reflective process as a component of relationship-based, developmental care in the neonatal intensive care unit (NICU). I thank my many colleagues in Illinois who are bringing reflective practice to the front doors of early intervention, and with three of whom I had the privilege to write a chapter: Theresa Atchley, Sonja Hall, and Sarah Martinez. Deep thanks to my colleagues at Erikson's Fussy Baby Network and Infant Studies Program and my students, who are the source of continuing growth, and to my husband, Don Lamb, who became so intrigued with RS that he incorporated it into another field about early beginnings—astrophysics, and to our son, Mike Lamb, who has known since day one that listening leads to learning.

Linda Gilkerson

INTRODUCTION

GETTING STARTED

Linda Gilkerson and Sherryl Scott Heller

A gently made observation can acknowledge a parent's pain and make it safe to speak; support from co-workers and supervisors strengthens a practitioner's ability to act effectively.

—Emily Fenichel (2001, p. 2)

This guidebook is written for two audiences: (a) administrators who have decided to initiate reflective supervision (RS) in their early childhood program and (b) the professionals who will fulfill the important role as reflective supervisors. In some programs, the administrator will also serve in the role as reflective supervisor, assuming the dual functions of mentor and monitor. In other programs, administrative supervision and reflective supervision will be carried out separately by different persons. Whichever model you choose, this book will help guide you during the first year of bringing RS to your program.

Here are the assumptions that underlie the book:

1. You are in charge or have been given the role by the decision makers in your setting to bring RS to the setting.

2. You will be the reflective supervisor or you have someone in mind who will serve in this role and will work with you to implement and maintain an RS program in your setting.

3. Your program is in a period of relative stability.

4. You have secured the resources to implement RS: that is, commitment from administration, financial resources, and adequate staff support.

Each chapter addresses a critical question that will help you launch RS in your setting, and provides you with a reflective tool to help structure the developing process. Here is a brief description of what you will learn in each chapter and what you will be able to do. We invite you to think of us—the chapter authors—as your partners on this journey toward RS. As Jeree Pawl, past president of ZERO TO THREE, has said: Never do hard things alone. So together, with your team, let us join you on the path toward RS, a path that we continue to walk and learn from each step of the way.

CHAPTER 1: WHAT IS REFLECTIVE SUPERVISION?

Rebecca Shahmoon-Shanok

This chapter introduces RS, describes its profound purposes (the whys of RS), and highlights the essential components. Here you will learn that the main goal of RS is to improve program quality and practice by cherishing strengths and partnering around vulnerabilities to generate professional growth (Shahmoon-Shanok, 1992). By the end of the chapter, you will be able to:

1. Define RS and explain its purposes within the context of early childhood work.

2. Understand the core processes of RS.

3. Use Reflective Tool 1 to begin your practice and reflection about working with young children and families.

Chapter 2: How Do I Develop an Implementation Plan to Begin Reflective Supervision in My Program?

Sherryl Scott Heller

Now that you have an understanding of your program's readiness for RS, you have choices to make about how to go about implementing RS. This chapter discusses some of the options to consider when designing an RS model for your program and ways that you can organize the planning effort. By the end of the chapter, you will be able to:

1. Identify a coordinator and organize a planning committee.

2. Develop an implementation plan.

3. Use Reflective Tool 2 to help you evaluate your implementation plan at different stages and from different staff perspectives.

Chapter 3: How Do I Introduce Reflective Supervision to My Program?

Neil W. Boris and John C. Grabert

Here you will learn about what we call the "discovery phase": that is, how to enter the system, introduce staff to the concept of RS, and—through active listening and reflective dialogue—develop an enhanced understanding of the organization's current level of reflective functioning and support. You will learn how to use strategies such as focus groups and informal conversations to collect staff perspectives relevant to the implementation of RS. By the end of the chapter, you will be able to:

1. Define and describe the skills used in active listening.

2. Understand the role of active listening in assessing your program's readiness to implement RS.

3. Use Reflective Tool 3 as a guide to structure and conduct a discovery focus group.

Chapter 4: What Does a Reflective Supervisory Relationship Look Like?

Deborah J. Weatherston and Carla Barron

In this chapter you, as the reflective supervisor, will learn how to establish and maintain the type of nonjudgmental climate that allows reflective partners—supervisor and supervisee—to explore the supervisee's vulnerabilities as well as his or her strengths. We focus on what the supervisor and supervisee each should bring to the supervisory relationship to better assure a mutually satisfying partnership, and we offer vignettes that illustrate the dialogue that might occur at different points during the first year of a supervisory relationship. By the end of the chapter, you will be able to:

1. Describe the actions that the supervisor takes to create a safe environment for supervision and the actions that the supervisee takes to ensure active participation in supervision.

2. Participate more confidently in a new, reflective supervisory relationship.

3. Use Reflective Tool 4 to remind each partner, supervisor, and supervisee of his or her important contribution to the RS relationship.

Chapter 5: What Are the Phases of the Reflective Supervision Meeting?

Theresa Atchley, Sonja Hall, Sarah Martinez, and Linda Gilkerson

One of the core elements of RS is regularity. Regularity refers not only to RS sessions occurring at a set frequency and time but also to the predictable routines that contribute to the creation of a safe, trustworthy environment. In this chapter, you will learn about the phases of the supervisory session: preparation, greeting, opening the dialogue/finding the agenda, information gathering/focusing on the details, formulating hypotheses, considering next steps, closing, and reflection. Each phase is described in detail, and vignettes are used to illustrate the phases in both individual and group supervision. By the end of the chapter, you will be able to:

1. Picture and describe one approach to the structure of a supervision meeting.

2. Consider how you will structure supervisory sessions.

3. Use Reflective Tool 5 to guide your reflection after supervision meetings.

Chapter 6: How Do I, as a Reflective Supervisor, Repair Ruptures in the Supervisory Relationship?

Angela W. Keyes, Amy E. Cavanaugh, and Sherryl Scott Heller

Like all relationships, the RS relationship will have times of synchrony and dysynchrony. This chapter helps you see ruptures in the RS relationship as a breakdown in the collaborative process (Safran & Muran, 2006). We describe some of the tensions that we have encountered in RS relationships (e.g., frequent cancellations, silences, supervisor overtalking), and offer ways that you can explore the meaning of these behaviors and begin to repair the relationship. A central premise is that if ruptures are addressed sensitively and effectively, these challenges can strengthen the supervisory relationship and provide a unique opportunity for mutual growth. By the end of the chapter, you will be able to:

1. Understand the role that rupture and repair can play in strengthening the supervisory relationship.

2. Increase your comfort in exploring tensions within the relationship.

3. Use Reflective Tool 6 to help you process times when your relationship with a supervisee is out of sync and consider ways to repair the relationship.

CHAPTER 7: HOW CAN ADMINISTRATIVE AND REFLECTIVE SUPERVISION BE COMBINED?

Judith Bertacchi and Linda Gilkerson

RS is often contrasted with administrative supervision. In this dichotomy, administrative supervision is about accountability and RS is about staff development. Here, we present how these two roles can be effectively combined into an integrated model of RS, called the "mentoring/monitoring (M/M) approach." We describe the values of the M/M approach, qualities of the M/M supervisor, and some of the advantages and challenges of the dual role. A central thesis is that both administrative tasks and direct service responsibilities benefit from reflection. By the end of the chapter, you will be able to:

1. Describe the M/M model of supervision, its strengths, and its challenges.

2. Contract with a supervisee for supervision using the M/M model.

3. Use Reflective Tool 7 to build your capacity to use supervision to work through performance issues in an honest, direct way.

CHAPTER 8: BEYOND REFLECTIVE SUPERVISION: HOW CAN MY ORGANIZATION SUPPORT STAFF WELL-BEING?

Brenda Jones Harden

Although RS is arguably the most important vehicle for enhancing staff practice, there are other mechanisms that support staff development and optimize staff interventions with children and families outside of RS. We propose that a staff-oriented infrastructure, in concert with RS, is essential to support early childhood practitioners who often work with highly vulnerable and stressed families, and, too often, without adequate preparation for this psychologically demanding work. In this chapter, you will learn how an organization can support early childhood staff, in conjunction with RS, in order to allow them to deliver services in the most effective manner. By the end of the chapter, you will be able to:

1. Make a case for the importance of a staff-centered organizational structure, in concert with RS, to support effective early childhood practice.

2. Describe the elements of a staff-centered organizational structure and the resources needed to support it.

3. Use Reflective Tool 8 to assess staff well-being and select staff-centered strategies to promote safety, nurturance, and competence.

CHAPTER 9: WHAT STAFF DEVELOPMENT ACTIVITIES CAN BE USED TO BUILD REFLECTIVE CAPACITY?

Gerard Costa and Lorri Sullivan

Staff differs in their experience with reflective process and their comfort with it. Because we view the capacity for reflection as a basic human capacity, we believe that reflection is an ability that can be nurtured and strengthened. In this chapter, you will learn about engaging activities to practice reflection that can be used in the discovery phase but also can and should be used (and reused) as you and your staff members become more skilled in the reflective process. The message you will be conveying is that reflection is a process that we all are learning and relearning at every point of our professional lives. By the end of this chapter, you will be able to:

1. Talk with staff about the role of feelings in the helping relationship.

2. Create a safe space for staff to play with and engage in eight reflective activities.

3. Use Reflective Tool 9 to collect the lessons learned about reflection from the leader and participants.

This guidebook provides you with a map for initiating RS in an early childhood program. You can share the guidebook with your fellow travelers and work through the chapters as a team. As you read the chapters, try out the ideas, and use the reflective tools, you will be writing your own guidebook to RS. Best wishes on this rich journey!

REFERENCES

Fenichel, E., (2001) Editor's Note. Infant mental health and Early Head Start: Lessons for early childhood programs. *Zero to Three, 22*(1), 2.

Safran, J. D., & Muran, J. C. (2006). Has the concept of the alliance outlived its usefulness? *Psychotherapy, 43,* 286–291.

Shahmoon-Shanok, R. (1992). The supervisory relationship: Integrator, resource and guide. In E. Fenichel (Ed.), *Learning thru supervision and mentorship to support the development of infants and toddlers and their families: A sourcebook* (pp. 113–119). Washington, DC: ZERO TO THREE.

CHAPTER 1

WHAT IS REFLECTIVE SUPERVISION?

Rebecca Shahmoon-Shanok

One sees clearly only with the heart.
Anything essential is invisible to the eye.

—Antoine De Saint Exupery (1943, p. 63)

Reflective supervision (RS) is a collaborative relationship for professional growth that improves program quality and strengthens practice. RS builds the capacity of individuals, relationships, and organizations by cherishing strengths and partnering around vulnerabilities (Shahmoon-Shanok, 1991, p. 18). This chapter explains this idea by introducing RS, describing its profound purposes (the whys of RS), and highlighting the essential components. By the end of the chapter, you will be able to:

1. Define RS and explain its purposes within the context of early childhood work.

2. Understand the core processes of RS.

3. Use Reflective Tool 1 to begin your practice and reflection about working with young children and families.

HISTORY OF REFLECTIVE SUPERVISION

Let's start at the very beginning.
A very good place to start.

—Hammerstein and Rodgers (1959, The Sound of Music)

We start with a brief summary of the development of RS in the field of early childhood intervention. The term *reflective supervision* is deeply linked to clinical supervision that mental health workers (social workers, psychologists, psychiatrists, psychoanalysts, marriage and family therapists, psychiatric nurses, arts therapists, and others) experience in their pre-degree training and later in their workplaces. In the late 1980s and early 1990s, as the birth-to-3 field was in its infancy, ZERO TO THREE (then the National Center for Clinical Infant Programs) identified elements of training important to all work with infants, toddlers, and their families. The workgroup involved in that effort, which included leaders from across several different disciplines, became increasingly convinced that clinical-like supervision, different from administrative supervision that tracks level of service, chart writing, and the like, is necessary for any provider working with very young children (Fenichel, Eggbeer, & the TASK Advisory Board, 1990). There was some hesitancy about advocating for this kind of supervision as it could feel like an imposition of mental health practice onto all of the other disciplines in early childhood intervention. However, ZERO TO THREE's workgroup recognized that what does stem from the field of mental health is a way to think about and begin to manage the enormous range of interpersonal situations with which all providers are confronted, as well as a method of learning how to use personal impact in a positive way—no matter what one's profession (Pawl, 1995).

RS AS A FORM OF APPRENTICESHIP

All kinds of work are learned through experience. Sometimes it's called "on-the-job training." The more formal term is apprenticeship. From designers to dancers, from plasterers to pilots, from Webmasters to waiters, all human occupations have apprenticeship periods during which people learn by doing while receiving guidance from those who have had experience doing their job (Shahmoon-Shanok, 1991, 2006). Within apprenticeships in the human services, RS provides a recurring time for providers[1] to step back from their interpersonal work to think alongside a more experienced partner. Stepping away from practice to contemplate what has been both experienced and done enables the provider to plan and become ready for next steps in practice. RS, then, is a component of apprenticeship. "As functioning families are for growing children, so apprenticeships are for (workers): small human groups responsible for imparting the skills necessary to become something" (Shahmoon-Shanok, Lapidus, Grant, Halpern, & Lamb-Parker, 2005, p. 457). Similar to how families teach their offspring behaviors and attitudes, along with myriad bits of information, apprenticeships are the age-old social medium for knowledge transfer about work from one generation of adults to the next. In RS, a relationship is formed between a provider—*the supervisee*—and someone else who has either more or a different kind of experience—*the supervisor*. Sharing knowledge, ideas, and experiences helps providers analyze what happened in their interchanges with parents and with children, and figure out next steps while simultaneously learning and growing in their careers. Now that I have given you the background and a context for RS, I turn to providing a definition.

DEFINITION

As noted, RS is a collaborative relationship for professional growth that improves program quality and practice by cherishing strengths and partnering around vulnerabilities to generate growth (Shahmoon-Shanok, 1991). A reflective supervisor tailors learning opportunities to each individual supervisee by providing a reliable, respectful relationship over time, one in which the reflective supervisor listens deeply, a capacity that sets the tone between them and allows the supervisor to come to know the unique qualities of the particular provider before her. Together, reflective supervisor and reflective supervisee pay attention, developing and deepening shared attention to the same phenomena that, not incidentally, are a fundamental developmental capacity for individuals and within relationships (Fonagy, 2001; Greenspan, 1992). A safe, protected, reliably recurring space is created as context in which there is authenticity and genuine interest in exploring emotional experience in order to support a nondefensive willingness on the part of the supervisee to share strengths and allow his vulnerabilities to be seen. The reflective partners discuss what each one notices, exchange perspectives, widen each other's

---

[1]Provider *is the word used throughout this book to denote anyone who works with young children and their parents, from daycare provider, to nurse, to child welfare worker, to home-based occupational, physical, speech-language, or expressive arts therapist, to paraprofessional.*

horizons, and, often, plan the next steps for the supervisee to take. The shared thought, care, awareness, and planning experiences between supervisee and supervisor grow over time to become a cornerstone in the foundation for the supervisee's practice. See Reflective Tool 1 Ten Questions to Foster Your Journey Toward Self-Reflection, for a list of probes to consider in RS.

It is also important to note that RS is characterized by three key elements: reflection, collaboration, and regularity (Fenichel, 1992, p. 9). *Reflection* is the stepping back to consider the work from multiple perspectives, including from what one and others observe, feel, and think. *Collaboration* is the respectful, mutual exchange that relies on the full participation of the supervisor and supervisee. *Regularity* refers to predictable routines and sufficient frequency to create the interpersonal safety necessary for authentic interaction around strengths, vulnerabilities, and the intrinsic problems of practice. Regularity often refers to a mutually determined, set schedule for supervision. However, it also refers to the expected, consistent nature of the relationship (see Weatherston & Barron, this volume, p. 63, for more on the importance of this) and to the routines of the supervisory sessions (see Atchley, Hall, Martinez, & Gilkerson, this volume, p. 83, for more on the importance of routine).

PURPOSE OF RS: IMPROVES PROGRAM QUALITY AND STRENGTHENS SKILLS THROUGHOUT A CAREER SPAN

The overall aim of RS is to improve practice and thereby increase the quality of early childhood services for young children and families. RS accomplishes this goal in two ways: (a) by building overall organizational capacity and (b) by strengthening provider competency (Gilkerson & Shahmoon-Shanok, 2000). In terms of organizations, incorporating RS implies that each worker has someone to whom she can turn, someone upon whom she can lean, someone who serves as teacher. The program or agency also has the opportunity to transform itself to become a

> learning organization, where open communication and idea-development can flow in
> several directions, not merely from the top down . . . The changes required will not be
> only in organizations, but in ourselves as well . . . organizations work the way they
> work, ultimately, because of *how we think and how we interact*. Only by changing how we
> think can we change deeply embedded policies and practices. Only by changing how
> we interact can shared visions, shared interactions, and new capacities for coordinated
> action be established. (Senge, 1990, p. XIV, italics in original)

Senge was writing about for-profit organizations from massive, worldwide corporations to small local businesses. If businesses of all sizes can reinvent themselves by attending to reflections and connections between people, not-for-profits serving the youngest children and families can similarly flatten hierarchies to integrate new perspectives and ideas.

> Although there are often tensions in coming together . . . , thoughtful, relationally (and
> reflectively) oriented facilitation can turn tension into a learning experience . . . .
> When people, disciplines, and roles join together in a training and service partnership
> (such as what can occur in reflective practice programs) to undertake a substantial
> endeavor that has meaning to them in terms of conjoined . . . goals, vision and mission,

a sense of greater possibility and promise emerges that boosts the sense of the possible and—not incidently—of hope. (Shahmoon-Shanok et al., 2005, pp. 474–475, parentheses added)

The box Benefits of Reflective Supervision highlights key purposes and processes that facilitate RS and support achieving its goals.

....

Benefits of Reflective Supervision

Builds Organizational Capacity

- Diminishes scale

- Models parallel process

- Supports ethical practice

- Builds shared understanding of program philosophy

- Facilitates implementation of administrative requirements

- Improves program quality and accountability

Strengthens Professional Competence

- Supports cross-cultural responsiveness

- Begets initiative and effective, engaged practice

- Nourishes self-knowledge and responsibility

- Develops the capacity to remember

- Encourages critical thinking and trial action

- Amplifies self-regulation and responsibility

- Contributes to professional identity and career development

—Adapted from Gilkerson and Shahmoon-Shanok (2000)

....

Although RS is usually conceived of as a form of apprenticeship for newer providers, it is also an essential component of practice for experienced providers, including program managers and reflective supervisors themselves. Some, or more likely many, who have the position of reflective supervisor may never have received RS themselves. This is just one of the reasons that reflective supervisors benefit from a reflective forum in which they can step back and refresh their thinking and clinical skills. About 3 years ago, for example, I realized that I had become too involved in work with a mom who had been severely abused sexually and psychologically beginning in her early childhood. I sought RS from someone with extensive experience and knowledge of recent advances in work with traumatized adults. Over time, this relational, reflective learning experience helped me develop greater steadiness and skill in what had earlier been a deep wish to rescue, my over-responsiveness to the woman's great distress, neediness, alternating extreme states of mind and emotion as well as to her horrendous childhood.

Rather than getting set in our ways or ignoring our own blind spots with certain individuals, families, or situations, people who have been in this work for decades, no matter their professions, need partners with whom they can be straightforward, with whose partnership their own perspectives and awareness can be broadened and vitalized. Like the providers they lead, senior leaders also need someone to listen to them "with generosity" (Toomey, 2004). Each of the disciplines that works with children from pregnancy to 6 years old and their families, plus the cross-pollinating world of earliest childhood itself, is enjoying a period of rapidly evolving knowledge to be integrated. Over the decades-long course of a career, reflective individual, group, or peer supervision becomes the space in which to slow down time to remember, to reflect, to reorganize, to reintegrate, to recharge, and to renew. Its reward is dawning awareness of patterns in children, families, colleagues and ourselves.

PROCESSES OF RS

Although RS is always shaped by the individuals involved, there are core processes that characterize RS across relationships and across settings. These processes are described below.

Parallel Process: Passing on Emotional Tone

> *If you sow corn, you reap corn.*
> *If you sow beans, you reap beans.*
> *Why do we have to go through so many*
> *trials before we realize this?*
>
> — *Thich Nhat Hanh, (2007, p. 31)*

By definition, RS is a relationship whose aim is to improve professional practice. Given all that is known by now about the effect of early attachment relationships upon young, growing children (Sroufe, Egeland, Carlson, & Collins, 2005) and on their parents (Galinsky, 1981; Mayes, 2002; Shahmoon-Shanok, 1997, 2000a, 2000b; Slade, 2002)—that is, given the fact that all human beings have grown and been formed in both parent–child and apprenticeship relationships—it is unsurprising that a very deep form of learning takes place in the special relationships created together in RS. Furthermore, what happens in one set of asymmetrical relationships—relationships where there are differences in relative power between the players—often has a deep effect on the other relationships of each player, perhaps especially those of the more junior one (Shahmoon-Shanok, 1997). So, for example, the establishment of safety and connections (or of fear and disconnection) in RS establishes a powerful set of parallels between

- The supervisee and the supervisor
- The parent and the supervisee as his provider
- The baby and her parent

This factor is powerful enough that it has a name; it has come to be known as *parallel process*. It could also be called the "pass-it-on" factor or "ripple effect." When a boss yells at a manager, it becomes more likely that the manager will send off messages of criticism and impatience to her workers. Workers, in turn, may bleed that stress into interactions with coworkers or clients even if they try not to do so. Conversely, the positive also holds true: As we are nurtured, so we are enabled to nurture. Jeree Pawl (1995) put it so well about RS, "Do unto others as you would have others do unto others" (p. 43).

RS is a set of caring conversations co-constructed over time by supervisee and supervisor, improvised or created in the moment, yet deepening their connection as together they develop their history and knowledge of one another and of the children and families in their conjoined care. Although interchanges between the provider and parent or child are created similarly to those that occur in RS, it is RS that provides the awareness, so those improvisations in engagement generate positive change. Thus, RS provides the safe and nurturing environment that supports learning and growth in the provider and in turn the client; hence, the term parallel process.

A Sense of Safety Is Vital

> *Everyone needs help from everyone.*
> —Bertolt Brecht (*Famous quotes and authors.com*)[2]

RS is stepping back from the immediate experience to become aware of and sort through thoughts and feelings about what one is observing and doing with children and their parents (Shahmoon-Shanok, Gilkerson, Eggbeer, & Fenichel, 1995). The atmosphere generates investigative thinking within which the supervisee is usually stimulated to recognize more about his own motives, emotions, and behavior than previously. Simultaneously, he comes to focus on what it feels like to be the parent or the child. When the supervisory relationship is growing as it should, the supervisee feels like he can let himself— the different dimensions of his selves—be seen, allowing his supervisor in on both the domains of which he is proud and those of which he doubts or feels badly, ashamed, or even mortified.

"One of the deepest longings of the human soul is the longing to be seen" (O'Donohue, 1997, p. 25). To get to the point of such openness in the RS relationship, it is essential for the supervisee to feel safe about exposing both the positive and the negative aspects of herself and her work. By modeling both openness and trustworthiness, by being simultaneously tactful and honest, by discussing confidentiality, and by manifesting a commitment to the supervisee's growth, the supervisor helps set a contract for safety. Thus, when necessary, RS paradoxically enables the supervisee to feel safe enough to explore even acute discomfort (Stitt, 2009). Examples of such discomfort include the supervisee's feelings, such as anger at or envy of a child, physical attraction to a parent, shame about what the supervisee said or did in a session with them, fear of home visiting in a particular neighborhood, or racist attitudes.

It may seem even more paradoxical to those new to RS to realize that it is possible to feel safe in a supervisory relationship within a practice setting or graduate school, even while the supervisor holds the power of evaluating and/or grading (Shahmoon-Shanok, 1991, 2006) and may also be responsible for making sure that the supervisee's charts and levels of services are adequate. The reason that a supervisee can be secure when the supervisor holds the power of evaluating or grading the provider or provider in training is that the supervisor makes crystal clear that his goal is to partner the supervisee for growth across all dimensions of the supervisee's job. Supervisor and, gradually, supervisee alike understand that continual growth of awareness and skills are a career-long goal. Moreover, it is intrinsic to the interest of each that the supervisee becomes the strongest possible provider, which includes the meeting of agency

---

[2] *For well-known, poetic quotations which introduce some sections of this chapter, Web site citations are offered to assist the reader who wants to learn more about the context of the particular author's thought.*

and field assignments. To share the power, the reflective supervisor and supervisee usually discuss, and some in fact write, the supervisee's evaluation together. Furthermore, in several programs, the supervisee is invited to give written feedback to the supervisor (Shahmoon-Shanok, 1991, 2006). The goal of evaluating in both directions is a deep exchange of reactions and ideas about how the relationship between them is serving the growth of the supervisee as a generative, maturing provider (Heffron, 2005; Shahmoon-Shanok, 1991, 2006).

Engaging with an experienced, emotionally attuned senior partner, the supervisee is enabled to grasp aspects of her work about which she might not have thought otherwise. For example, what prompted the parent to get a manicure or stay on the phone during her child's session? The supervisee is no longer alone with what she feels are the most difficult aspects of the work or the worst parts of herself.

Observation Is Key

Our sense of touch connects us to the world in an intimate way.
As the mother of distance,
the eye shows us that we are outside things.

—John O'Donohue (1997, p. 73)

All providers who touch the lives of young children and their families are trained to observe certain phenomena. In so doing, however, they also become trained to ignore other phenomena (Shahmoon-Shanok, Henderson, Grellong, & Foley, 2006). A pediatric nurse practitioner, for example, learns to notice skin tone and the color of the whites of the eyes. A speech-language therapist "sees" speech prosody, pragmatics, and the nuances of articulation. Teachers concentrate on the behavior, skills, and knowledge a child demonstrates, and how that youngster interacts with others. In RS, by definition, two or more people focus on the same phenomenon over time. As no two people see alike, the mere fact of discussion and exchange expands viewpoints. Furthermore, it is usually the case that the reflective supervisor has more or a different experience than the supervisee does. Once again, there is an enlargement of perspective.

This effect is maximized when RS takes place across disciplines. We can think of supervision as *super* vision: Just like a superhero, super vision enables us to see deeper, wider, and further (Shahmoon-Shanok, 2006). Indeed, there are "invisible"—out of awareness—areas that work with a reflective supervisor is meant to bring into focus. What transpires in the relationship between child and parent—including preverbal and nonverbal elements—and consideration of the representations of the parent(s)—parental memories and predispositions that represent patterns internalized from the time and the ways they were raised (Shahmoon-Shanok, 2006)—are examples of such invisible areas.

Focus on Process

What is being addressed together in RS is process, which is "a natural phenomenon marked by gradual changes that lead towards a particular result" (*Merriam-Webster's New Collegiate Dictionary*, 1963, p. 678). As partners, it is the responsibility and goal of both reflective supervisor and supervisee that the process leads toward growth in the supervisee and, in parallel, in his clients. It has been said that all behavior has meaning; the challenge is to figure out what a set of behaviors and displays can tell observers. Paying attention to process—that is, carefully observing and reviewing what happened, what occurred next, and, then again, what transpired after that—allows professionals to link occurrences, thoughts, and ideas over time so that they come to perceive more and then more of the story. What was previously in peripheral vision moves into focus. With increasing awareness, the story becomes elaborated, increasingly complex and rich. As the reflective pair slows down to pay attention to the effect of one set of interactions on others over time, they are becoming aware of process.

Another way to become aware of process is to realize that the focus of the RS session may be, on one hand, client centered or, on the other, provider centered. An example of client-centered process follows where the focus is on developing a deeper understanding of a child's feelings and experiences in order to make adjustments to better meet his needs. This is followed by an example of provider-centered process, in which the focus is on clarifying a social worker's own contribution to a set of interactions with her own supervisee. More often than not, client and provider experiences are intertwined, and RS process examines themes in both domains.

Client-centered process. A preschool teacher asked her reflective supervisor for help in handling a 3-year-old boy's daily tantrums that always seemed to occur midmorning, at almost the same time every day. In response, the supervisor posed many questions whose answers would be based on information gathered from both the preceding and succeeding observations by the teacher/supervisee:

> How does the boy seem as he comes into school? What does he do and how does he seem between arrival and his collapses? How have they tried to help him? Who usually drops him off? What happens between them and how does he say "bye" to that person? How is that person with him? Has the teacher ever asked if the boy eats breakfast, what he eats, and how he sleeps?

With his queries and their conjoined reflection on the responses, the reflective supervisor is launching a process that bridges observations to foster the building of a story—the child's and parent's realities, the patterns of their relationship, and the child's in-school experiences—over time. In so doing, supervisee and supervisor co-construct a sense of the process leading to the boy's upsets, and co-conjecture about possible reasons for the pattern. The supervisor might bring up a discussion of state regulation and invite the supervisee's sense of how to help children—and the supervisee—stay or become calm.

Contemplating process in this way assists in deciphering what can be seen and uncovering what is hidden. In the previous example, to explain why a child might break out crying at his child care center every day at about the same time, the supervisor and teacher-supervisee look for continuities and breaks in the story of what the teacher sees, and together build hypotheses, consider linkages, and consider new possibilities. They continue to do this until they reach sufficient understanding to plan new actions on the teacher's part. These actions might include ways to reach for collaboration with the boy's parent(s) and/or strategies to support the boy, even before he cries, so that his pattern of upsets can diminish and he can become better regulated more of the time.

Provider-centered process. The prior example of the preschool teacher struggling with the young boy and his daily outbursts illustrates the client-centered form. The reflective supervisor inquired about the child and the context of his difficult behavior. Together, the supervisor and teacher/supervisee reflected on her responses more deeply for what they could discover about the boy. On the other hand, in listening to a supervisee, a supervisor may notice certain patterns in the supervisee that are having an impact on interactions with clients or coworkers. These could be points that are emphasized or left out or themes that are repeated. A provider-centered focus on process is also an essential part of RS. In the example that follows, the supervisor helps the supervisee see a pattern in her own behavior—her hesitance to say what she really thinks—that is influencing her interactions not only with her boss but also with her own supervisee.

> In an early supervisory session, a reflective supervisor named Miriam invited her new supervisee, Stephanie, to contemplate what she would like to concentrate on in supervision. Stephanie was a seasoned social worker in her early 50s who supervised famiy workers in a Head Start program. This was her first experience with RS. She tentatively suggested that maybe she could discuss her difficult relationship with her boss, a person she described as set in her ways and often defensive. When asked how she usually handles her boss, Stephanie responded that she always goes along with her because she loves her job and wants to keep it. They continued to consider the possibility of placing Stephanie's boss on their regular agenda for a few minutes and then moved on to other ideas. Toward the end of the same appointment, the pair began to think about the possibility of Stephanie choosing one of her four family workers to place on their regular agenda. As it was not obvious to Stephanie which of the four she should choose, Miriam asked her to give a thumbnail description of each.

> As Miriam listened, she noticed that the descriptions of all the relationships seemed positive and that Stephanie felt she was helpful to all of them. Nevertheless, as she described one of the family workers, Lizette, Stephanie mentioned, almost in passing, that she had not told Lizette that she does not like the fact that this family worker has taken a second job. After asking a few questions to be sure that she understood the situation correctly, the supervisor told Stephanie that she thought that there might be a parallel between what Stephanie had said in relation to her boss and what she had said in relation to Lizette. When Stephanie responded by asking Miriam to continue, Miriam added that with both the boss and Lizette, it seemed that it was sometimes difficult for Stephanie to find a way to speak her mind.

> Seeing Stephanie nod her acknowledgment, Miriam wondered aloud what she might want to say to Lizette and what would be difficult about that. Stephanie replied that she valued Lizette and knew that she needed the extra money. Stephanie did not want to burden Lizette by revealing that she hated Lizette's second job because Lizette always had to leave immediately at the end of her shift and even occasionally had to make phone calls during the day for that other job. By asking some questions, Miriam helped Stephanie join her in brainstorming ways that Stephanie could broach the topic with Lizette that would likely invite Lizette's own feelings on the topic of her second job.

Excited by this possibility, Stephanie remarked that she would do it that very after-noon. Following the process a bit further, Miriam placed herself in Lizette's position and asked Stephanie to do the same. The supervisor suggested that because these comments would not be about what they usually discussed, but instead about the new demands on Lizette's time and attention, perhaps it would be gentler as well as more effective to help Lizette anticipate that their next conversation would be different from their usual supervisory sessions. They agreed that Stephanie would slow down the planned pace of her discussions with Lizette. Today she would suggest to Lizette that the next time they meet they hold a step-back-and-assess-how-things-are-going meeting, with Lizette invited to participate first.

As it was still early in their relationship, before they ended their appointment that day, the supervisor, Miriam, checked out what today's interchange was like for Stephanie. Stephanie replied with enthusiasm, "I feel like I learned so much!"

In ways like these, reflective supervisors invite reflective supervisees to notice and pay thoughtful attention to their own experiences and those of others as they unfold. Reflective supervisors simultaneously model attending to the process unfolding within the supervisee and between the supervisor and supervisee themselves.

Conscious Use of Self

By paying attention to and tracking phenomena over time, awareness of both process and context—of the self and of the other—evolves and becomes stronger. Becoming aware helps people go beyond being nice. Being nice is necessary, but far from sufficient to assist people in their growth process. Becoming aware enables professionals to make selections in how they use themselves within their relationships, which is called "the conscious use of self." In the previous example of Stephanie and Lizette, Stephanie did not consider bringing up her feelings about Lizette's second job because she wanted to be nice; that is, she hesitated to let Lizette know and be burdened by the knowledge that she, Stephanie, hated Lizette's other occupation. In making that decision, however, Stephanie had eclipsed the possibility of learning what it was like for Lizette to juggle two jobs and of exchanging perspectives on that topic. This decision to "be nice" had implications for how Lizette carried out her job in the organization to which Stephanie and Lizette were both responsible. What can seem like kindness may, instead, result in staying on the surface during interchanges. In contrast, growth is assisted by taking steps toward awareness in increments the person can handle and reflect upon.

Stephanie later told Miriam in RS that her conversation with Lizette had gone well. In fact, Stephanie shared that Lizette had told Stephanie that she was feeling "left out" because Stephanie seemed more distant and less supportive. Miriam noticed that Stephanie now seemed more comfortable with Lizette's relative unavailability, concentrating instead on a plan Stephanie and Lizzette were making for a new parent group that the two of them would lead together. As a result of the discussion between them, Stephanie and Lizette were able to move forward in their work together with an increased awareness and appreciation of each other's perspectives and concerns.

Explore Differences

*Possibility and change become growth within
the shape of time that we call a day . . . .
To engage with honor the full possibility of your life
is to engage in a worthy way the possibility of your new day.*

—*John O'Donohue (1997, p. 129)*

It is within these deeply significant RS relationships that supervisor and supervisee can also explore and deepen their understandings about differences across culture, class, race, ethnicity, immigration, gender orientation, and family styles. Together, they have a better chance than either of them do alone of appreciating "the meaning and consequences of multiple categories of identity, difference, and disadvantage" (Cole, 2009, p. 170) as well as "social categories [which] jointly shape experiences and outcomes" (Cole, 2009, p. 171). They can raise questions (e.g., "Seeing her sitting alone in the crowded playground, the only Black mom in a sea of White people, I wondered what it was like for her to be alone, especially given her 4-year-old who has so few words"), learn from each other, recognize when they do not know enough, and figure out how to find out more either from the clients themselves or from other resources. Together they can also assist the supervisee in learning how to identify the supervisee's areas of comfort and discomfort, contemplate difference related to social categories, and consider ways to raise questions about differences with his or her clients in order to solicit their clients' experiences and deepen their connections (see Keyes, Cavanaugh, & Scott Heller, this volume, p. 99, for more on addressing cultural differences).

Use Reflection as Trial Action

*We don't stop playing because we grow old;
We grow old because we stop playing.*

—*George Bernard Shaw (ThinkExist.com)*

One way that Sigmund Freud (1958, 1964) wrote and spoke about thought was as "trial action." So too in RS, a kind of trial action, even playfulness of ideas, emerges. That is, the supervisor and supervisee play with options as they try to discover possibilities that lie below the surface. Together they hover over scenes that the reflective supervisee tries to bring to life in his recollections. The reflective partners are never quite sure where they are going to land, but recognize that, on the way, their conjoined vantage point will allow them to see more deeply. Reflective supervisee and supervisor try to imagine themselves into each person and situation. Each scene is a revelation as both supervisor and supervisee investigate what may seem like secrets that lie just below the surface of the story. Questions may be raised: "Why is the dad now working late and not getting home until after his son has gone to sleep? Where does the mom go during your session with her baby? How might it be possible to reach each of them?" Even when the images are rich, sometimes they are left with a lack of clarity or a sense of indecisiveness. The supervisor may ask for further detail: "What did you see? Then what happened? Please describe it so I can visualize it, like it's a movie." Considering actions before acting allows supervisees to learn to take multiple perspectives and contain their impulses toward premature action.

Being Held in Mind

Children spell love T – I – M – E.

—David Wagner (2002, p. 55)

As they consider trial actions, the reflective supervisory pair gaze both at what is illuminated and toward the shadows, hunting for clues to clients' unfolding narrative, visualizing the actors whose roles deliver awareness of their level of development and sense of meaning, or not, in the world. Such co-concentration tends to foster a relationship in which the reflective supervisee feels respected, nurtured, remembered, and safe. The supervisee knows that they are on the same wavelength, that they are sharing contents of mind; the supervisee feels understood and partnered. In the context of children and their parents, Siegel and Hartzell (2003) put it well when they wrote, "In this manner [each of the partners] comes to feel felt. They come to feel as if their mind[s] exist in the mind of the other" (p. 83). Experiencing a holding environment in supervision builds supervisees' capacities to hold others in mind—the parents, children, and colleagues—and to create safe spaces that encourage their growth and development.

Regulation of Emotion

In doing this work together, reflective supervisee and supervisor find their way to co-regulation. What is sometimes an agitated state for the supervisee gradually becomes one within which she can think, plan, and grow. Her state shifts from one in which she may have felt hopeless or horrified, anxious or angry, envious or excited, embarrassed or cocky, to one in which she is calmer, readier to constructively engage once again. As the supervisee's emotional state downshifts, she becomes readier to use her mind and her ideas. She is better able to gain access to the full range of her experience, insight, and ideas, to become a more resourceful helper for her clients in the moment. Thus, the first step to reflection is regulation.

Every birth-to-6 professional learns of painful histories and circumstances almost every day he is at work. Some stories—the actual realities of people's lives—are gruesome. It is in RS that a supervisee finds a safe harbor within which he can dare and bear to explore ugly or provocative situations in order to find effective interventions in very trying circumstances. In so doing, he activates thinking that allows contemplation, resourcefulness, and planning to surface in the face of very serious challenges.

While discussing anxiety and other emotional reactions on the part of providers, Rothschild and Rand (2006) wrote,

> It is advisable to make sure that you are always able to think clearly when working with clients (and probably in most other aspects of your life too). This means paying attention to your own levels of arousal and making sure it stays low enough that your hippocampus does not shut down. It is the function of the hippocampus, for example, to help you to distinguish whether an internal experience stems from something occurring now or something that occurred in the past . . . when the hippocampus is suppressed you can no longer think clearly as space and time become confused. (p. 162)

"It is impossible to keep one's mind blank and remain completely objective when facing a client's emotions. Even the best trained and most experienced psychotherapist is vulnerable to being touched or stirred by his clients" (Rothschild & Rand, 2006, p. 16). "The goal of putting on the brakes is to become calmer so that you can think clearly" (Rothschild & Rand, p. 117). In writing these words, Rothschild and Rand were addressing the need for self-awareness in order to know when to use self-care strategies for managing the stress of vicarious trauma. In fact, RS helps providers to become aware of and manage the anxiety, helplessness, anger, envy, attraction, or other intense emotions that often arise as professionals involve themselves with cases of every conceivable kind, from transient problems to traumatic situations within which some children and parents in their care are entangled.

Relationship, Rupture, and Repair

If we all hold hands, we can't fight.

—Fabian, age 6, Brooklyn, New York

When RS is going as it should, it usually feels good to both the supervisee and the supervisor to participate together. Through the purpose-centered partnership they nurture, supervisor and supervisee are deepening insight and awareness about the supervisee's case responsibilities to promote expansion of the supervisee's understanding and skills to serve clients well. Together they are making meaning (Kegan, 1982).

Yet, between people, there are almost always misunderstandings and conflicting perspectives or desires. The supervisory journey is not without hazards. Indeed, it is not unusual for there to be periods when supervisee and supervisor each feel that she is searching for a path with, or to, the other and, in some instances, not finding it. There are times when a rupture of some sort occurs, either between supervisee and supervisor or between supervisee and someone on his or her caseload. When there are mismatches, the supervisor models dedication to discovering repair and asks the same of the supervisee. She searches her internal process and asks the supervisee to do the same (see Keyes et al., this volume, p. 99, for more about repair in the supervisory relationship). Repair requires negotiation, and negotiation leads to greater awareness and learning both about the self and others. Previously unspoken feelings get aired through emotional displays, actions, sounds, or words. Sometimes they hurt in one or both directions.

In what can be intense interchanges, supervisee and supervisor both feel they make an impact upon one another. Each discovers more about his own ideas and how to negotiate for the vantage point he feels to be correct. "It is the depth of engagement of these highly motivated (re)negotiations that often propel" the dyad to greater understanding through more vital emotional expression and effective communication, even when under stress (Shahmoon-Shanok, 2000a, p. 234). When such intense interchanges occur in RS, they actually can become precious practice for both supervisee and supervisor in what Rothschild has called "putting on the brakes" (Rothschild & Rand, 2006, p. 112) that is, staying (or getting) calm, thoughtful, and open to another's perspective—essential skills that are often crucial to generative work with children, parents, and coworkers alike.

SUMMARY

RS is a relationship for learning. The partnership nurtures a process of remembering, reviewing, and thinking out loud about a specific child, family, or people who surround them and what happens (or does not) between them. RS "enhances vision, clarifying what is seen and even what is see-able. In a real sense, the effect of reflective supervision is that it nourishes 'super vision'—a nuanced, co-constructed vision that penetrates further, deeper and more" (Shahmoon-Shanok, 2006) and leads to more attuned, more effective practice.

In RS, a commitment is made, a dedication of space, time, and trust to foster transformations that motivate and become growth—growth of providers, parents, children, and programs so that they may flourish. In the rush, rush, rush of modern daily life, many who have had RS report that they experience it as a respite, wherein the passage of time shifts to the background as the foreground emerges as a sanctuary. Taking the time seems to transform time. RS partners focus their conjoined efforts on deep human yearnings—to connect and share vital interests, to do work well, and to help others grow. Together, these aspirations coalesce and gain ascendance.

REFERENCES

Atchley, T., Hall, S., Martinez, S., & Gilkerson, L. (2009). What are the phases of the reflective supervision meeting? In S. Scott Heller & L. Gilkerson (Eds.), *A practical guide to reflective supervision* (pp. 83–98). Washington, DC: ZERO TO THREE.

Cole, E. R. (2009). Intersectionality and research in psychology. *American Psychologist, 64*(3), 170–180.

De Saint-Exupery, A. (1943). *The little prince*, Orlando, FL: Harcourt

Fenichel, E. (Ed.). (1992). *Learning through supervision and mentorship to support the development of infants, toddlers, and their families: A source book.* Washington, DC: ZERO TO THREE.

Fenichel, E. S., Eggbeer, L., & the TASK Advisory Board. (1990). *Preparing practitioners to work with infants, toddlers and their families: Issues and recommendations (four related documents) for parents, the professions, policymakers and educators and trainers.* Arlington, VA: National Center for Clinical Infant Programs.

Fonagy, P. (2001). *Attachment theory and psychoanalysis.* New York: Other Press.

Freud, S. (1958). *The standard edition of the complete psychological works of Sigmund Freud: Firmulations on the two principles of mental functioning* (Vol. XII). London: The Hogarth Press.

Freud, S. (1964). *The standard edition of the complete psychological works of Sigmund Freud: Formulations on the two principles of mental functioning* (Vol. XII). London: The Hogarth Press and the Institute of Psycho-Analysis.

Galinsky, E. (1981). *Between generations: The six stages of parenthood* (pp. 30–47). New York: Times Books.

Gilkerson, L., & Shahmoon-Shanok, R. (2000). Relationships for growth: Cultivating reflective practice in infant, toddler, and preschool programs. In J. D. Osofsky & H. Fitzgerald (Eds.), *The WAIMH handbook of infant mental health* (pp. 33–79). New York: Wiley.

Greenspan, S. (1992). *Infancy and early childhood: The practice of clinical assessment and intervention with emotional and developmental challenges.* Madison, CT: International Universities Press.

Hammerstein II, O., & Rodgers, R. (1959). "Do-Re-Mi" [Sung by J. Andrews]. *The sound of music:* Williamson Music Co.

Hanh, T. N. (2007, Summer). *International Deep Memory Association Newsletter, 2,* pp. 1–40.

Heffron, M. C. (2005). Reflective supervision in infant, toddler and preschool work. In K. M. Finello (Ed.), *Handbook of training and practice in infant and preschool mental health* (pp. 114–136). San Francisco: Jossey-Bass.

Kegan, R. (1982). *The evolving self: Problem and process in human development.* Cambridge, MA: Harvard University Press.

Keyes, A. W., Cavanaugh, A. E., & Scott Heller, S. (2009). How do I, as a reflective supervisor, repair ruptures in the supervisory relationship? In S. Scott Heller & L. Gilkerson (Eds.), *A practical guide to reflective supervision* (pp. 99–119). Washington, DC: ZERO TO THREE.

Mayes, L. C. (2002). Parental preoccupation and prenatal mental health. *Zero to Three, 22*(6), 4–9.

Merriam-Webster's new collegiate dictionary. (7th ed.). (1963). Springfield, MA: Merriam Webster.

O'Donohue, J. (1997). *Anam cara: A book of Celtic wisdom.* New York: Harper Collins.

Pawl, J. (1995). On supervision. In R. Shahmooon-Shanok, L. Gilkerson, L. Eggbeer, & E. Fenichel (Eds.), *Reflective supervision: A relationship for learning* (pp. 41–49). Washington, DC: ZERO TO THREE.

Rothschild, B., & Rand, M. (2006). *The psychology of compassion fatigue and vicarious trauma: Help for the helper (self-care for managing burnout and stress).* New York: W.W. Norton.

Senge, P. (1990). *The fifth discipline: The art and practice of the learning organization.* New York: Doubleday.

Shahmoon-Shanok, R. (1991). The supervisory relationship: Integrator, resource and guide. *Zero to Three, 12*(2), 16–19.

Shahmoon-Shanok, R. (1997). Giving back future's promise: Working resourcefully with parents of children who have severe disorders of relating and communicating. *Zero to Three, 17*(5), 37–49.

Shahmoon-Shanok, R. (2000a). Infant mental health perspectives on peer play psychotherapy for symptomatic, at-risk, and disordered young children. In J. O. Osofsky & H. Fitzgerald (Eds.), *WAIMH handbook of infant mental health* (Vol. 4, pp. 197–253). New York: Wiley.

Shahmoon-Shanok, R. (2000b). *The action is in the interaction: Clinical practice guidelines for work with parents of children with developmental and learning disorders* (pp. 333–371). Bethesda, MD: Interdisciplinary Council on Developmental and Learning Disorders.

Shahmoon-Shanok, R. (2006). Reflective supervision for an integrated model: What, why and how? In G. M. Foley & J. D. Hochman (Eds.), *Mental health in early intervention: Achieving unity in principles and practice* (pp. 343–381). Baltimore: Brookes.

Shahmoon-Shanok, R., Gilkerson, L., Eggbeer, L., & Fenichel, E. (1995). Reflective supervision. In Shahmoon-Shanok, R., Gilkerson, L., Eggbeer, L., & Fenichel, E. (Eds.) *Reflective supervision: A relationship for learning: Discussion guide* (pp. 7–15). Washington, DC: ZERO TO THREE.

Shahmoon-Shanok, R., Henderson, D., Grellong, B., & Foley, B. (2006). Preparation for practice in an integrated model: The magic is in the mix. In G. M. Foley & J. D. Hochman (Eds.), *Mental health in early intervention: Achieving unity in principles and practice* (pp. 383–422). Baltimore: Brookes.

Shahmoon-Shanok, R., Lapidus, C., Grant, M., Halpern, E., & Lamb-Parker, F. (2005). Apprenticeship, transformational enterprise, and the ripple effect: Transferring knowledge to improve programs serving young children and their families. In K. M. Finello (Ed.), *Handbook of training and practice in infant and preschool mental health* (pp. 453–486). San Francisco: Jossey-Bass.

Siegel, D. J., & Hartzell, M. (2003). *Parenting from the inside out.* New York: Jeremy P. Tarcher/Penguin.

Slade, A. (2002). Keeping the baby in mind. *Zero to Three, 22*(6), 10–16.

Sroufe, L. A., Egeland, B., Carlson, E., & Collins, W. A. (2005). *The development of the person: The Minnesota study of risk and adaptation from birth to adulthood.* New York: Guilford Press.

Stitt, S. (2009, February). *Work with a challenging client.* Remarks made as a panelist at interdivisional training, Jewish Board of Family and Children's Services, New York.

Toomey, M. (2004, June). *What is leadership? Create, listen, sustain, and develop.* Rowe Leadership Program. Rowe, MA: Rowe Camp and Conference Center.

Wagner, D. (2002). *Life as a daymaker.* San Diego, CA.: Jodere Group, Inc.

Weatherston, D. J., & Barron, C. (2009). What does a reflective supervisory relationship look like? In S. Scott Heller & L. Gilkerson (Eds.), *A practical guide to reflective supervision* (pp. 63–82). Washington, DC: ZERO TO THREE.

Reflective Tool 1

Ten Questions to Foster Your Journey Toward Self-Reflection

Self- and other-awareness are essential to thoughtful practice. By being asked questions or asking them of ourselves, such interpersonal intelligence grows. Felicitously, such inquiry also promotes calmness and focus. These are questions that one can ask of oneself or may also be asked in by peers who trust one another.

1. **What does it feel like to be in this situation?**

2. **With whom do I identify in this family?**

3. **Does this case press any "hot buttons" for me? Is there an emotional trigger in this for me?**

   - Thinking about differences as well as similarities often reveals some hot buttons.

4. **What are my perspectives, assumptions, and frames and how might they be making an impact on my choices around treatment goals and strategies?**

5. **Do I think I should play a particular role in this situation?**

   - In other words, what expectations do I have for myself (as a teacher, social worker, home visitor, or the like) with this case?

   - What other roles could I assume and other ways could I be?

   - How would it change my work with the family to shift my role and way of being?

   - How might the experience shift for the family?

6. **How do I explain the child's/family's/other professional's behavior?**

   - What are alternative explanations for the behaviors in question?

7. **How might the process occurring between me and my agency or supervisor be reflected in the process between me and the parent, and be reflected in the process between the parent and child?**

   - Could this question be asked in the other direction, too?

8. **Given who I am, what do I bring to this family?**

   - How might I be influencing or having an impact upon this family in ways not at first apparent?

   - What hidden assumptions might I be working under in this case?

9. **What might I be taking for granted in this case?**

10. **How might I be getting in my own way with this case?**

CHAPTER 2

How Do I Develop an Implementation Plan to Begin Reflective Supervision in My Program?

Sherryl Scott Heller

Change has a considerable psychological impact on the human mind.
To the fearful it is threatening because it means that things may get worse.
To the hopeful it is encouraging because things may get better.
To the confident it is inspiring because the challenge exists to make things better.

—*King Whitney, Jr., President, Personnel Laboratory, Inc.*
quoted by Wall Street Journal, June 1967

Developing your implementation plan is a little like going to eat at a buffet: Some people choose a lot of one or two items, others sample a little of everything, and some people choose to skip the buffet altogether. None of these approaches is necessarily right or wrong. In launching reflective supervision (RS), you want to choose the strategies that best fit your program. In this chapter, we describe (a) how to organize the planning process, (b) how to determine the key features of the RS model, and (c) what to consider when designing an RS program for your organization. By the end of the chapter, you will be able to:

1. Identify a coordinator and organize a planning committee.

2. Develop an implementation plan.

3. Use Reflective Tool 2 to help you evaluate your implementation plan at different stages and from different staff perspectives.

PROGRAM CONDITIONS

Because the addition of RS is a systems intervention, you have the best opportunity to bring change when the system is in relative balance and when communication is reasonably open. Some of the characteristics that you want to have in place before implementing RS are relatively open communication, staff members who feel like they can voice their opinions and concerns to administration, and administrators who feel like staff are invested and committed to the mission of the organization. It may sound that to launch RS you already need to be a healthy functioning organization. To a certain extent, this is true. However, some level of distrust exists in many organizations—the key is to get a handle on the degree of distrust and how it impacts communication within the organization. If your program is in a period of major disequilibrium, if there is a significant degree of mistrust, or if the decision makers are not supportive of RS, then this may not be the time to implement RS program-wide.

If there is a significant lack of trust, it is important for the program to work on improving it before you attempt to implement RS. This may mean bringing in a consultant to work on systems issues, implementing RS at a slower pace, holding question and answer sessions with staff to address their concerns about the purpose of RS, or holding team-building sessions. If these issues are not addressed prior to RS, then the RS sessions have a tendency to turn into gripe sessions as opposed to focusing on enhancing professional development. It is important to point out that one can always begin to use the principles of RS in your own practice, as a provider or a supervisor of providers.

In addition to a relatively healthy organization you, as an administrator, need to have a clear idea as to your own goals for RS and how you think implementation will impact staff. Much of this will become clear in the discovery phase (see Boris & Grabert, this volume, p. 41, for in-depth discussion of the discovery phase). However, it is good to review a few key questions before moving forward in the implementation phase (see box Ten Questions for Leaders to Foster Implementation).

Ten Questions for Leaders to Foster Implementation

This set of questions is for leaders to help you contemplate implementation of reflective supervision (RS) in your program and to jump-start it once you have begun to go ahead. For example, it could be a way to help you think about how to focus a presentation to staff on RS and its benefits and purposes within your setting. Consider the following queries:

1. In your own words, describe the mission of your program.
2. Briefly describe RS and its purposes.
3. How do you see RS supporting your agency's mission?
4. What benefits do you hope RS will provide your program?
5. What benefits do you hope RS will provide for your staff?
6. What challenges will need to be addressed in the implementation of RS in your program?
7. What fears or concerns do you have about implementing RS in your program?
8. What fears or concerns do you think your staff will have?
9. What are the first steps you want to take to move this forward in your program?
10. What are you looking forward to when RS gets under way within your agency?

—*Sherryl Scott Heller with Rebecca Shahmoon-Shanok*

PACING IMPLEMENTATION

Implementation of RS needs to go at a "just right" pace so it can be absorbed into the work of all the parties involved. The press to rush to implementation is typically related to limited resources and time (especially in nonprofit organizations), a fear of staff resistance, a desire to improve services as quickly as possible, or an expectation that slowly introducing RS will require too much energy and resources. These types of pressures often lead to the misconception that implementing RS quickly will save money and time. Unfortunately, this approach often backfires and the implementation becomes even more burdensome then anticipated; thus reinforcing everyone's fears of and resistance to change. On the other

How Do I Develop an Implementation Plan to Begin
Reflective Supervision in My Program?

27

hand, spending too much time planning can frustrate everybody involved, and that will, in turn, negatively affect the success of the project. In the next several sections, we provide some steps to ensure a steady pace of implementation (neither too slow nor too fast).

Identify a Key Person

To maintain communication with staff, and adhere to a reasonable timeline, it is helpful to identify a staff member or individual who is responsible for the RS implementation. An essential aspect of this person's role is to be the energy that moves this process forward—implementing projects that support staff development often gets sidelined when client or organization crises arise. As she will be central to the success of implementation, it is very helpful if this person has some experience with reflective processes so that she will be able to model reflective process and collaborative decision making. In other words, the person should:

- Be skilled at active listening (as described in Boris & Grabert, this volume, p. 41)
- Incorporate staff suggestions (when appropriate)
- Be able to mediate, support, and model healthy conflict resolution (Parlakian & Seibel, 2001)
- Possess the leadership skills to move the process forward
- Have the full support of the decision makers or is one of the decision makers

Form a Planning Committee

The role of the planning committee is to review the information collected in the discovery phase (Boris & Grabert, this volume, p. 41) and to use it along with committee members' own knowledge of the organization and staff to determine how to best integrate RS into the program, including how to introduce it to staff, the policy for participation, and the specifics of what the RS program will look like (Reflective Tool 2 at the end of this chapter lists the kind of questions the committee will need to consider).

If you have a smaller organization in which staff members have the time to meet as a group, you can involve your entire staff in the process of plan development. However, if yours is a larger organization, this may not be an option. In that case, it is useful to form a committee to focus on the incorporation of RS into your organization. It is important to ensure that all levels of your organization are represented within this committee, and if there are multiple sites, that each site is represented. Staff members who tend to be the spokesperson in the discovery phase focus group are often ideal for this role. Remember this is not necessarily the most outspoken person but rather the one who seems connected to the others and trusted by them to represent their perspectives. For example, in the focus group transcript presented in chapter 3 (Boris & Grabert, this volume, p. 41), Karen would be a good candidate to consider for this role: She speaks up, yet also responds to and thinks of other staff members' perspectives. In that same transcript, LaKeisha is also outspoken, however, she tends to represent her own point of view and get stuck on her own agenda. Although she may be seen as a leader she is not one that necessarily represents the perspectives of everyone, especially when their opinions are different from hers, and probably would not be the best candidate to be a committee member.

Develop a Timeline

Consider your resources (financial and personnel) when developing a timeline. Select goals that are both doable and sustainable. Staff members and administration should agree that the timeline (for implementing and maintaining) is realistic. For example, the RS training of managers will occur within 6 months, and then the managers will receive RS for 6 months before beginning to provide it; the committee will meet again in 8 months to discuss how the plan is progressing and plan the next phase; and the individual leading the RS program will have introduced RS and active listening to the staff at trainings throughout the year (see Costa & Sullivan, this volume, p. 149, for activities to use). It is useful for this committee to come together on a regular basis to discuss not only the implementation but also the maintenance and growth of the RS program (see Heller, Jazefowicz, Redmond, & Weinstock, 2004, for an example of how three Early Head Start programs at three different stages of RS implementation/ maintenance use a mental health consultant to support their RS program's growth and development).

Create a Formal Way to Solicit Staff Involvement

This committee should continue to seek input from the larger group of staff throughout the implementation process (Norman-Murch & Ward, 1999). Some of this information will be gathered during the discovery phase as discussed in chapter 3 (Boris & Grabert, this volume, p. 41). If you need additional information, it is advisable to obtain staff members' opinions in a formal as opposed to an informal manner (i.e., catching someone in the hallway or lunch room). By soliciting staff's opinion in a formal manner you are (a) validating the importance of this new program plan, (b) reinforcing the importance of staff input to the organization, and (c) increasing staff buy-in and minimizing staff resistance to the impending change. It is also important to keep the staff informed about the timeline and implementation plan (and keep them updated on progress and changes in the timeline). This can be done via memos, newsletters, or staff meetings. You can distribute a short survey (with a checklist of options for each item) for staff members to fill out anonymously. Be sure to leave space for additional comments, and set a deadline for the forms to be returned. You might also talk with staff members periodically about their experiences with RS and ask their opinions on changes under consideration.

Review Lessons Learned From Discovery Interviews and Focus Group

Here you can present the feedback gathered during the discovery phase and then discuss how to incorporate this feedback into the implementation plan (see Boris & Grabert, this volume, p. 41, for an in-depth discussion of the discovery phase). For example, one topic raised by the participants in the focus group transcript from chapter 3 (Boris & Grabert, this volume, p. 41) was frustration regarding the current level of supervision. Some participants felt that the current supervisors had too many other duties to provide adequate supervision, others said the focus of supervision was on paperwork rather than on what happened in the classroom, and some of the newer teachers wanted more supervision. How these important issues will be addressed in and with RS would be important to discuss not only with the committee but also with the current supervisors and the future RS supervisors.

Develop the Implementation Plan

There are a number of questions to consider when developing an RS protocol that best fits your organization's needs. It is important to keep in mind the tenets of RS as well as the unique needs of your organization and staff members when developing your protocol.

How often should RS occur? As with many of the decisions related to RS, the answer is often dependent upon or limited by the resources available. The key is to provide RS at a frequency in which it is consistent and productive.

Regular schedule. It is essential that RS happens regularly and in a predictable manner (Fenichel, 1992). Participants come to depend on the occurrence of RS and will hold topics or decisions until they get a chance to reflect on them in a session. It is disruptive to the reflective process to have two sessions occur a week apart and then another a month later, or to leave a session unsure of when the next session will occur. Approaching it from a more theoretical perspective, providing RS irregularly or unpredictably or both, is not adhering to the platinum rule ("Do unto others as you would have others do unto others"; Pawl, 1995, p. 43) and breaks the contract of safety. Predictability and regularity in regard to home visits, therapy sessions, or child care are essential to good service provision. This is also true of RS sessions. Typically RS sessions should not occur more often than once a week. Reflection and introspection are taxing, and participants need time and space to process what was discussed during the RS session. Conversely, meeting less often than once a month limits the impact of RS and can be detrimental to maintaining a solid rapport. Ideally, RS should occur weekly or every other week.

Predictability. The partner of regularity is predictability. Staff members need to know not only how often RS will occur, but also when it will occur. It is not a good idea for managers to catch staff members in the hallway and suggest an RS session that afternoon. The supervisor's goal may be to be sure that sessions occur weekly (regularly) but not necessarily at a scheduled time (predictability). This unpredictability is detrimental to the process of RS. Predictability allows the recipient to choose which issues she or he wishes to reflect upon and to prepare to process reflectively—a behavior that a frontline staff member typically does not have the time and luxury to perform. Of course, informal or as-needed reflective sessions can be very helpful for staff members; however, they should not occur in lieu of scheduled sessions.

Length of individual sessions. One rule of thumb is that the further apart in time sessions are scheduled, the longer each individual session should last. For example, weekly sessions can last 45 to 60 minutes, whereas monthly sessions may need to last closer to 90 minutes. When sessions occur too far apart, the tendency is to spend a lot of time reporting facts as opposed to processing interactions, behaviors, and responses. For group RS, longer sessions can be helpful in order to allow everyone the opportunity to participate.

Staff and client characteristics. It is important to take into consideration the characteristics of both your staff and clients when determining how often to schedule RS sessions.

Staff experience level is a factor to take into consideration. Ideally, all staff should have weekly, individual supervision available to them. However, because of resource availability, the schedule may need to be less frequent. One criterion to consider when determining the schedule is experience. Experience here includes experience within the field as well as experience with reflective processing and supervision. A more experienced individual may do well with bimonthly or monthly sessions, whereas a less experienced individual may need the intensity of weekly sessions. If resources are tight, you might provide a new employee with 6 months of weekly sessions before shifting to a bimonthly schedule used by the rest of the staff.

Also, take into account the population your organization serves when you decide on session frequency. If your organization works with a population that is difficult to serve (i.e., hard to engage, limited resources, trauma-exposed), then staff members may require more frequent sessions to decrease burnout or turnover. Another example is a population whose needs change seasonally (e.g., school or migrant population). In this instance, staff members may need more frequent sessions at certain times of the year than others. If this is the case, then plan the shift in RS session frequency ahead of time and discuss it with all staff members.

Who Should Provide the RS?

Some organizations have the direct supervisors provide RS, whereas other organizations use mental health staff members or external mental health consultants to provide RS. Typically, the overall goal is to have the direct supervisors provide the RS in order to enhance the relationship between staff and management, to support the development of a relationship-based or reflective organization, or to reflect what the budget will allow (see Bertacchi & Gilkerson, this volume, p. 121, for a discussion on how to handle the dual roles of being a reflective supervisor and a direct supervisor). As with many of life's journeys, the path to this destination differs for each individual or organization—and the final destination may be revised along the way.

Some managers and administrators may feel that they do not have the skills to provide RS. This is especially true when they have not received any type of RS themselves. One approach is to provide the managers or administrators with RS for a set period of time (e.g., 6 months) from someone who has experience providing it. After this trial period, the planning committee should feel more confident in discussing RS and how to incorporate it into the organization.

It is at this point that shifting some of the RS responsibilities to internal staff may be more realistic. However, it is important to respond to any fear or insecurities your management staff may have about providing RS. In some instances, a manager may not have the skills or traits necessary to provide quality RS. If this is the case, then allowing this person to do so can be detrimental to the staff at many levels (see Bertacchi & Gilkerson, this volume, p. 121, for more details about the qualities important for a reflective supervisor).

Finding an experienced external provider is not always an easy task. In addition to the characteristic or traits described in chapter 7 (Bertacchi & Gilkerson, this volume, p. 121), there are professional qualifications to consider. At a minimum a reflective supervisor should have:

HOW DO I DEVELOP AN IMPLEMENTATION PLAN TO BEGIN
REFLECTIVE SUPERVISION IN MY PROGRAM?

31

- Training and experience in some area of mental health, preferably infant and early childhood mental health.

- Worked with the population your organization serves and with organizations similar to your own.

- Experience and training in providing RS.

Unfortunately, having these qualifications does not always ensure a qualified provider. For example, one of the best reflective supervisors that I had the good fortune of supervising did not have a mental health degree. Thus, keeping an open mind is important. (See box Interviewing Reflective Supervisor Candidates for items to use when interviewing potential reflective supervisors.)

Finding a professional within your community with these qualifications can be difficult. One solution is to contract with a consultant who is not local to provide distance supervision. The consultant should come on-site to conduct in-service training on RS to your staff and then provide RS to select personnel via the phone (see box The Pros and Cons of RS Over the Phone).

Interviewing Reflective Supervisor Candidates

Along with the basic inquiries regarding experience providing reflective supervision (RS) and experience working within settings similar to your organization, it is helpful to get a sense of an applicant's reflective capacity. You want to get a sense of the individual's ability in the following areas:

1. Provide thoughtful support as opposed to problem solving; that is his ability to sit back, observe, and try to help the supervisee understand a situation fully as opposed to responding as "the expert."
One way to get an idea of this is to provide vignettes of issues from your program and ask the applicant how he would respond to this in an RS session. For example, you could provide the candidate with the following vignette:

> **In a reflective session, a teacher states that she has a child in her class who will not sleep when he is supposed to sleep. This child has just moved up to the 2-year-old classroom and did not exhibit this behavior in the prior classroom. How would you respond to this teacher?**

Responses will be varied. However, you do want the applicant to demonstrate some of the following processing abilities:

- Consider multiple contexts, such as what is going on at home or how the setup in this classroom is different from the prior classroom.

- Consider multiple relationships—for example, what the prior teacher did to get the child to sleep or what his parents do to get him to sleep.

- Inquire about the meaning of this behavior, and child, to the teacher, asking about (a) how the teacher has dealt with this type of behavior in the past, (b) how this child's behavior is affecting the class, or (c) what this means to the teacher (e.g., child is manipulative or spoiled).

- Probe the teacher about her thoughts on solutions, and wonder about the possibility of using other specific solutions—for example, the candidate would say something such as "I wonder what would happen if the child napped in the younger class for a while" or "I wonder what would happen if you rocked the child to sleep?"

2. Demonstrate an ability to be reflective regarding his own professional experiences. As indicated above, you want to get a sense of the applicant's thought process. Providing open-ended questions is a good way to assess this. Some possible probes are as follows:

- Tell me about the most difficult client you have had to work with, why he or she was so difficult, and how you handled it. Would you handle it differently now?

- Tell me about the most difficult person you had to supervise, why it was so difficult, and how you handled it. Would you handle it differently now?

- Tell me about your favorite supervisor (reflective supervisor if he or she had one). Why was this person your favorite?

3. Has some background or experience in RS. Prior experience providing or receiving reflective supervision is not an absolute necessity, but it is certainly preferred. Here are some suggestions as to probes regarding prior experience with RS. As indicated above, it is not an exhaustive list, but a sample of possible questions.

- Define RS. Here you want the applicant to demonstrate a familiarity with RS and it tenets.

- What strengths do you find in the RS model?

- What challenges do you have in implementing it? How have you addressed those challenges?

The goal is to get a sense that the applicant has experience with this model and has thought about it and provided it successfully.

Alternately, a consultant could train local infant mental health or mental health professionals as reflective supervisors and then supervise them by phone. Although not ideal, we have used this model successfully to train local reflective supervisors when shortages exist. In these instances, the consultants were provided with a packet of readings on RS (good readings for mental health professionals include Fenichel, 1992; Gilkerson & Shahmoon-Shanok, 2000; Heffron, 2005; Heffron, Ivins, & Weston, 2005). This was followed by phone consultation on RS and its implementation at the given organization. Once it was clear that the local consultant grasped the essential features of RS, then the consultant began to provide RS to staff while receiving RS herself on a regular basis, depending upon how often she provided RS. In some cases, she received RS weekly; in other cases, she was provided with RS twice a month.

The Pros and Cons of RS Over the Phone

There are many similarities between phone and face-to-face RS sessions; however, there are some subtle differences. During phone RS:

- Silences can be difficult to interpret as there is no cueing from facial expressions or body language.

- It is difficult to be sure that the sessions are occurring in a quiet and secluded spot, free of interruptions.

- It usually takes more time to develop a comfortable pace in regard to turn-taking so that the facilitator and participant are not interrupting each other.

- It is more important to attend to tone of voice, changes in pace of speech, and speech volume as there are no cues from facial expression or body language.

- The facilitator needs to become more dependent on the use of her speech as a facilitation tool because both facial expression and body language are not available.

- Miscues and misinterpretations are more likely on either end of the line.

The facilitator can help by:

- Including an inquiry about the participant's level of privacy with the standard start-up questions (e.g., How's your week going?).

How Do I Develop an Implementation Plan to Begin
Reflective Supervision in My Program?

33

- Inquire directly when unsure about the speaker's intent or affect and ask the participant to do the same. Set it up as part of the features of phone supervision. Some examples are:

    - "You are being silent. Tell me what that means? Are you not agreeing or are you processing?"

    - "I hear a change in your voice. I am wondering if this line of inquiry is frustrating you?" Or "Boy, you sound really excited about ..."

- Inquire about changes in environmental sounds, remembering that if the person is being overheard he may prefer Yes/No inquiries.

- Give the participant permission to clarify your silences, tones, or background noises.

Phone RS has definite advantages (i.e., scheduling sessions is easier as both people don't have to be in the same location or same city) and can be just as beneficial and rewarding as face-to-face sessions.

What Format Should We Use for RS?

It is important to consider feedback from your staff and RS provider, just as it is with many of the other decisions discussed in this chapter. In addition to staff preferences, it is also important to take into consideration the realities of finances (What can your organization afford?) and geography (Is your provider local?).

Group versus individual. Not all staff members should or need to receive the same type of RS, nor do all staff members have to receive only one type of RS. Determining what format is the most useful (and realistic) for staff is usually a process that is revamped or enhanced over time given staff input and changes in the organization's and staff members' needs. The options are many. For example, everyone can receive one type (individual or group), the format each staff member receives can depend upon different factors (i.e., role in organization or level of experience), or individuals may participate in both formats (individual and group). When deciding whether to use group or individual RS sessions at your site, you should consider the following:

- *Resources:* Can your organization's budget cover the cost of individual sessions? Can your organization provide staff coverage during RS (especially with group RS sessions)?

- *Staff role:* If there are a large number of people who fill a specific role, they may benefit from reflecting together as a group, or if you have multiple sites where one group (e.g., director or case manager) may benefit by coming together regularly.

- *Level of reflective experience:* Typically, individuals with less education have less experience with reflective process as a form of professional development. For these persons, starting RS in a group format may be less intimidating, whereas individuals with extensive reflective experience may benefit from a peer-facilitated group.

- *Time and resource constraints:* Is there a time the staff or groups of the staff meet regularly that could include RS? You can schedule group RS during staff meetings, but be sure to set clear boundaries so that it is not pushed aside because of administrative issues (see Fenichel & Eggbeer, 1992; Norman-Murch, 2005, for suggestions on how to handle this dilemma).

Phone versus face-to-face. Ideally, RS is provided face-to-face. However, this is not always a viable option. Phone RS is a reasonable option when using individual supervision (see box The Pros and Cons of RS Over the Phone). For this type of RS to work, it is helpful for the facilitator and participant to have had contact prior to starting phone sessions. Ideally the two know each other. However if this is the first interaction between them, then it is best to try to hold at least a couple of sessions face-to-face. Familiarity with each other or with RS eases the transition to phone supervision. Having had prior contact with each other allows for familiarity with speaking styles and aids in interpretation of silences.

It is especially important that the RS provider be physically present in a group format if this is the first time individuals are experiencing or providing RS. It is very difficult to interpret body language, silences, or manage a group discussion via the telephone. As technology advances, providing supervision via video conferencing—where all parties see each other and can converse in real time—may become a viable option (Wajda-Johnston, Smyke, & Nagle, 2005).

When providers and supervisors have experienced RS, it is possible to provide group supervision via the phone. In this situation, it is helpful to keep the numbers small (four to six participants) and provide some type of formal format or structure. During the first group session, you can decide how to set up the format. Begin with the supervisor checking in with each participant. If there is no crisis or critical need that has to be handled, then the group can move forward. There are a number of formats that can be created. Here are a few examples:

- Each participant is given time to present a case or challenge for discussion.
- Use a case conference type structure in which one or two people are the main focus for each group (see Copa, Lucinski, Olsen,& Willenburg, 1999, for a model of reflective case presentation).
- The group selects a topic for discussion as it relates to its practice (e.g., cultural differences, working with fathers, or the importance of talking to infants).

Where Should RS Occur?

One essential feature of RS is that the session must occur in a location that provides solitude—that is, uninterrupted time and space. The purpose of RS is to allow the participant to step back from the immediate experience and process thoughts or feelings about what he is observing and doing. For this to occur, the participant needs to feel safe and unrushed. One way to support a sense of safety and the ability to step back is to ensure privacy. The participant needs to feel comfortable that his discussions will not be overheard. Interruptions should be an exception—ideally, they should not occur at all.

Interruptions can take two forms: incidental and intentional.

- *Incidental form:* The room or its contents are what the interrupter is seeking. This type of interruption usually occurs when the RS room is also used for other activities such as storage or breaks. One simple strategy in addressing this type of interruption is to place an "RS Session in Progress: Please Do Not Disturb" sign on the door of the room in use.
- *Intentional form:* It is one of the RS participants that is being sought out. This type of interruption usually occurs when a manager or administrator is one of the RS participants.

To ensure that sessions remain uninterrupted, it is important that staff members see the administration recognizing and supporting, in action and word, the importance of uninterrupted RS sessions. Your organization can emphasize the importance of uninterrupted time in many ways:

- State it in any procedural policies written about RS
- State it at meetings that introduce or discuss RS

How Do I Develop an Implementation Plan to Begin
Reflective Supervision in My Program?

35

- Model it
- Formalize recommended practices for unavoidable scheduling changes

Administration can also support RS by:

- Limiting the expectation that RS should be cancelled or interrupted for other activities such as meetings or trainings
- Providing a quiet and secluded spot for RS
- Respecting the "RS Session in Progress: Please Do Not Disturb" sign

Follow through is one of the essential ways to convey the importance of providing privacy for successful reflective processing. This is most often seen in day-to-day interactions. For example, when an administrator, who is often rushed and pressed for time, needs to contact a staff member, she should not request that an RS session be interrupted. This type of request not only interrupts the current session but also gives the message to staff that the administration does not truly support RS. "Actions speak louder than words," as they say, and staff members tend to hear administration on two levels: what is said and what is seen. Staff members tend to give more weight to the administrator's behavior, especially when it contradicts what is stated.

Should RS Be Mandatory?

RS should be required for key administrators and all direct service staff. The expectation for participation in RS should be included in the policy and procedure manual as well as in job descriptions. The individual's capacity to use RS to strengthen practice should be a component of performance appraisal. Requiring staff to participate in RS and evaluating their capacity to use RS may seem counter to the spirit of RS. However, there are ways to help staff feel safe and comfortable in participating. Typically, once staff begins the process of RS, they are amazed that the program ever existed without it.

If your program is just starting, then including RS within staff members' job descriptions makes the expectation clear from the beginning. RS can be described during the interview process, and the candidate's willingness and reflective capacity can be assessed. However, in most situations, the RS model is being introduced into an existing program. Staff attitude about RS, as in any new program feature, is largely dependent upon how it is introduced. Allowing staff or representatives of the staff to be a part of the process that develops the RS protocol helps to increase staff members' interest and willingness to participate in RS (Gilkerson & Shahmoon-Shanok, 2000; Norman-Murch, 2005; Norman-Murch & Ward, 1999). You can decrease some of your staff's hesitance by helping them see RS as a tool that supports their professional development, and that enhances the services the organization provides. This process is something that should start in the discovery phase (see Boris & Grabert, this volume, p. 41, for more details). You can explore with the individual his feelings about RS and listen with acceptance. You can shape the sessions in the beginning to focus on areas in which he is most comfortable using supervision (e.g., planning lessons for individual children or problem-solving around parents). You can also go slowly, gradually adding staff to the RS system. You can ask staff regularly for feedback on the process and work on increasing the goodness of fit between the supervisee and supervisor match.

Is RS Necessary for the Supervisors?

It is not an absolute requirement that the facilitators receive RS. However, the process is much better when this level of supervision is integrated into the model (Parlakian, 2001). Providing the supervisor with an opportunity to slow down and process the interaction and emotional climate of the reflective sessions, especially group sessions, enhances the facilitator's ability to provide a calm setting and gentle probing. One of the most challenging aspects of RS is holding the anxiety and negative affect of the participants in order to allow them the space to process through their affect to the situation being discussed (Norman-Murch, 2005). Furthermore, supervisory structure acts as a form of parallel process; that is, the supervisor of the RS facilitator provides the same nurturing space that the facilitator, in turn, provides the staff. Thus, the model is enhanced at the verbal level via the discussions between the supervisor and facilitator, and at the experiential level via the provision of a safe and calming space in which to contemplate the emotional context of the reflective sessions (Gilkerson & Shahmoon-Shanok, 2000; Pawl, 1995; Pflieger, 2002).

SUMMARY

Any programmatic change produces significant and varied responses in staff members, as is captured by King Whitney, Jr.'s quote at the beginning of this chapter. Although it is important to ensure that the RS provided by your program is high quality (topics covered in chapters 4 to 7 of this book), it is just as essential to plan how to introduce and structure that change to best meet the unique needs of your organization. Often the focus of program change is on the outcome or impact of the change (i.e., improved organizational functioning or enhanced client services) and not much time is spent on the planning stages (i.e., discovery phase and implementation plan) or on matching the important aspects of the change to the needs of the program's staff. In this chapter and in chapter 3 (Boris & Grabert, this volume, p. 41), the authors argue that the implementation and planning phases are not only important but also essential aspects to be attended to if any programmatic change is going to be successful, specifically the implementation of RS. For RS to be successfully implemented, it must be individualized to meet the needs of the program and of the participants.

How Do I Develop an Implementation Plan to Begin
Reflective Supervision in My Program?

37

REFERENCES

Bertacchi, J., & Gilkerson, L. (2009). How can administrative and reflective supervision be combined? In S. Scott Heller & L. Gilkerson (Eds.), *A practical guide to reflective supervision* (pp. 121–134). Washington, DC: ZERO TO THREE.

Boris, N. W., & Grabert, J. C. (2009). How do I introduce reflective supervision to my program? In S. Scott Heller & L. Gilkerson (Eds.), *A practical guide to reflective supervision* (pp. 41–61). Washington, DC: ZERO TO THREE.

Copa, A., Lucinski, L., Olsen, E., & Willenburg, K. (1999). Promoting professional and organizational development: A reflective practice model. *Zero to Three, 20*(1), 3–9.

Costa, G., & Sullivan, L. (2009). What staff development activities can be used to build reflective capacity? In S. Scott Heller & L. Gilkerson (Eds.), *A practical guide to reflective supervision* (pp. 149–181). Washington, DC: ZERO TO THREE.

Fenichel, E. (1992). *Learning through supervision and mentorship to support the development of infants and toddlers and their families: A source book.* Washington, DC: ZERO TO THREE.

Fenichel, E., & Eggbeer, L. (1992). Overcoming reflective obstacles to reflective supervision and mentorship. In E. Fenichel (Ed.), *Learning through supervision and mentorship to support the development of infants and toddlers and their families: A source book* (pp. 18–26). Washington, DC: ZERO TO THREE.

Gilkerson, L., & Shahmoon-Shanok, R. (2000). Relationships for growth: Cultivating reflective practice in infant, toddler and preschool programs. In J. Osofsky & H. Fitzgerald (Eds.), *WAIMH handbook of infant mental health: Early intervention, evaluation and assessment* (Vol. 2, pp. 33–79). New York: Wiley.

Heffron, M. C. (2005). Reflective supervision in infant, toddler and preschool work. In K. M. Finello (Ed.), *The handbook of training and practice in infant and preschool mental health* (pp. 114–136). San Francisco: Jossey-Bass.

Heffron, M. C., Ivins, B., & Weston, D. R. (2005). Finding an authentic voice. Use of self: Essential learning processes for relationship based work. *Infants & Young Children, 18*(4), 323–336.

Heller, S. S., Jazefowicz, F., Redmond, R., & Weinstock, J. (2004). Starting where the program is: Three infant mental health consultants discuss reflective practice. *Zero to Three, 24*(6), 10–19.

Norman-Murch, T. (2005). Keeping our balance on a slippery slope: Training and supporting infant/family specialists within an organizational context. *Infants & Young Children, 18*(4), 308–322.

Norman-Murch, T., & Ward, G. (1999). First steps in establishing reflective practice and supervision: Organizational issues and strategies. *Zero to Three, 20*(1), 10–14.

Parlakian, R. (2001). *Look, listen, and learn: Reflective supervision and relationship-based work.* Washington, DC: ZERO TO THREE.

Parlakian, R., & Seibel, M. L. (2001). *Being in charge: Reflective leadership in infant/family programs.* Washington, DC: ZERO TO THREE.

Pawl, J. (1995). On supervision. In R. Shahmoon-Shanok, L. Gilkerson, L. Eggbeer, & E. Fenichel (Eds.), *Reflective supervision: A relationship for learning* (pp. 41–49). Washington, DC: ZERO TO THREE.

Pflieger, J. (2002). Reflective supervision. *Head Start Bulletin, 73,* 31–36.

Wajda-Johnston, V., Smyke, A., & Nagle, G. (2005). Using technology as a training, supervision, and consultation aid. In K. M. Finello (Ed.), *The handbook of training and practice in infant and preschool mental health* (pp. 357–374). San Francisco: Jossey-Bass.

Reflective Tool 2

Reflective Supervision Implementation Process Plan

Reflective Tool 2 is meant to be used as a worksheet to guide you, as the person responsible for developing the reflective supervision (RS) protocol for your program, through the development and implementation phases. The first two rows (Organizational Level and Staff Level) contain items that will be answered during the discovery phase (see Boris & Grabert, this volume, p. 41); these are yes/no questions. When you answer no to any of the items, it is important that you address that item before continuing. The next three rows (RS Preparation, RS Program and Format, and RS Supervisors) provide you with items to consider as you fine tune the RS protocol to best meet your organization's needs and realities. The final row (RS Continuity) presents questions regarding evaluation of the RS program by the staff within your organization.

		QUESTIONS	CHECKLIST

AREAS OF IMPLENTATION	Organizational Level	• **Is your organization ready to implement RS?**	• Does the administration support the philosophy of RS?
			• Is the administration willing to commit resources to RS?
			  — Monetary, for example, pay for someone to provide RS.
			  — Staff time, for example, allow staff to participate during work hours.
			• Is there a moderate level of trust between staff and administration?
			• What individual within your organization is willing to take on the oversight, implementation, and maintenance of RS?

	Staff Level	• **Does the staff know what RS is?**	• Have you provided brief readings to the staff (e.g., Pflieger, 2002)? • Have you presented a brief overview of RS to the staff allowing and encouraging questions and discussion? • Have you created an RS committee that represents all roles within your organization (ideally these are volunteers from the staff)?

	Preparation	• **What should the committee think about first?**	• Who is going to receive RS (e.g., everyone or management only)?
			• What is a reasonable timeline?
			  — How will the rollout look (e.g., does everyone begin RS at the same time or do some groups get it first and others later)?
			• How will different individuals/groups respond to RS:
			  — Who will welcome RS and be eager to participate?
			  — Who will be more cautious and need time/support?
			  — Who might find this objectionable?
			• How can the staff's views be heard?
			• What kind of support will be needed for those who are cautious or object to RS?

continued

		QUESTIONS	CHECKLIST
AREAS OF IMPLENTATION	**RS Program and Format**	• **What is our RS program going to look like?**	• Will we use individual RS? If yes, have you: — Created a list of recipients? — Determined who will provide RS to whom? • Will you use a group format? If yes, have you: — Created a list of who will receive it? — Decided how groups will be formed (e.g., by role)? — Decided who will provide group RS? — Determined who will provide coverage for staff while in RS? • Will anyone receive both formats? If yes, have you: — Created a list of who will receive both formats? — For each format and session have you: – Decided which session will be phone, face-to-face, or a combination? – Determined how often the sessions will occur? • Decided where the sessions will occur?
	RS Supervisors	• **What about the RS supervisors?**	• Who will provide RS? (The following list is from the least to most costly.) Is there someone: — On our staff who has the training and availability to provide RS? — In the community who has the training and availability to provide RS? — Who can train our staff to provide RS as a consultant? • How will we support our supervisors? — Will they receive RS? If yes, – How often? – Who will provide it?
	RS Continuity	• **How is RS going?**	• When will staff have the opportunity to provide feedback about RS? — How often will this opportunity be provided (e.g., annually, monthly)? • What form will these feedback sessions take? — Occur during staff meetings? — Occur via anonymous surveys? • What did staff report? • Does the staff feel RS is helpful? — Do they like the: – Format? – Supervisor? – Frequency? • Do they feel the need for any changes? If yes, what? • How does the staff feel about options currently under consideration? • How is your organization going to incorporate the staff's feedback?

CHAPTER 3

HOW DO I INTRODUCE REFLECTIVE SUPERVISION TO MY PROGRAM?

Neil W. Boris and John C. Grabert

Listening creates a holy silence. When you listen generously to people they can hear truth in themselves, often for the first time.

—*Rachel Naomi Remen (1996, p. 220)*

Now that you have a basic understanding of reflective supervision (RS) and the implementation process, the next step is to develop a deeper understanding of your organization's current level of readiness for participating in RS. We call this the "discovery phase." What is learned in the discovery phase is important to guiding decision making during the implementation phase discussed in chapter 2 (Scott Heller, this volume, p. 25). During the discovery phase, two key components to a successful implementation occur: (a) you learn through exploration and clarification about the organizational climate and current views of administrators and frontline providers about supervision and their readiness to make change, and (b) staff find out through firsthand experience through individual or group discussions what the reflective process is. The understandings gained in the discovery phase will guide you in the planning and implementation stages (see Scott Heller, this volume, p. 25). This chapter provides you with a conceptual framework for the discovery phase and a practical guide to active listening. By the end of the chapter, you will be able to:

1. Define and describe the skills used in active listening.

2. Understand the role of active listening in assessing your program's readiness to implement RS.

3. Use Reflective Tool 3 as a guide to structure and conduct a discovery focus group.

DISCOVERY PHASE: LEARNING THROUGH LISTENING

The word *reflect*, at least as applied to reflective practice, means "to think, ponder or meditate" (*The American Heritage Stedman's Medical Dictionary*, n.d.). You might ask, "But who has the time?" Most early childhood programs face limited budgets, experience high client loads, and serve highly stressed families. Permitting program directors or frontline personnel time to reflect would appear to be a luxury that no one can afford. However, as stated in chapter 1 of this volume (Shamoon-Shanok, this volume, p. 7), RS is an investment. The ultimate goal of RS is to help early childhood programs provide high-quality services in a supportive environment while maintaining qualified staff; RS is a tool for enhancing professional practice through ongoing support.

Let's assume that you have been asked to develop the protocol to bring RS into an early childhood program either as a consultant or as a staff member already in the organization. Your program (or the program to which you are consulting) is already convinced that RS is worth the investment of resources. Now you ask yourself, How do I begin?

The first part of the answer to this question is that you begin by listening. Listening is an important component of the reflective process. As will become clear, the kind of listening you'll use is about learning through exploration and clarification; whereas listening is essential to the creation of a reflective environment, it is only one of many important components. For listening to be truly reflective in nature it needs to support the construction of a caring environment (Shamoon-Shanook, this volume, p. 7) and investigative thinking (Shamoon-Shanook, this volume, p. 7) which can only be done in a climate of respect and trust. Thus, a reflective relationship cannot be developed overnight or after one sitting.

For early childhood programs, everything is delivered through relationships. A reflective supervisor's job is to create sincere positive relationships that beget sincere positive relationships. RS allows you, as a supervisor, to model the importance of positive relationships. From the beginning, you need to understand the challenges to creating and sustaining positive relationships that exist in the program you will be serving.

For example, consider Michelle, a woman with an associate's degree in child care entering her first job at an early childhood program as a home visitor. In her first month on the job, Michelle is charged with working with a young, stressed mother and her 6-month-old infant. If Michelle wants to help the mother cope with her stress and understand her baby's needs, she will need to spend some time creating a common understanding with this mother. You would hope Michelle would be trained to use empathy and education in equal measure, to read the mother's signals, and to learn about the mother's world. However, if Michelle is to grow in her job and become a highly skilled home visitor, then many things within the program will need to be in place for her. She will likely need the support and direction of more experienced colleagues or perhaps the encouragement of the program director. If she senses the mission of her program is to enhance her own learning and development, then she will get more from trainings meant to develop her skills. If she is empowered instead of overwhelmed, she will develop rather than retreat. What will empower her most is a web of caring relationships at work—a program with just enough support to lift her up when the going gets tough. In the discovery phase, you will want to meet Michelle and understand the degree to which the program is currently lifting her up. You will also want to listen to her supervisor, her program director, and her colleagues.

Listening

There is a Turkish proverb that reflective supervisors find useful: "If talking is silver, then listening is gold." It is not that talking is not valuable; it is that listening can be more valuable. Careful, thoughtful, and empathic listening is the foundation of reflective supervision. Silence isn't the same as listening. Many people consider listening to be nothing more than hearing someone say something. The kind of listening used in RS is called "active listening." *Active listening* is a term that encompasses more than hearing what is said. In fact, active listening involves understanding another person's perspective through empathic inquiry.

In the discovery phase, active listening is a precursor to the development of a reflective relationship. Whereas active listening is an important component to RS, it is not the whole of RS; it is the starting point of the reflective relationship. In the discovery phase, active listening aids you in enhancing your understanding of staff members' readiness for RS. In addition it introduces staff members' to the experience of being listened to (and heard). But for active listening to be truly reflective in nature it needs to occur within a climate of trust, respect, and empathy. In this section the techniques or behavioral components of active listening are described; using them in an empathic manner is demonstrated in the vignette at the end of this chapter.

The core components and associated skills include the following: (a) inviting dialogue through the use of questions, (b) promoting shared understanding by paraphrasing, (c) discovering feelings, and (d) moving dialogue forward by summarizing and prioritizing (Grabert, 2009). These same components, summarized in Table 3.1, will guide your assessment process with the organization and the individualized encounters with staff.

Table 3.1. Communicating Through Active Listening

COMMUNICATION COMPONENTS	COMMUNICATION SKILLS
Inviting dialogue	Asking open-ended questions Asking closed-ended questions (when appropriate, typically for clarification purposes)
Promoting shared understanding	Paraphrasing to acknowledge, clarify, and check accuracy
Discovering feelings	Acknowledging feelings expressed Eliciting feelings Identifying feelings not expressed
Moving the dialogue forward	Summarizing and synthesizing information Prioritizing information

Inviting Dialogue

Inviting dialogue involves the use of single open-ended questions to encourage the respondent to tell a story. For instance, you will want to know about the degree to which frontline personnel trust administration, the nature of current supervision, or the availability of supervisors. Open-ended questions are the broadband approach; they invite dialogue. Table 3.2 provides a few examples of general (open-ended) versus specific closed-ended questions.

Table 3.2. Examples of Questions That Promote and Inhibit Dialogue

PROMOTES DIALOGUE	INHIBITS DIALOGUE
How is supervision provided to you in this program?	How often is supervision provided to you in this program?
What are the ways that staff communicate with the program director at this site?	Is the program director regularly available to speak with you when you have questions?
What kind of support do you receive to address challenging families?	Do you ever have challenging families?
What's going well in your program? What are the challenges currently in your work?	Is the nature of your work stressful?

Promoting Shared Understanding

Promoting shared understanding involves paraphrasing, which is restating key phrases to acknowledge information is being heard. Paraphrasing serves as an opportunity for clarification and is a strategy for checking understanding. It allows staff an opportunity to provide you with corrective information about inadvertent mistakes in listening or from false assumptions. When you are interacting with staff, you want to be sure they know you understand and are really interested in what they have to say. Here is where closed-ended questions are useful in the discovery process. The box So What You Are Saying Is That . . . lists some examples of using paraphrasing and closed-ended questions for promoting shared understanding.

> **So What You Are Saying Is That . . .**
> - Although you like the idea of RS, you don't think there is enough time to meet regularly?
> - Your staff has varying levels of experience and you wonder how RS can be successfully applied when they have different skill levels?
> - You think that some of the staff who have worked here longest may be the least receptive to any kind of change?
> - You are wondering how RS works across so many disciplines?

Discovering Feelings

Discovering feelings focuses on the affective part of the message shared, which includes acknowledging feelings expressed, eliciting feelings not readily stated, and identifying feelings associated or embedded in content. Labeling feelings can be complex, especially when trying to interject a feeling that is not readily expressed. This is like listening closely to a song to hear the tones accompanying the words.

Discovering feelings requires that you be alert to nonverbal communication. Often this is about reading clusters of signals. For instance, if a frontline staff member averts her eyes, sighs, and crosses her legs as a discussion of trust in the organization is opening up, then you will want to find a new opening to suggest that the topic of trust is one that brings up emotions for many people and then ask her about her own feelings. If you are a skilled interviewer, you are probably used to seamlessly interpreting nonverbal signals already. Regardless of your skill level it is a good idea to read about nonverbal communication in preparation for leading RS sessions—capturing nonverbal communication is just that important. Developing relationships is about internal experience (how people feel and think)—your own as well as others. Nonverbal signals give you an "external" clue about where you may want to explore more, with openness, curiosity, and a willingness to be surprised.

Attending to other's body language is only part of the process; you must also be aware of the message you are sending with your own body language. A smile or leaning in toward a speaker can be reassuring and communicate to the speaker that you are listening and interested in what is being said. Whereas looking at your notes or sitting with your arms folded can relay the message that you are uninterested or disagree with what the speaker is saying. Just as open-ended questions are important to promoting dialogue, so is your own body language.

Discovering feelings is not all about nonverbal cues. Often enough feelings will come up directly, and you will want to create an opening to hear more about those feelings. The box It Appears to Me That . . . lists statements or questions that exemplify the kind of "reflecting back" that is at the core of RS and can be especially powerful with the attuned body language.

It Appears to Me That . . .

- You have been *worried* for several months that your most experienced staff member wants to leave the program, and you think it might be due to burnout (you pause and look toward group for confirmation or clarification).

- You look *perplexed* by the questions I am asking (you pause and lean forward with an inquisitive expression).

- Even though you have not said it, can it be that you are *nervous* about talking about your recent supervisory experience (you pause and look toward the group with inquisitive look)?

- You are *upset* with the way children who show aggressive behaviors are managed at this center (you pause and look toward the group for confirmation or clarification).

Moving the Dialogue Forward

Moving the dialogue forward involves summarizing and synthesizing chunks of information to facilitate discussion. It allows one to create a sense of closure for one piece or several pieces of information. Summarizing also helps everyone stay on topic. As you will be focusing on perceptions of barriers to creating and maintaining positive relationships in the program, making sure you understand each person's perspective by clarifying or summarizing is important. It can also be helpful to prioritize; it is useful to know if there are discrepancies in what's viewed as the most important issues facing the program. In fact, creating a list of issues or topics that come up as you assess a program and speak to those who work there is valuable (see the box So What You Are Saying Is . . . for examples of these types of statements).

So What You Are Saying Is . . .

- You have seen a good deal of staff turnover in the past 3 years and that makes your job more difficult because there is not enough staff continuity.

- You think RS is a good idea, but you are not sure that there will be administrative support for the time needed because other suggestions have been made in the past without follow-through.

- You think that this is a great time to introduce RS because there is a new team forming, and you are already looking for ways to better manage challenges that present themselves.

If you have been asked to provide RS in a program, it is likely you already use these communication skills. On the other hand, making a concerted effort to build your active listening skills is important. In fact, we recommend role-playing a session with a colleague as a way of preparing for meeting with a program director or frontline staff member. The more you develop these basic communication skills, the more you will make program personnel feel understood and valued. Feeling understood builds trust, and trust is the oil in the engine of reflective practice.

In the prior section we reviewed the importance of active listening to the discovery process as well as the two-way nature of nonverbal communication. Whereas these are important skills, it is essential to remember that the various skills and techniques described do not by themselves create a reflective environment.

THINKING ABOUT THE "PORT OF ENTRY"

The purpose of the first set of meetings is to better understand the climate of the agency. Your goal is to begin to understand staff relationships with each other and with their clients, and how these relationships influence staff member's level of reflective functioning. Understanding these factors will guide the decision-making process regarding the RS implementation plan. One factor to consider as you prepare for discovery phase meetings is the "port of entry" through which you have come into the organization. Although the core features of RS would not change based on whether you are an outside consultant or a program insider, you will need to be aware of the advantages and disadvantages associated with each situation.

Outside Consultant

As outside consultant, you have the advantage of not having prior relationships with the administration or frontline staff. Your fresh perspective on ways to collaborate between administrative and frontline personnel can be beneficial. You can generate new ideas without being confined by preconceived system limitations or internal conflicts. On the other hand, you do not know the individual history or "ghosts" of the organization. Furthermore, staff might be suspicious about an "outsider" who may be perceived as being brought in because work needs improvement. As an outsider, you need to guard against being perceived as an instrument of the program director. You will need to take more time to explain the goals of your work and to build trust with each employee. You will want to talk about your own background and about what motivated you to be a reflective supervisor, and to tailor this discussion to each level of employee you work with.

Current Staff Member

As insider or current staff member, you have the advantage of having a sense of the dynamics of relationships in the program and the challenges the program faces. You might know only too well that there are tensions between some staff members and may have experienced firsthand the resistance or hostility that can flare up between colleagues. Having a sense of these fault lines will help you as you listen and probe for understanding. On the other hand, you may have the disadvantage of being viewed by some with resentment for being "promoted" to reflective supervisor. You may even experience the change in roles as a loss in some ways. You will need to guard against accepting the job without negotiating for the kind of support you will need to do the work well. If you are being asked to add the job of being reflective supervisor to your responsibilities without adequate time or training, then it is likely you will not be successful. It can be difficult to negotiate a "new position" with someone who is already your boss; this is especially true if your program director has gotten a mandate to add RS without really understanding why it might help the program and what it takes to do the job well. Listen carefully to what the program director is hoping for and be sure to generate shared understanding about what you will need to do the work. When you meet with colleagues, spend time up front describing your new role and understanding their perceptions about the supervision they already receive. Whether you come from inside or outside the organization, you will need to approach the discovery phase in an organized fashion. It is important to start at the top with the program director, but you will also need to meet with middle managers and frontline personnel on the way to formalizing RS in the program.

FROM THE TOP TO THE FRONT LINES

Early childhood programs have quite varying organizational structures. Typically, though, there is someone in charge of day-to-day operations, a person familiar with how the program functions and who works with personnel at all levels. This is the person to meet with first as you begin the discovery phase. Even if someone in upper management has approached you about provision of RS, it is critical to understand the perspective of the program director about how his or her program functions. Chapter 1 in this volume (Shamoon-Shanok, p. 7) can help you define RS and describe its benefits for the organization.

Program Director

In the initial meeting with a program director, you will be beginning to understand the program well enough to gauge organizational commitment to your work. A helpful place to start is to talk about the program's stated mission. If you can, write the mission statement down before you meet with the program director and bring a copy to the meeting. Remember that your overarching goal is to help the program create and sustain nurturing relationships, be it within the organization or with the clientele. For now, you need to understand what challenges the program faces that affect relationships at any level.

Your initial meeting with the program director should include a dialogue focused on understanding program function from the director's viewpoint and where she sees RS fitting. You will need to take enough time to understand the program director's point of view and to generate support to begin to assess other employees at various levels of the program.

Middle Manager and Frontline Personnel

Once you have met with the program director, you will want to meet with middle managers and frontline personnel to gather more data on program functioning. It is important that the program director actively support you in organizing these meetings. Having the program director explain who you are and why you are meeting with staff ahead of time is important. If you are not an external consultant but rather a current employee of the organization, it is important to have the director clarify to the staff that your role at the organization has shifted and that you will now be responsible for both the creation and monitoring of an RS program in your program. It is not critical to meet with one group before another, nor is it essential to conduct individual rather than group meetings; there are benefits and challenges to each approach. However, if you are going to hold group meetings, then you should have some familiarity with how to conduct focus groups.

Goal of a Focus Group

The goal of focus groups is to elicit opinions in an organized fashion from a group, typically six to eight individuals at a time. A good guide to designing and moderating focus groups (Morgan, Krueger, & King, 1998) is essential for those with limited experience leading focus groups. You will find that preparing for a focus group will reinforce some of the principles reviewed in this chapter: Good focus groups require active listening and careful attention to laying out questions that are open-ended. Focus groups offer a chance to build up knowledge through facilitating exchange among members of a group. In fact, focus groups are not only efficient (because you can meet with eight people in the time it takes to meet with one or two), but they also offer staff a chance to reflect on what others are saying, which often leads to new insight and deeper discussion. On the other hand, conducting the groups requires some skill, particularly in making sure that everyone feels comfortable enough to disagree and debate. Furthermore, it is difficult to attend to what is being said while monitoring nonverbal signals and thinking of when and how to probe for more information. In other words, conducting focus groups alone can be overwhelming at first. It is a good idea to consider audiotaping the group for review or asking a colleague to join you and take notes. In either instance, you will need to explain carefully to the group at the outset what you plan to do with the information. Free exchange comes with trust, and building trust in groups requires taking the time at the outset to give participants a sense of who you are and how you wish to help them. If you have the program director introduce you in a positive way, you should carefully prepare an introduction for the group, as well as have a strategy for exploring themes as they develop. The focus groups will then give you a wealth of information and save you some time. Reflective Tool 3, provided at the end of this chapter, contains sample items to use when holding a focus group.

Positive First Impression

Whether you choose to use group meetings or individual ones, the way you introduce yourself is important. Aside from arriving on time and greeting people warmly, you need to start out by clearly laying out the goals of the discovery phase in a positive way. For example, "I am here to observe and talk with staff to determine how we can build on the good work currently being done here." You need to communicate by action and words that everyone is vital to the organization; one way to do this is to show sincere interest in all staff members—from the person answering phones, to the bus drivers, to the program staff, to the executive director. Respect for individuals is a theme at the core of RS. By introducing yourself to everyone you meet and by learning something about who they are and the role they play in the organization, you are underscoring respect. It has been said that a fundamental principle for reflective supervisors is to "do unto others as you would have others do unto others" (Pawl & St. John, 1998, p. 7).

Define RS

Once you have started with introductions, it is time to shift into active listening mode. Especially early on, you want to answer questions directly about who you are and what RS is. Defining how RS is different from other types of supervision that managers or frontline staff may have had can be challenging. Start with finding out what staff know about RS, as well as their thoughts about how RS might fit into their current work and their schedules. Everyone knows that change of any kind tends to elicit reactions. Introducing this new process might bring about excitement for those thinking about professional growth, natural hesitation to those who may not be informed about this form of supervision, and resistance from others who might even present barriers that block or cloud your momentum. Be prepared to educate the staff with handouts or publications (see box An Introduction to Reflective Supervision for a brief handout describing RS) that describe RS.

Listen and Model: Accept People Where They Are

The discovery phase is about listening and modeling, not about guiding and intervening. In this phase it is important to accept people where they are. Accepting the staff where they are may be difficult, but remember that staff members' reactions are well grounded in beliefs and previous experiences. Inquire about their earlier and current supervisory experiences. Be open and curious to their thoughts. Do not dismiss or provide glib reassurance to concerns they express. Do not judge and do not advise. Instead, you want to understand, affirm, and support their interest. You want to role model the very skills that you ultimately want them to learn.

Make Culture a Topic

As you develop trusting relationships with staff by eliciting and defining their perspectives, you will need to look for openings to talk about issues like race, class, and culture. Although race, class, and culture are sensitive issues, the power of RS can only be unleashed when staff members sense that talking about sensitive issues is acceptable. In some programs, cultural diversity is embraced; whereas in others, the ways in which cultural issues play a role in the organization are not talked about or are only given lip service.

An Introduction to RS

As defined by Shahmoon-Shanok, "RS is a collaborative relationship for professional growth that improves program quality and practice by cherishing strengths and partnering around vulnerabilities to generate growth" (2009, p. 8). But what exactly does that mean? Why is it important? How is that going to happen here?

These are the questions many people new to reflective supervision ask, some excitedly and others more warily. This handout will help clarify the whats and whys, however, the hows are specific to each organization. Although there are central elements and characteristics of RS that are essential, there are also features that are flexible (i.e., who, when, and where).

What Is RS and Why Is It Important? RS . . .

- Is the practice of staff members meeting regularly with an experienced supervisor to discuss their experiences, thoughts, and feelings related to their work.

- Is a place where critical judgment is suspended so that staff are supported to explore their thoughts and feelings related to the challenging work with young children and families.

- Enhances staff members' professional growth and personal discovery.

- Involves thinking about how relationships affect the ability of an organization to meet its mission and to provide quality care to children and families.

- Focuses on relationships and solutions to challenges that come up in serving parents and young children, such as:

  – Dealing with burnout

  – How emotions impact your work

  – Celebrating successes

  – Addressing challenges in the relationship between staff and families served by the program

  – Building teamwork among staff members

  – How administration and staff communicate

RS Has Three Central Elements[1]

- *Regularity*: An established and consistent time/day and routine for meetings that are protected from unwanted interruptions; these meeting can occur individually or in a group.

- *Reflection*: Establishing a trusting relationship among participants to foster reflection or thinking out loud about emerging work challenges.

- *Collaboration*: Listening, asking questions that promote personal reflection, being supportive and nurturing, and being emotionally open to talking with others.

—Neil W. Boris and John C. Grabert with Sherryl Scott Heller

---

[1]*Fenichel, E. (Ed.). (1992). Learning through supervision and mentorship to support the development of infants, toddlers, and their families: A source book. Washington, DC: ZERO TO THREE.*

Listen for What Is Said and Not Said

As the focus group facilitator, it is important that you are aware of how issues such as race, class, and culture may be influencing individual's responses. Oftentimes when cultural diversity is an issue, it is unsaid and thus may not come up in a discussion. However, if you notice, for example, that all of the African American staff members have offices in the back of the building, this may be a topic to raise for discussion. Or perhaps you find that when you speak to the frontline staff they imply that everything is fine and that they have no issues, yet not much more is said. It may indicate that there are indeed class, or role, differences, and the frontline staff does not feel safe or empowered enough to speak about these issues.

Although these are not the first topics to raise, the discovery phase is not complete until you open topics like race, class, and culture for discussion. Not only should you consider the impact of culture within an organization, but you also should ask questions to determine how staff members think their cultural background plays a role in their work with clients. For example, you should ask how differences in race or class influence relationships with families or how differences in staff backgrounds are used as an asset in their work with clients. By being forthright and open, you are both modeling openness and probing areas in which unspoken attitudes or pockets of resentment may exist.

Resist the Urge to "Fix" During Discovery Phase

Remember your job is not to suggest a "fix" to these issues. In fact, often the most difficult part of RS is resisting the urge to talk about solutions when topics that bring up powerful emotions are touched upon. For now, in the discovery phase, it is enough to say things such as: "It sounds like you think that there are times when people with different backgrounds aren't given the same kind of respect in this program. This is a tough issue, and your willingness to talk about it today means a lot." As there is a natural tendency to avoid topics that are loaded, noting when issues like race, class, and culture are opened up is important. The next section is a focus group sample transcript. This transcript provides an example of using active listening skills to learn about an organization as well as the importance of beginning the discussion of RS and its purpose early.

HOW TO ORGANIZE AND LEAD A DISCOVERY FOCUS GROUP

A discovery focus group with staff covers five key areas: (a) introductions, (b) mission of organization, (c) definition of RS, (d) invitation to share experiences about supervision, and (e) exploration of the group's experience with change.

The following transcript is from a focus group with seven teachers at a medium-sized early child care program serving inner-city children birth to 4 years old. The group facilitator's job is to start the process of discovery as smoothly as possible. Joanna, the group facilitator, is an outside consultant who has worked at a sister agency. She was invited to this organization by its director to help bring an RS program to the center. The respondents had been excused from their classrooms to meet with Joanna. She arranged the chairs in a circle, and all but one person scheduled to be in the meeting have arrived and are seated. Recognizing that it is 5 minutes past the hour, Joanna decides to begin:

• • •

Open With Introductions

Joanna (facilitator): "Good morning, why don't we get started? First, let me thank you all for coming this morning. I'd like to start out by letting you know more about who I am and why Ms. Kennedy [*program director*] has asked you to meet with me. I know we're expecting one more of your colleagues, I expect she'll be here soon, and since the goal this morning is to have some open conversation about this program, she'll have plenty of chances to add to the discussion. I've met most of you, but if you're like me, remembering names takes a few, or more than a few, repetitions. I'm Joanna Stemps, and I started out in this field about 15 years ago as an early childhood educator. After several interesting and challenging years as a preschool teacher, I went back to school for my master's in social work and have since worked in one way or another as a supervisor or manager at programs like this one. It's been a real joy for me to start doing consulting work as a reflective supervisor. I started working as a reflective supervisor about 3 years ago, and it's in that capacity that I come here today. I'm hoping to learn more about your program because Ms. Kennedy is interested in starting RS here as well. I'm guessing some of you know something about RS, and I hope to have a chance to talk about what RS is in a minute. But it'd help me to start off by having each of you introduce yourselves and remind me what you do here and how long you've been with the organization. Who'd like to start?!"

[Pause]

Michelle: "I guess I will. I'm Michelle, and I've been a teacher here for almost 2 years—and long ones at that!"

[A few chuckles from the other teachers]

Lawana: "Yeah, but you're not a teacher, you're an early childhood specialist, remember?!"

[More laughter]

Joanna (facilitator): "Hi Michelle. I want to get back to what's made your years here long, but first let me let the rest of you introduce yourselves. Early childhood specialist is a nice title—I like it!"

Lawanna: "I'm Lawanna, and I've been here for nearly 4 years, though I took time off after my baby was born—about 2 years ago. I'm also a teacher if you don't want to use the fancy title."

The rest of the group members introduce themselves (Candace, Shelly, LaKeisha, Tanya, and Karen) as Joanna jots names on paper corresponding to a diagram of the seating arrangement she'd made up before the group. She also notes in an area on her pad the words "titles" and jots down "long years" next to Michelle's name as a reminder to get back to that comment. The final participant has arrived now and taken a seat.

Ask Group to Describe the Mission of Organization in Their Own Words

Joanna (facilitator): "Well, I've jotted down names just to help me remember you all. Ms. Kennedy told me you were an experienced group—she's right about that. Karen, thanks for coming, you missed me introducing myself, I'm Joanna and I'd like to hear more about your day-to-day work here. One way to start the conversation is to ask you about the mission of this center: How would you all describe the mission of the organization?"

[Pause]

Candace: "You mean our mission statement? It's posted in the office, isn't it?"

[Looking at her colleagues for confirmation]

Shelly: "Yeah, but I don't remember it exactly! Something about providing a learning environment, respecting differences, and other stuff."

Joanna (facilitator): "Right. Mission statements tend to be a bit lofty. If you all could put into your own words what this program is aiming at—who you serve and what the philosophy is—that'd help me get a sense of the program's mission from your perspective."

Joanna senses some hesitancy in the room as the participants tend to glance tentatively at each other when they respond. She is unclear whether this is because a focus group is something new to the group or because they are wary of her, or whether it is indicative of communication at the center. Right now she makes an effort to attend to her body language and tone to be sure she is purveying a positive and calm demeanor.

Candace: "Well, we serve poor families, and most of the moms go to school or work two jobs. We really try to not just be day care, but to give our kids a real learning environment, like it says in the statement. We have family advocates that help with job training and that kind of stuff for the families. It's a good program, and a lot of the kids come here when they're on a bottle and leave when they're out of diapers."

Shelly: "Yeah, but some of the families don't act like they see us as anything but babysitters!"

LaKeisha: "I don't feel like a babysitter. My kids spend more time with me than some of them do with their mommas . . . see we get a lot of young ladies here who don't always know how to be raising kids. Yeah, they work and everything, but it's the grandmas that raise the kids mostly and some of the mommas march in here like they all that when they don't spend enough time with their kids from what I see."

Joanna (facilitator): "I hear you all saying a few things that are important: The first is that part of the mission of this program is to provide a learning environment for the children and to go beyond that and really provide services to the whole family. Most of the children you serve come from low-income families, it sounds like, and many of their parents share caregiving with one or more of the child's grandparents. You work with babies until they are almost ready for school, so by definition you are in the business of shaping young children's brains! But it sounds like there are times when Shelly feels like she's seen as a babysitter. LaKeisha even feels like some of the parents can be judgmental toward you all. I'd like to hear from some more of you if I've heard things correctly so far."

Lawana: "Keisha's just mad 'cause she got the two meanest mommas!"

[Laughter]

Joanna (facilitator): "I sure remember a few tough moms—that can be exhausting—and it can be easy to lose sight of the program's mission when parents are challenging."

LaKeisha: "No, see, I do my job. They can be trifling, but they not gonna make me change my game."

Lawana: "Keisha, wait 'til Ms. Kennedy hears that you been calling people trifling!"

Tanya: "Lawana, who's gonna tell Ms. Kennedy, you? See, I'm being quiet until someone tells me why we are talking about all this. I don't know anything about reflecting supervision, and I feel like we spend enough time in supervision already. Are we supposed to be having regular meetings like this in groups now, too?"

Restate Confidentiality

Joanna (facilitator): "You raise a couple of key issues, Tanya. I apologize for not being clear about what RS is. In a moment, I'll send around a handout I've made that we can discuss to get into RS a bit more. I'm glad you jumped in here, and I get the sense that since you don't know me very well and don't have a good sense of what this meeting is about that you're not sure you want to talk openly. I can understand that! First, let me say that I made it clear to Ms. Kennedy that I would not be reporting back to her who said what at this meeting. I think it is very important to protect everyone's confidentiality here and would ask that each of you respect each other's confidentiality as well."

Confidentiality was discussed with the staff prior to participating in the focus group. However, it is not unusual for staff to lack clarity about confidentiality, thus it is often worthwhile to repeat.

Joanna (facilitator): "My goal today is pretty simple—to learn more about you all and this program as a way to begin the process of designing a plan for RS here. Neither Ms. Kennedy nor I are sure yet what would work best in terms of that plan, Tanya. Too much supervision is like too much of anything else. For me in my career, the biggest issue has been about quality of supervision. And it wasn't until I learned about RS through being supervised this way when I was a teacher that I really got into it."

Karen: "Don't mind Tanya, Ms. Stemps, she don't trust no one." *[Laughter, Joanna notices that Tanya is laughing as well.]* "Plus, Ms. Kennedy treats us right mostly anyway. I'm okay with more supervision, but I don't want to have to stay later than we do already for it, I know that much. I think our program is one of the best ones around here. Us teachers need more breaks, and they never should have gotten rid of the floater like they did, but I got a friend who works not too far from here and I would much rather be at our program. It's true that some of the young moms we deal with here got a chip on their shoulder, but some of 'em come from families where there's too much chaos. I never thought of it before, but maybe that's one reason why the mission statement here has that line about respect in it, 'cause I do believe we're trying to teach some of our families about respect." *[The facilitator makes a note that this staff member seems to be a leader or spokesperson for the group.]*

Joanna (facilitator): "As far as I'm concerned, trust is earned and since Tanya doesn't know me, I feel like I know where's she's coming from. You just said something else interesting, too, Karen. That part about how maybe the mission statement has something in it about respect because giving respect can be an issue for families who experience a lot of chaos. I know when I was a teacher for a program serving high-risk kids, a lot of times it seemed like it was the parents that I worked the hardest to gain their respect, that I ended up having the closest relationship to over time. It seemed like they respected me more in the end than I ever thought, but boy, for some I can remember, that was one long hill to climb."

Joanna was aware that this was more personal information than a facilitator typically provides. However, she felt that she needed to help some of the respondents, especially Tanya, feel more comfortable with her.

Michelle: "Yeah, and I haven't reached the top of the hill with most of mine . . ."

Candace: ". . . and I got some who ain't even ready to climb." *[Laughter]*

Define RS

Joanna (facilitator): "Right, and how do you get a parent who sees you as a babysitter and maybe also sees their 3-year-old as a troublemaker, or even worse, well how do you get them to start climbing—to start respecting and learning from you? Or to see their son or daughter in a different way? Turns out that RS is about finding a way to answer questions like these. The tough questions—the ones that exhaust you at the end of the day. I guess I should give you all this handout now. At the top, you'll see that RS is really a tool for what is called "professional development." I suppose that's why you all are called early childhood specialists—you're professionals and so you get the title to go with it. Why don't you all take a minute to look over the handout now?"

[Silence as the group looks at the handout. As heads raise from reading, Joanna begins again.]

Explore What Current Supervision Is Like

Joanna (facilitator): "Now, I know that there is a supervisory system here already. I'm wondering if the kinds of challenges you've talked about in the last 10 minutes—from trust in the organization to dealing with parents who view you as babysitters—come up for you in supervision."

LaKeisha: "Not for me. We mostly talk about how to deal with the kids better. Like I have a biter right now—he's almost gonna be kicked out 'cause he won't stop. He's started 3 months ago, and it hasn't stopped yet. Ms. Robinson *[assistant director at the center]* been working with me on trying to get him in time out before he goes to biting again. But he's smart and he does it mostly when I'm dealing with somethin' else. Then she also reminds me to change the learning materials in the room and how to manage the kids in the hallway, stuff like that. I ain't worried about trust 'cause I know if I do my job, everything will be all right and when the mommas of my kids 'dis' *[disrespect]* me, I pretty much ignore it."

Tanya: "You need to get that boy's momma to work with you on the biting—I heard her laughing about it the other day when they was walking out."

LaKeisha: "Yeah, but she don't take anything serious, and that's why he's such a mess."

Joanna (facilitator): "Sounds to me like just the kind of situation that supervision was created for. You've got a tough problem with that little boy, toddlers who bite are always a challenge, and if his momma is really not taking it seriously, then it might be an even tougher problem to solve. Ms. Robinson has lots of experience. Do each of you feel like your supervisors are available enough to support you when you need them?"

Candace: "We can try to call for help when we need somebody for a kid with a problem, but it ain't like our supervisors are around for stuff anytime—they got work to do, too. They need to tell that boy's momma that the next time he bites, he's going home for the day—then she's gonna start to take it seriously!"

Michelle: "I don't get to talk to my supervisor more than once a week when she comes to my building to meet with me and Rita. But I'm always asking other people for advice because I've only been doing this for 2 years now. I wouldn't know what to do with a kid who kept on biting for months like that!"

Joanna (facilitator): "Michelle, I used to have a teacher tell me that the biggest paradox about teaching is that you don't learn how to do it in school. You learn how to do it when you start working. I remember you said your first 2 years have been long ones—I think most people find that to be true! So what about those of you who've been around longer, what's your experience with supervision been like over time?"

Karen: "For me, supervision is mostly just talking 'bout what's going on with the kids and stuff. I can see from this paper here how what you're talking about is different I guess. I got put on the training committee last year because I been complaining that we need more good trainings around here. Like talking about learning materials for the classroom—that should be in a training at the start of the year. Then you just plan out how to teach about things in creative ways by changing it up every month or so. I'm not sure how to make supervision better, but most of the supervisors I've had, they just worry about paperwork and the like. Plus, you get new ones just about every year anyway, and I've had supervisors who didn't have as much experience as me, they just went further in school. So I guess I'm saying that it could be good to try some new things."

Joanna (facilitator): "Mmm, having supervisors change so often can be really disruptive. One major goal of RS is to focus on ways to help you feel more effective as a professional. The focus is less on classroom materials or teaching approaches and more on thinking through challenges you face. So you might choose to spend time talking about how to build better connections with the mother of that biter or even better connections with your supervisors!"

Joanna senses some hesitancy in the teachers about supervision and uses this time to educate them a bit about RS and how it is different. By responding to some of the concerns that they raise she is validating their view, letting them know that she hears them, and educating them a bit on how RS can be a tool to address some of their concerns.

Karen: "I don't know. I guess, well, like I'm not one to be going for new stuff. I tend to mind my own business and just do my work. But like with that biter, it is true that you got to have the momma work with you on that. And like people have said already, some of the young ladies whose babies come here, they feel like they don't have to listen to anything. You know, Ms. Kennedy ain't going to want to kick that kid out of the program, so then it is gonna be about finding a way to get him to stop. And a lot of these kids do come in in the morning already wound up. I guess I always thought we had to deal with this stuff ourselves, and if our supervisor couldn't help or wasn't around, so be it."

Tanya: "If I have a problem like that with one of my mommas, then I'm gonna ask Ms. Connelly [one of the family advocates] to talk with her."

Candace: "But how's that going to help you, Tanya?"

Tanya: "It probably isn't gonna help me, but I ain't got the time or the patience."

Shelly: "Yeah, sometimes, to me, we have too many things we gotta worry about."

Joanna (facilitator): "Sounds like you do have a lot to worry about, lots of responsibility and more than enough challenges. It sounds like there have been limits to supervision here—and ones that I'm familiar with such as limited time with your supervisor and, if I hear you correctly, maybe even limits on what you focus on in supervision. I can't tell yet what you all think of the potential shift toward RS, but I hope we can continue to talk about this."

Exploring Change in the Organization

Joanna (facilitator): "This has been some great discussion, and it brings me to an important issue: Every organization grows and changes. I'm wondering about how you view this organization—how does growth or change happen in this program?"

Tanya: "Seems like nothing much changes around here—people come and go and that, but I stay in my classroom with my kids. Ms. Kennedy or someone might come along and tell us that we got to change our lesson plans or work without a floater, but you know that's gonna happen so you just got to deal with it."

Shelly: "Amen. You deal with it whether you want to or not."

Joanna (facilitator): "It sounds to me like Tanya and Shelly see change as something that happens to you rather than something that you get to participate in or guide. I get the sense that that can be frustrating, from what Shelly says."

Karen: "What frustrates me is new things we have to do that don't click with what we are dealing with every day. Like, we are now supposed to be filling out monthly progress reports on language and basic skills in my classroom, and then we give them to the parents. Most of the time, they get this glazed-over look when I give them the report, and then we got no time to talk about it with them anyways. So, what are the reports going to do? Besides giving me more paperwork!"

Joanna (facilitator): "Boy can I relate to that example as an ex-teacher! And your example, Karen, is again about how changes here feel like they happen to you rather than with your input."

Candace: "Since we're only the teachers, we are the low man on the totem pole. So, if something's gonna change, it's gonna change and we don't have much say."

Michelle: "I know I did put a note in our suggestion box that we should cut out the quarterly assessments if we are going to have monthly reports, and I heard from Ms. Robinson [*assistant director*] that Ms. Kennedy [*program director*] thought that was a good idea."

Candace: "You used the suggestion box, Michelle? I didn't think anything got put in there ever?!"

[*Group laughs*]

LaKeisha: "I got some more suggestions we could make! But seriously, about those monthly reports, when it came to dealing with little Malcolm who's been biting, Ms. Connelly *[family advocate]* and me met with his momma together 'cause I think one reason why he bites is 'cause nobody can understand what he wants 'cause he isn't talking yet, and he just gets so mad. So his momma said she's going to go to get him evaluated at speech and hearing, and it was the only time those sheets ever did something but drive me crazy."

Joanna (facilitator): "Wow, LaKeisha, that's a nice example of how teamwork can really make a difference. And I think Michelle's use of the suggestion box is about teamwork, too. It can be hard for program directors to really understand how change affects you all—the frontline workers. And it can seem even harder to find the time to communicate about change—about, for instance, why Ms. Kennedy thinks monthly reports are needed or about how these reports affect you. I'm struck by two things that you all have said: One is that having change happen without good communication can breed frustration. The other is that when you find new ways to communicate, that's when the real change happens and problems in the classroom can get solved. RS is about communicating ideas. My hope would be that as this organization grows and changes that your input would be a big part of what drives the change here."

Karen : "Yeah, 'cause nobody knows the families better than us."

Joanna (facilitator): "That's right, Karen, and that's exactly why I wanted to hear from you all directly—and you all have given me some very helpful insights into both strengths and challenges that your program faces."

•   •   •

Each program is different, but the types of issues brought up in this sample transcript are representative. Still, this transcript likely only represents about 15–20 minutes worth of discussion! As this transcript suggests, focus groups create opportunities to use all of the key active listening skills from inviting dialogue, to using open-ended questions and probes, to discovering feelings. Often, you will promote shared understanding by synthesizing information just presented and then move the dialogue forward with another probe. You will sometimes work around resistance, especially early in the process, and you may have the sense of the group getting stuck on issues (e.g., the discussion about the child who is a biter). Still, each issue of interest to the group can be reframed in light of one of your goals for the group. For instance, in this group, the moderator tried to have the issue of the child who was biting serve as a way of both exploring how supervision works at the site and then providing some further understanding of what makes RS different. However the facilitator, an experienced teacher and social worker, refrained from providing or suggesting any solutions beyond the use of RS. As you grow as a reflective supervisor, you will be able to use the discovery phase as not just a time for gathering information but also a time for modeling what RS is at its core. Using active listening skills and moderating a focus group by guiding and directing the discussion give you a great deal of insight into program dynamics.

You will find that the discovery phase brings up many issues, and it can be useful to give a brief oral or written summary of topics or issues that came up to the program director. The key in doing so is to protect confidentiality by not revealing specific issues or statements that might be linked to an individual. Instead, you might note how change is experienced by this group of teachers, by using the example of the monthly progress reports, and work with the program director to anticipate how best to introduce RS as a change that is embraced rather than viewed as another thing being added to the teachers' burden.

Summary

The discovery phase of RS is about learning through respectful and empathic listening. Meeting with personnel at all levels of the organization provides a foundation for the work. Ideally you start with the program director. The goal of this meeting is to review the director's understanding of RS and to dialogue about the strengths and challenges the program faces in creating and sustaining positive relationships (both among staff and between staff and families). From there, you will solicit the program director's active involvement in introducing you to middle managers and frontline staff. In meeting with middle managers and frontline staff, you will explore their understanding of RS and emphasize its role in professional growth. You will dialogue further, priming discussion with open-ended questions about the central role of supportive relationships in working with families and identifying barriers to creating and sustaining such relationships both with colleagues and families.

Being a student of active listening and learning how to conduct focus groups will serve you well as you move through the discovery phase. Role-playing with colleagues and formulating questions you would like to explore before you meet with individuals or groups are essential. Taking notes and defining themes are standard practice. Having simple and clear handouts about what RS is and who you are will help build understanding. From the very beginning, you will bring modeling into conscious awareness, respectfully engaging others is your mantra. You will open up difficult issues such as race, class, and culture both to gain important information about how these issues affect staff and as a way of making it clear that such issues are important to struggle with openly.

As your work evolves in an organization, and as sessions with staff at all levels of the organization build, the way in which RS can best serve the organization will become clearer. In the discovery phase, you will do little guiding. RS is no quick fix. However, when the three essential elements of reflective practice—regularity, reflection, and collaboration—are followed, its power to strengthen programs is realized (Fenichel, 1992). In chapter 2 (Scott Heller, this volume, p. 25), the process of structuring and implementing RS was laid out. The information you learn in the discovery phase is vital for guiding the implementation phase. Change is inevitable, and you are beginning to be an agent for changing your early childhood program through building and sustaining positive relationships.

REFERENCES

Fenichel, E. (Ed.). (1992). *Learning through supervision and mentorship to support the development of infants and toddlers, and their families: A source book.* Washington, DC: ZERO TO THREE.

Grabert, J. (2009). Integrating early childhood mental health into early intervention services. *Zero to Three, 29,* (6), 13–17.

Hill, C. (2007). *Helping skills: Facilitating exploration, insight, and action.* Washington, DC: American Psychological Association.

Morgan, D. L., Krueger, R. A., & King, J. A. (1998). *Focus group kit.* Thousand Oaks, CA: Sage.

Pawl, J., & St. John, M. (1998). *How you are is as important as what you do…in making a positive difference for infants, toddlers and their families.* Washington, DC: ZERO TO THREE.

Remen, R. N. (1996). *Kitchen table wisdom: Stories that heal.* New York: Penguin.

Scott Heller, S. (2009). How do I develop an implementation plan to begin reflective supervision in my program? In S. Scott Heller & L. Gilkerson (Eds.), *A practical guide to reflective supervision* (pp. 25–39). Washington, DC: ZERO TO THREE.

Shamoon-Shanok, R. (2009). What is reflective supervision? In S. Scott Heller & L. Gilkerson (Eds.), *A practical guide to reflective supervision* (pp. 7–23). Washington, DC: ZERO TO THREE.

The American Heritage Stedman's Medical Dictionary. (n.d.). Retrieved April 11, 2009, from http://dictionary.reference.com/browse/reflect

H O W   D O   I   I N T R O D U C E   R E F L E C T I V E   S U P E R V I S I O N
T O   M Y   P R O G R A M ?

61

Reflective Tool 3

Discovery Phase Meetings: Areas for Exploration and Sample Questions

Reflective Tool 3 lists central areas of inquiry when meeting with individuals or leading focus groups. Within each area in the table below, the information that is important for you to understand is listed along with sample questions. Although this is not an exhaustive list, it provides you with ideas on how to elicit staff members' perspectives in key areas that will impact the development and maintenance of the RS program. As you lead your focus groups or interviews, it is important to keep in mind the core components and skills associated with active listening: (a) inviting dialogue, (b) promoting shared understanding, (c) discovering feelings, and (d) moving dialogue forward (Grabert, 2009).

		INFORMATION TO COLLECT	SAMPLE QUESTIONS
AREAS OF EXPLORATION	Organization Mission and Structure	• Understand the mission of the organization and how it is perceived by staff. • Identify the organizational beliefs or values that guide staff and daily interactions with families. • Determine if there is a shared program vision among staff.	• In your own words could you tell me what the mission of your program is? • How do the mission statement or program goals guide your day-to-day activities? Tell me more about that? Could you give me examples? • How do you (or your program) communicate this mission or belief to parents and families? • How have new policies or program changes been introduced in your organization?
	Team Relationships and Supports	• Assess whether the agency supports relationship-based, reflective practices in management and staff interactions, as well as in service delivery.	• Do you consider yourself part of a team? • How does your program celebrate staff successes? • In what ways does your program support you to do your job effectively? Are there ways you would like the program to increase its support? Tell me how? • Do you feel like the program recognizes the demands of the work? Tell me more about that? • How are challenges and difficult conversations with staff managed? Can you give me an example?
	Current Supervision	• Develop a picture of how staff receives support and how supervision is currently provided across all positions in the organization.	• How are you currently supervised? Is this regularly scheduled? • What kinds of work challenges get discussed? What's the focus? • How do you get supervisory support during the day to deal with work challenges? Is that support often enough available? • How would you like to see supervision change?
	Training Opportunities	• Identify current opportunities for training, professional development, and personal development that come from the program and whether outside training is sought after.	• What kind of professional training does your program provide for staff? • Do you attend professional trainings outside of the agency? • In what areas would you like to see more training? • Do the current training opportunities meet your needs? If not, what topics would you like to see addressed?
	Reflective Supervision	• Understand knowledge and experience with RS across all levels of staff as it can relate to quality of services delivered and to professional and personal development. • This is an opportunity to educate and dispel misconceptions about RS.	• Do you know what RS is? Have you had experience with it? Could you tell me how the experience was for you? • From what you have heard about RS, as a supervisor, do you think you have the knowledge and skills to provide RS? • From what you have learned, what might get in the way of establishing regular meetings for RS?

CHAPTER 4

WHAT DOES A REFLECTIVE SUPERVISORY RELATIONSHIP LOOK LIKE?

Deborah J. Weatherston and Carla Barron

*The most basic and powerful way to connect to another person
is to listen. Just listen. Perhaps the most important thing we ever give
each other is our attention. A loving silence often has far more power
to heal and to connect than the most well-intentioned words.*

—*Rachel Naomi Remen (1996, p. 143)*

Supervision has been described in many ways. To some, it relates to administrative oversight for the purpose of reviewing paperwork, reviewing program policies, monitoring productivity, and setting goals. To others, it is a clinical meeting to review casework, develop intervention strategies, review progress, and problem solve. Although reflective supervision (RS) may incorporate administrative and clinical tasks, and also include attention to collaboration within learning relationships, its primary focus is the shared exploration of the emotional content of infant and family work as expressed in relationships between parents and infants, parents and practitioners, and supervisors and practitioners (Michigan Association for Infant Mental Health, 2007). The exploration occurs within the context of a trusting supervisory relationship that highlights strengths and partners around vulnerabilities (Shahmoon-Shanok, this volume, p. 7); it invites attention to the awakening of thoughts and feelings that occur in the presence of infants and families and lead to introspection and deeper understanding.

In this chapter, we explore what the supervisor and supervisee each bring to the supervisory relationship to better ensure a mutually satisfying partnership, the emergence of reflective capacities, and professional/personal growth. We offer strategies to support a supervisee's growing ability to expand understanding of infancy and early relationship dynamics while reflecting on the intersection of personal and professional experiences in the infant and family field. Of additional importance, we offer excerpts from reflective supervisory conversations that illustrate the dialogue that might occur at different points during the first year of a supervisory relationship.

By the end of the chapter, you will be able to:

1. Describe the actions that the supervisor will take to create a safe environment for supervision.

2. Describe the actions that the supervisee will take to ensure active participation in supervision.

3. Participate more confidently in a new and reflective supervisory relationship.

NATURE OF THE SUPERVISORY RELATIONSHIP

Mutually rewarding RS requires the construction of a secure and trusting relationship between people who have a commitment to best practice within the infant and family field and to each other (Eggbeer, Mann, & Siebel, 2007; Fenichel, 1992). Here we refer to the first person in the partnership as the supervisor and the second partner is the supervisee. Although each shares responsibility for the growth of the relationship, it is the supervisor who has primary responsibility for creating an environment in which the supervisee feels secure enough to have, as well as to explore, thoughts and feelings about her work with very young children and families and, as appropriate, about herself. The supervisee has primary responsibility for sharing what is on her mind during the supervisory hour. Together, they learn to explore what the supervisee has seen and heard, as well as the emotional content of the work. Over time, the capacity for reflection deepens as supervisor and supervisee demonstrate a willingness to be open, curious, and emotionally available to each other.

EMOTIONAL SAFETY

Emotional safety is extraordinarily important to a successful supervisory relationship. Safety allows the supervisor and supervisee to offer information, to ask questions, and to develop a shared agenda while remaining flexible. Emotionally secure in the relationship, the supervisee is able to use the supervisor as a safe base from which the supervisee is free to explore and to which the supervisee returns when frightened, vulnerable, or insecure.

The Supervisor's Role

Donald Winnicott's (1965) concept—holding—provides a concrete metaphor for the supervisor's role. By definition, holding describes the ways in which a parent supports the baby's physical and emotional needs, helping the baby to feel safe and secure, promoting confidence and trust (Weatherston, 2001). With Winnicott's concept in mind, the reflective supervisor establishes a routine, agrees to meet regularly with the supervisee, at a certain time and in a certain place, with few to no interruptions. The supervisor, like Winnicott's "good enough" parent, remains emotionally available to the supervisee and listens very carefully. Fully attentive to the supervisee for the supervisory hour, the supervisor sends a powerful message: "You are most important right now. You will get all of my attention." Emotionally present, the supervisor creates a context in which the practitioner feels protected and safe. He follows the supervisee's lead, attending to verbal and nonverbal cues, listening closely, offering affirmation, offering guidance, if appropriate, an empathic response, or a combination of these. Available and invested, the supervisor serves as a continuing source of support for the supervisee. He offers reassurance and praise, as appropriate, building the supervisee's confidence in responding to an infant and family's needs. These characteristic behaviors are particularly important to establishing a basis for mutual trust.

The attributes listed in Table 4.1 lead to a trusting relationship in which both the supervisor and supervisee may have and express thoughts and feelings to one another about the work of infant and early childhood and, as appropriate, about themselves. Although the relationship is a collaborative one, it is important to keep in mind that the supervisor has the primary responsibility to hold and contain the

Table 4.1. Supervisor Attributes That Support the Development of a Safe Holding Environment

ATTRIBUTES	MESSAGE TO SUPERVISEE
Safety	I will accept what you have to tell me. I will listen carefully and respond as I am able. I will set limits for you that are clear, firm, and fair. I will be available if you need me.
Consistency	I will explain the work as I understand it and respond to you with care and concern. If something is not clear to me, I will ask you to tell me a little more.
Dependability	If we have scheduled a meeting, I will make every effort to be there when I said I would be there. I will try to let you know where you can find me or when I am going to be away.
Respect/ Confidentiality	I will accept you and all that you tell me. I won't be judgmental. I will keep what you tell me between us and not share it with others without your permission.
Honesty	I will be open with you. I will let you know when I think things are going well for you and for the families you are working with. I will also let you know when I have concerns.

emotional content of the supervisee's reflections and experiences. The task is a challenging one for most supervisors whose own thoughts and feelings are awakened while listening closely and containing the emotional content of others.

The Supervisee's Role

Although the supervisor sets the tone for the developing reflective supervisory relationship, the supervisee is not without responsibilities. The supervisee's observations, ideas, feelings, and worries provide the essence for the reflective conversation. This requires a certain amount of trust that the supervisor will follow the supervisee's lead, which is to listen and value what is offered. For both, but particularly for the supervisee, it is a courageous step and requires a leap of faith that the supervisor can be trusted.

Supervisees come into this relationship with a variety of educational, work, cultural, therapeutic, and supervisory experiences. They also come with expectations about what RS means to them and what they might need from a supervisor. It is essential that the supervisee enters into the supervisory relationship with an open mind: that is, (a) open to meeting regularly, open to talking about her work, (b) open to responses from the supervisor, and (c) open to identifying what it feels like to be with vulnerable infants, young children, and families. The conversation may not come easily, and it may not come immediately. However, learning to stay open to the emotional content as part of every supervisory meeting will open the door to reflection and deeper meaning. The box Supervisee's Tasks That Guide Entry Into a Reflective Supervisory Relationship offers suggestions for attitudes/actions that a supervisee should bring/take in the supervisory relationship.

Supervisee's Tasks That Guide Entry Into a Reflective Supervisory Relationship

TASK	BEHAVIOR
• Allow your supervisor to support you through consistent supervisory meetings.	• I will come on time, prepared to share detailed observations, thoughts, feelings, and concerns.
• Explore the relationship of your feelings to the work you are doing.	• I will be open to becoming aware of my feelings as they relate to what I see and do.
• Think more deeply about your work with infants, young children, and families, and yourself.	• I will ask questions that challenge my assumptions, values, and beliefs.
• Increase attention to "self" and "other" and wonder about the relationship between personal and professional.	• I will explore and share thoughts and feelings, increasing my awareness of self and enriching my understanding of others.
• Take in and use new awareness and insights, personal and professional, which emerge through the reflective supervisory relationship.	• I will act on my new awareness and learning to strengthen my practice.

In the beginning, a supervisee may experience feelings very similar to those expressed or felt by families who are newly referred or enrolled in services—overwhelmed, uncertain, incompetent, and wary of entering into a new relationship, no matter how positively it is presented. A supervisee may require extra outreach, a gentle reminder of the upcoming supervisory hours, and extra sensitivity on the part of the supervisor. The parallels between supervision and intervention are many. It is imperative that the supervisee understands that the supervisory relationship will provide a safe place to think, which is especially important when feeling stressed or overwhelmed by the challenges of relationship-based work.

As the reflective supervisory relationship deepens over the first year, the supervisee begins to increase attention to "self" and "other," paying close attention to the emotions awakened by the intensity of her work with infants and families. Further exploration of the relationship between personal and professional helps the supervisee to reach a deeper understanding of the emotional content of the work. As the supervisee increases capacity to share thoughts and feelings within a trusting supervisory relationship, she will increase the ability to offer the same to families, too. The reflective supervisory relationship provides the model for relationship work and reflective practice between the supervisee and families with whom she is engaged.

CORE ELEMENTS OF THE REFLECTIVE SUPERVISORY RELATIONSHIP

From the first session throughout the reflective supervisory relationship, there are four core elements that fuel the development of this relationship: curiosity, thinking/feeling, compassion, and shared

Table 4.2. Four Core Elements of Reflective Supervision

CORE ELEMENT	SUPERVISOR BEHAVIORS THAT REFLECT THESE ELEMENTS
Curiosity	I will remain attentive, inquisitive, and open to what the supervisee says, exploring possibilities, while staying grounded in what the facts are.
Thinking/ Feeling	I will allow myself to have thoughts and feelings in response to "stories from the field," brought to me during the supervisory hour.
Compassion	I will remain nonjudgmental, patient, and empathic in response to what the supervisee tells me about the infant, the parent(s) or caregiver(s), the nature of their interactions, or feelings awakened in the presence of the developing relationship.
Shared Attention	I will notice, wonder about, and respond to the experiences of the infant, the parent(s), and the practitioner as I observe and listen to what the supervisee tells me.

attention (W. Schafer, personal communication, 2002). The supervisor who keeps these elements in mind will promote a supervisee's ability to be reflective (see Table 4.2).

BEGINNINGS: THE START OF A REFLECTIVE SUPERVISORY RELATIONSHIP

Beginnings are important to the success of a reflective supervisory relationship. It is important for the supervisor to allow plenty of time for the supervisee to talk. It is equally important to listen. Time and attention are significant ingredients in practice that promotes infant mental health; time and attention are essential for developing a strong and meaningful supervisory relationship that invites reflection. The first conversations set the tone for other meetings. To the extent that the supervisor can model a thoughtful beginning with the supervisee, it will serve the relationship very well.

Ask About What Brings the Supervisee to This Work

The supervisor might first ask the supervisee to talk about experiences she has had with infants or very young children and families. These may be personal experiences with siblings or young children at home, or they may be professional experiences in child care, school, clinic, or hospital settings. Of additional interest, the supervisor might ask, "What brings you to this program now? What intrigues you about working with babies and families?" The supervisor may offer a snapshot of his own experience, including how he entered the field, what excites him, or what has fueled his enthusiasm for the work.

Many practitioners enter the infant and family field with general training in social work, psychology, or family counseling. They are well prepared to think about mental health issues and responses. However, their experience with children birth to 6 years old and parents may be limited. On the other hand, some professionals enter the infant and family field as child care professionals, educators, or nurses. They understand early development and are capable observers. However, they may have limited training or experience with infant and parental mental health. The supervisor needs to ask about and be aware of a new supervisee's strengths and "gaps" in preparing for relationship-based infant–family work.

Ask About Past Experiences With Supervision

First meetings offer a time to talk about a supervisee's education, training, and work experiences. First meetings also allow a supervisor to ask about other supervisory experiences: "Have you met regularly for supervision before?", "Can you tell me about it?", "Was it helpful for you?", "Are there things you would like me to help you with?" The supervisor may offer more information about her own work experiences or invite questions about her training or beliefs about young children. As in chapter 3 (Boris & Grabert, this volume, p. 41), in which the authors discuss the discovery phase in regards to learning about an organization, here the first session or two are the discovery phase regarding the individual or group.

Explain the Supervision Format

First meetings allow the supervisor to explain what the supervision format will be. "We will meet every week for about an hour. I find it helpful to keep a set time and day. I will try very hard not to let anything get in the way of our time together." If the supervisee is relatively new to the work, the supervisor may suggest looking at some video material together or reviewing articles together about the promotion of infant mental health. The supervisor can then discuss the supervisee's first meeting with a family:

> After you have met with a family, we can talk about your experience: what you observed, what you learned, what you experienced when you were with them. I will listen as carefully as I can to what you have to tell me so that I can be helpful to you. For me, supervision is a lot like going on a journey together, not quite sure where we are going and open to discovery as we go.

Explain How RS Relates to Staff Evaluation

For a supervisor who has administrative responsibilities in addition to reflective and clinical responsibilities, it will be important to review the evaluation process in initial supervisory meetings, too. (See Bertacchi & Gilkerson, this volume, p. 121, for a more in-depth discussion on balancing administrative and reflective responsibilities within the reflective relationship.) If there are evaluation forms, the supervisor and supervisee can look at them together. If the supervisee has questions about expectations and the reflective process, she can ask them then, too.

The Work Gets Under Way

The supervisor may have many questions in mind about the baby, the parents, the conditions that place them at risk, but, as in the supervisee's work with families, follows the supervisee's lead. He might ask, "Is there something on your mind today that you would like to talk about?" or "Where would you like to begin today?" The supervisee who finds her voice in response to this, and shares observations about her experiences with a family, will begin to feel anchored or grounded by the supervisory relationship. As the relationship deepens, supervisor and supervisee will grow in their capacity to wonder about a baby, mother, or father, and the conditions that place them at risk for relationship failure, developmental delays, or disorders. Together, they will acknowledge the feelings aroused in the presence of vulnerable infants and families, reflect on them, and share new insights as they emerge during the supervisory hour.

Who each is, what their life experiences have been, and the stage of life that each is in affect the nature and content of RS. The exchange is likely to be quite rich if each can remain open to the other, listening carefully and responding thoughtfully from a personal perspective.

The Relationship Deepens

The supervisee's values and beliefs about babies, parenthood, childbearing, and child rearing will undoubtedly be awakened in the daily work of prevention and intervention programs. Basic caregiving practices may challenge new and seasoned providers alike. How a parent holds, feeds, dresses, or diapers a baby evokes a host of responses. The haphazard care of a baby by a very young mother may arouse deeply held beliefs about the proper care and feeding of babies and adolescent parenthood. The birth of a new baby may awaken longings that a provider has for a baby of her own but rarely speaks about with family and friends. Memories of other mothers or fathers and babies may come into consciousness and take a supervisee by surprise. A mother's harsh tone of voice or rough handling of her toddler may remind a supervisee of her own mother's angry outbursts, leaving her frightened and unable to cope. Overwhelmed by intense emotional experiences such as these, the supervisee may shut down and distance herself from the family or become quite active and overinvolved in the work on behalf of the child. Of equal interest, the supervisee may use the supervisory relationship as a place to act out feelings by distancing herself from the supervisor, canceling supervisory meetings, neglecting to bring details to supervision, and resisting reflective work. Refer to chapter 6 (Keyes, Cavanaugh, & Scott Heller, this volume, p. 99) for a detailed discussion of both challenges encountered in RS and potential strategies for addressing these challenges.

The Supervisor's Challenge

It is the supervisor's challenge to hold and contain the emotional content of the work. The supervisor works hard to maintain a reflective position: to be fully present and listen without interruption to what the supervisee has to say and to refrain from interrupting or offering guidance or advice prematurely. This is often difficult, but very important, in terms of establishing a reflective context within the supervisory relationship. It is the supervisor's job to create a place where the supervisee will feel safe enough to be curious, to ask questions, and to reflect on what is seen and heard. It is the supervisor's responsibility to refrain from asking too many questions and to listen without judgment or criticism. It is the supervisor's responsibility to be emotionally available and responsive to the thoughts and feelings awakened in the presence of a vulnerable infant or a very fragile parent and offered during the supervisory hour. It is the supervisor's responsibility to recognize and wonder about the supervisee's feelings of helplessness, vulnerability, and confusion, as well as her strengths. In responding to these feelings with empathy and compassion, the supervisory relationship will deepen, offering opportunities for the supervisee to explore these feelings more personally as well as the meaning of many relationships—past and present—and the emotions aroused in each.

RS offers unexpected treasures and rewards; it affords the supervisor many opportunities to learn and grow, too. She may discover new strengths as she opens herself up to a new relationship with a supervisee. She may have to work very hard to engage the trust of a supervisee who is new to the work and uncertain about reflective process. In the process of encouraging reflection, she may learn to listen more intentionally. She may gain new insights about infant and family work that come as a result of working thoughtfully with a supervisee who sees things from a unique cultural perspective. She may remember other babies, other mothers, or other relationships as she listens to a supervisee reflect on struggles with families in the field and emotional struggles within. The supervisor may not share her thoughts and feelings openly with the supervisee, but uses them to fuel her understanding of the work, the supervisee, and herself. To enter into a relationship and to invite reflection, a supervisor needs to:

- Observe and listen without interruption
- Help the provider to feel competent
- Remain emotionally present and empathic
- Allow herself to wonder and "not know"
- Remain curious and tolerate uncertainty
- Respond to the feelings as appropriate
- Hold the supervisee in mind as she listens to the details of his experience
- Hold and contain the feelings expressed
- Invite the supervisee to express himself without criticizing what he said or did
- Allow the supervisee to have and express feelings about the baby, the parent, or the developing relationship

ENTERING INTO A MUTUALLY SATISFYING AND TRUSTING RELATIONSHIP: THE FIRST YEAR

Trust is fundamental to all relationship development; it is the cornerstone for reflection within the supervisory relationship. Trust grows out of the supervisor's ability to be consistently available, sensitive, and responsive to the supervisee. Trust grows out of the supervisee's ability to be emotionally present, open, and honest. Together, they build a mutually satisfying and trusting relationship that allows them to discover the possibilities and rewards of infant and family work.

Building Trust Through Observation

Both the supervisor and the supervisee play a role in the development of the supervisory relationship. Trust is of crucial importance and at the center of their work together. As the relationship gets under way, supervisor and supervisee enter with a leap of faith, each needing to believe that she or he can trust the other. As the supervisor listens, observes, reflects, and responds in a supportive manner and is at the same time culturally aware and sensitive, he is laying the foundation of trust for their supervisory relationship. At the same time, the supervisee has an important role, to be committed to sharing observations about the infant, the family, and, when able, personal responses awakened when with them. These things contribute to the building of a trusting relationship between them.

Listening: The Foundation for Relationship

As the supervisor provides a listening context for the supervisee, the supervisory relationship deepens. While quiet, the supervisor listens for themes that emerge in the details of the supervisee's work. The supervisor listens for the emotional experience that the supervisee is describing, acknowledging what it takes to be open and vulnerable when working with families. Discussing infants and families can be difficult, especially if there is much distress or if the supervisee feels confused about what to say or do or feels that she has not said the right thing to the family. The supervisee needs to give herself the opportunity to wonder about the experience, and the supervisor needs to create the opportunity for this to happen (e.g., following the supervisee's lead and meeting her where she is). This may mean that the supervisor remains very quiet and does not respond to the supervisee immediately. The supervisor holds the awareness of what the emotional experience is like for the supervisee, sometimes growing aware of a theme that emerges and waiting for the supervisee to take them where it will be most helpful to go.

Reflecting on Shared Vulnerability

As the reflective supervisory relationship deepens and a sense of safety is created between the supervisor and the supervisee, the supervisee grows increasingly aware of the emotional responses awakened and finds words to talk about and reflect on the work with families. What are these feelings that are so intensely experienced in the presence of a particular baby, a particular parent or even a particular colleague? The supervisor's gentle encouragement to explore thoughts and feelings that arise supports the supervisee's deeper understanding of the infant, the parents, and reflective practice. The supervisor wonders about the relationship of professional understanding to personal insights about oneself.

The supervisor may feel comfortable sharing her own experiences as they are relevant to the supervisee's experience. The supervisor does this with great care. She may offer stories about babies and families with whom she once worked. She may share her personal response to work that was deeply evocative for her or she may not. The supervisor must keep in mind the needs of the supervisee and share when it serves the needs of the supervisee, which are not necessarily the needs of the supervisor. The session should focus on the supervisee's experiences and growth, and although sharing is important to support this growth, too much or inappropriate sharing (i.e., excessive or unrelated stories of the supervisor's own experiences) can prevent or inhibit growth in the supervisee.

REFLECTIVE SUPERVISION TRANSCRIPTS: EXCERPTS FROM THE FIRST YEAR

What follows are three separate excerpts from real RS sessions between Deborah Weatherston (supervisor) and Carla Barron (supervisee). Taken together, the three excerpts illustrate many of the concepts presented in this chapter. When reviewing the narratives, each author added what she was thinking or feeling, but did not say, during the supervision; these reflections appear in italics. The dialogue and unspoken words are offered here to encourage your questions, comments, and reflections about the process.

• • •

The First Supervisory Meeting

Supervisor: The supervisor checks the time and wonders where the supervisee is. She is about 10 minutes late. "Could she have forgotten?" the supervisor wonders. The phone rings, the supervisor answers it and explains that she is waiting for a supervisee and will call back later. She checks her watch again. "I have so much to do."

Supervisee: The supervisee hurries up the stairs, knocks on the door, and enters, saying, "Oh, I am so sorry to be late. I was reading the manual you gave me and lost track of the time." *I can't believe that I am late for this meeting. My first week on the job and I'm late.*

Supervisor: The supervisor says, quite gently, "Oh, that's understandable. Come sit down." *I actually felt a little annoyed that she was late and had apparently gotten distracted.* "Let me turn the phone off and close the door."

Supervisee: "OK." *That was strange . . . why did she turn the phone off? I know that she is very busy. I felt even more anxious about being late. I was not sure what the meeting was about. I didn't really know what I was supposed to say. I had hoped that I would remember what I read in the manual.*

Supervisor: "We did meet before during your interview, but I wonder if it would be helpful for me to tell you a little bit about myself? I began as a home visitor a number of years ago—a lot of years ago. I loved parent–infant work. It was so different from working with adults and seeing clients in the office day after day. I have worked for a long time now as a supervisor." *I was feeling quite anxious. Beginnings are not easy. I felt unsure about how I would be received by this new staff person—what I might step into—if I would be able to give her what she needs.*

Supervisee: "I've done a little bit of home visiting work, but ummm, not with children this young and not for more than a few visits with each family. Babies and long-term work are new for me." *I felt a little relieved that the supervisor knows what it's like to be out there working with babies and families in their own homes.*

Supervisor: "I'm wondering what kind of supervision you had in your other jobs."

Supervisee: "Oh, we had a regularly scheduled time like this in the beginning, like now. We talked about policies and such. After my initial training, we saw each other if something important came up or there was a crisis." *I was actually thinking that this was a little unnerving. I definitely didn't have to sit and talk with my supervisor every week before, with the door closed and all that. What would we talk about for all that time?*

Supervisor: "Well, we have guidelines that we can go over together about RS and also a format that might help you organize your thinking about what you saw and what you heard, at least initially. Here, let me show you." *I was aware of a familiar dilemma—balancing teaching with listening. I felt pushed to offer guidelines and guidance rather than to invite the supervisee to let me know what was on her mind.*

Supervisee: "Well, having the guidelines will be helpful, I'm sure. So, would you want to hear about each family when we meet or just one or what? I have only been on a couple of home visits so far, but they were really overwhelming." *I was actually still thinking about one young mom I met. I felt so sad when I left there.*

[Knock, knock, knock. The two are interrupted by someone wanting the supervisor's signature. They are momentarily distracted.]

Supervisor: "Now, where were we? Interruptions are difficult." *It is so hard for me to get back on track when interrupted! I want her to feel engaged, and there is so much for her to know.*

Supervisee: [Hurriedly] "Well, I was thinking, I saw this woman this week. She was 8 months pregnant and has no support. I felt so bad for her. I wanted to say, 'I will be with you,' but I didn't. I really felt overwhelmed." *It's weird that I started talking about her without being asked what the home visits have been like so far. I'm not sure we can talk about this now, with all of the other training I need, like paperwork. It's not like there was a crisis with this young mom right now.*

Supervisor: "Oh . . . what a difficult spot for you to be in. Was there something in particular that worried you?" *I felt surprised. We hadn't been talking about a case. I realize now that I had overlooked the supervisee's urgent need to share what she had experienced this first week on the job. Instead, I had led with my own agenda to guide and inform.*

Supervisee: "Well, I wondered if an offer to be with her during labor and delivery was too intimate, too soon? I didn't really know her. She hadn't signed the paperwork yet. Then, what if I couldn't go? I wasn't sure really what to say or do." *I felt like I was babbling. I don't really know how to describe what I was feeling. It seemed like I didn't know what I was doing!*

Supervisor: "I wonder. Will you see her again?" *I knew that my task was to hold and contain this very new supervisee. Our time had run out. It felt very incomplete.*

Supervisee: "Oh, yes, by the end of our visit, she had agreed to be part of the program and asked if I would see her twice next week." *She didn't give me a straight answer! But I felt like she was really listening. She didn't look at me in a disapproving way when I was babbling . . . she just listened. It was nice to talk about that, even briefly. I must have been more overwhelmed than I thought. I needed to get that out.*

Supervisor: "That's a terrific start. You will have time to find out what supports exist for her and what resources she has. If you like, we can talk about this case next week when you come. Let's make sure we have the date and time in our calendars. I am so glad that you have joined our team. I really do look forward to working together."

● ● ●

Reflections

In this first meeting, the supervisory relationship is just starting. Each is becoming more familiar with the other, exchanging stories about their work experiences. They spend some time reviewing

....

The First Supervisory Meeting

THE SUPERVISOR	*THE SUPERVISEE*
• Asks about beginnings, including previous work, supervision experiences, and expectations.	• Appears slightly anxious and unsure.
• Protects supervisory time from interruption.	• Shares some observations, feelings, and concerns about the family referred.
• Listens for themes that emerge and emotions.	
• Shows curiosity about the process aroused.	

....

expectations of supervision and turn their attention to the supervisee's casework. This excerpt offers a window into early moments in an RS or consultation relationship. In the box The First Supervisory Meeting important attributes and behaviors demonstrated by the supervisor and the supervisee are listed.

Several Weeks Into the First Year of RS

The following is an excerpt from a reflective supervisory session that took place during the fourth supervisory meeting. As planned, the supervisor and supervisee had met each week to talk about the referrals that the supervisee had received and her beginning work with families. The relationship between supervisor and supervisee, as well as the relationship between the supervisee and family, is still very new. The dialogue is offered here to encourage the reader to think about beginnings, the feelings we have as we enter into new relationships, and what it takes to establish mutual trust.

• • •

Beginnings

Supervisor: "Where would you like to start?"

Supervisee: "Hmm. I don't really know." *It was difficult to find a place to start, as with this family there was so much going on. I couldn't quite place or name the feelings I had about this situation. I was nervous about getting it right, making sure that I brought the right information to her.*

Supervisor: "Well, just take a few minutes to think about where to begin." *I actually felt quite anxious because I knew very little about the baby and the reason for the referral. To reduce my own anxiety, I was tempted to give the supervisee more direction by suggesting that she begin by telling me about the baby. If I had done that, I would have taken the lead and shaped the initial part of our conversation, perhaps meeting my need rather than hers.*

Supervisee: "At first I was nervous because I had talked a lot to the grandpa on the phone rather than the mom. I was worried that maybe I had started out wrong. There were friends visiting when I got there, but they left right away. Then, this young, young girl—the mom—picked up the baby from the jump seat, put him on her hip, and walked over to me and said, 'Hi!' The baby gave me a big smile, and then got shy, and I felt relieved. They let me in. I felt really good about that. The grandpa started talking. He had a lot of concerns. The whole time, the mom was quiet. She kept the baby on her lap and gave him some toys. He seemed very content and then dozed off. I felt nervous though. The grandpa has cancer, and he's very worried about what will happen to his daughter and the baby when he's not here." *I felt like I was rambling on with no direction. There was so much to see and to attend to. It was nice, though, to just talk without being interrupted. I noticed that she didn't say anything for quite a while, even if I paused during my telling of the story.*

Supervisor: *I listened without saying anything for what felt like a very long time. I finally said,* "I wonder if grandpa brought you in to protect them?"

Supervisee: The supervisee nodded, but continued, saying, "He credits the baby with prolonging his life." *I didn't think of it the way she presented it, and frankly it scared me. I don't think I'm ready for that responsibility. I think I sort of ignored her comment.*

Supervisor: *I felt the weight of this and also the sorrow. My own sorrow, perhaps, as a grandmother and also as a friend of two women with recent diagnoses of cancer. It was hard to stay focused.*

Supervisee: The supervisee went on to say, "I told the mom that I felt it was important to see her again this week. I wanted the connection with her. I was very deliberate about wanting a relationship with them. I am not sure why I said what I said." *I didn't realize that I was being so deliberate or so different from other times that I have met families. As I was talking about this first meeting, retelling it, I began wondering about this. At first I thought that it was because I felt more comfortable in my role, that my experience has allowed me to better talk about what the work means. But as I continued on, I got more confused about things.*

Supervisor: Rather than let the supervisee answer her own question, I interrupted, saying, "I wonder if you felt some urgency about the grandpa's health?" *That didn't seem to be it.*

Supervisee: The supervisee shook her head. "I think it's something different. I wanted more clarity about how we'll work together, the mom and baby and me, who I am in relationship to them." The supervisee struggled and went on to say, "Maybe the clarity is really about me—who I am, what my role is, what my relationships are—that might be what this is about." Having said that, the supervisee then wondered if there might be a parallel there. "The teen mom might be wondering the same thing. Who am I? What is my role? What about my relationship with my baby and with my father? What the heck is going to happen when he gets real sick and needs care?" *As I thought more about it, part of me didn't want to admit that maybe she was right about the grandpa bringing me in to protect his daughter and grandson. I didn't want to admit feeling scared and apprehensive about entering into a relationship with this family. Maybe I'm keeping myself a bit distant by being deliberate about describing this work to them. It seemed almost forced, not at all like I usually enter into a relationship. By maintaining this distant professional role, I won't get confused about wanting to take care of this family and get too close to a family who will soon experience a great loss. She allowed me to sit with this and didn't interrupt my own thought process. I don't think I could have understood this if she* *didn't allow for some quiet time and if I didn't feel safe enough with her to wonder and to be confused. I also had a glimmer of understanding about the teen mom and how confused and even frightened she might be about her role as a mom and what will happen when her father needs more care.*

•   •   •

The supervisor and supervisee sat quietly. You could have heard a pin drop. The two had been on a journey together in the course of the hour. At the outset, neither had been sure about how to begin or where they would go. The supervisor had offered very little guidance about what to say or do or how to engage the family. Instead, she provided a time and place for both to have thoughts and feelings about a very young mom, her 7-month-old baby, and an aging grandfather.

Reflections

At this point, the reflective supervisory relationship is better established although the two partners are still learning about each other. The supervisee has become a bit more comfortable with the reflective process, yet it is still a new way for her to process her work with families. This excerpt presents moments in an RS or consultation that demonstrates some of the following attributes listed in the box Beginnings.

Beginnings	
THE SUPERVISOR	**THE SUPERVISEE**
• Is accessible, genuinely caring, emotionally available.	• Remains curious.
• Is able to talk and to listen.	• Comes prepared to share detailed observations, thoughts, feelings, and concerns.
• Is willing to "not know" and tolerate moments of confusion.	• Is willing to explore the relationship of her feelings to the work she is doing (at least internally).
• Observes and listens without interruption.	• Remains curious.

Several Months Into the First Year of RS

The third excerpt occurs 3 months later and continues with a focus on the same family who was at the center of the supervisee's concerns in the second excerpt. The baby is now 10 months old.

• • •

A Mutually Trusting Relationship

Supervisee: The supervisee arrives on time.

Supervisor: Greets supervisee warmly, saying, "Hi, come in! I am so glad to see you. How are you?"

Supervisee: "There is so much going on. It has been a very full week."

Supervisor: "What would be most helpful? Where would you like to begin?"

[There is a long pause.]

Supervisee: "Well, I haven't talked with you about this family in a while. I think we should begin with them." *I knew I had avoided talking about this family during supervision. They had been so unavailable the past few weeks. When I talked with the grandpa over the phone or was with them in their home, I experienced so many feelings. I didn't even know how to name them. I knew there was something going on. I had learned that my own behaviors and feelings are part of something called "parallel process," but I wasn't sure that I wanted to know my role in all of this.* "Do you remember the grandpa who has cancer and the young mom and her baby boy I began to see several months ago? We started to meet once a week at 1:00 p.m. for 2 hours, which was how we decided to do it. When I would come, either the mom was sleepy or distracted or the baby was sleepy or fussy. Her dad was there, too, the baby's grandpa. He would often begin our discussions about his daughter's irritability and her sleepiness. He wanted to refer her to a psychiatrist. I was worried about this. It didn't feel right. The mom wasn't talking. The grandpa did all the talking. He also talked a lot about the baby's development, but it was more like, 'What can we do to make sure that he learns to read?' Sometimes they were there; sometimes, not. The grandpa called to cancel several times, but also expressed his worry. On one phone call, I said, 'You're worried about your daughter and your grandson. I want to help you and your daughter, but it seems hard to engage her. She sometimes wants me to be there, but other times she seems tired or distracted. It has to be her wanting me to come.' I wanted to say that it was hard to talk with her when he was always there, too, but I didn't know how to do this without hurting his feelings. So, I suggested that we plan that he be there in the room half of the time and half of the time I would be with his daughter and her baby. He said, 'OK.' What is really bothering me is that I didn't ask to talk to *her*. I kept on talking to the grandpa. Why did I continue to talk with him? She was always right there!" *I felt like I was talking too fast . . . I felt rushed, like I needed to get something out, but I wasn't sure what. I wasn't making sense to myself. What was I trying to say about this family? What were my own worries?*

Supervisor: *I was puzzled. I couldn't figure out why the supervisee was so concerned about the grandpa and why she overlooked the mom and the baby.* I finally said, "It might help if you can remember what you were feeling as you were talking with the grandpa when he called to tell you not to come to the house but seemed to want to talk."

Supervisee: "I felt annoyed. Annoyed with him and annoyed with me, too, I guess. I also felt sad, so sad. He needs his own support and there doesn't seem to be a service for him." *I felt guilty, too. I understood where his worries were coming from. He wanted to be sure that things were in place for his daughter and his* *grandson. He might have been anticipating the loss of seeing his grandson grow up and seeing his daughter grow as a mother. In thinking about this now, I feel terrible about being annoyed with a man who is dying!*

Supervisor: "You are so good at recognizing and talking about your feelings—annoyed and sad, you said. I wonder if you can use those feelings to think about what each might have been experiencing as you were talking? Maybe the mom was annoyed and also sad. Annoyed with both of you for talking and leaving her out and sad because she faces the uncertainty of caring for herself and her baby without her dad some day, maybe soon." *Was I moving too quickly? Was I putting my own interpretation of the feelings on to the supervisee's? I was oddly impatient with the focus on the grandpa and was wondering myself about the mom feeling left out.*

Supervisee: "Well, maybe so. I hadn't thought about that." *Of course I had thought about it . . . I just couldn't name it. She did it, she talked about it, the parallel process. I don't think I'm ready to think about all of this. I had recently supported a good friend whose father died. My friend is much older and has a lot of family and social support, and it was still so hard. How will this young, isolated mom deal with the death of her father, her only consistent support?*

[There was a pause in the conversation.]

Supervisee: "There have been a lot of no-shows or cancellations. I missed seeing them for about 3–4 weeks. I couldn't find them! They had to move. I kept calling and finally the grandpa called me back. The mom has turned 18 and wants to apply for her own aid."

Supervisor: *She is rushing, not organized. What is she struggling with? I can't find the center of this. I can't find the baby either.* "It is often so confusing when a family disappears for a while like this family did. How old has the baby gotten to be? What is he doing now?" *I was struggling. I thought that if I asked about the baby, it might bring a focus to the conversation, plus, he had about disappeared from the dialogue and I was worried.*

Supervisee: "Oh, he's 10 months old now. When I finally met up with them this week, I saw that he's a confident crawler, getting into things, pulling up but staying pretty close to his mom. He seemed quite hesitant to move too far from his mom. I thought it was OK because it is a new house. He moved around and explored more at the other house."

[The supervisee's voice was quite emotion-filled and intense. The description was very poignant.]

Supervisor: The supervisor wondered aloud, "If you think about the baby for a moment, what might he be telling us?" Then, restating the supervisee's words, the supervisor said, "He's not ready to go off on his own." Then, she asked the supervisee, "Do you think it might be true for each of them—not ready to go, not ready to be separate? The grandpa is sick and the mom is barely 18 years old and the baby, at 10 months, is not quite ready to be so independent either."

[They remained quiet for a brief period.]

Supervisee: "That is a very powerful image for me. It is true, this mom is 18 years old and her father is going to leave her. He's dying right in front of her. How can she even think about separating from him and moving out on her own? What is it like for her to watch her baby begin to move away from her? Will she be able to support him enough to allow him to separate from her when the time comes?"

In thinking about this, I felt sad and helpless. They were going to experience a profound loss and separation when the grandpa died. How were they going to manage it?

Supervisor: "Separation is a life theme—for children, for parents, for all of us—we continuously struggle with separations and often losses and have to learn to handle the feelings that come along, too. Separation and loss may be at the center of the case right now—on the grandpa's mind or the young mom's mind or the baby, for that matter, and on your mind, too." *I wasn't certain how far to take this. I felt fairly sure that it was something for the supervisee to think more deeply about. I wanted to recognize her feelings, to help contain them, and be empathic. I wanted to help her use what she was thinking about and experiencing to explore how these thoughts and feelings might help her in her work, but I didn't want to intrude. It is a tricky balance for me. But, then, I have to ask myself if this is on my mind because separation and loss are themes I am sensitive to or because I experienced the untimely deaths of two grandmothers as new grandbabies were born just this past week? I wonder.*

Supervisee: "I think that separation is on my mind . . . more than I even realize." *I am blown away by my own fear of this discussion of separation and loss. My most recent experience with death was a friend's father who was the same age as my parents are. I know that I am thinking of my own experience, my own separation from my parents, and the possibility of losing them one day. I am amazed at how a description of a baby learning to crawl, but not straying too far from his mother, was the beginning of a discussion about separation, loss, and relationships. I know that this theme will resound in our work and that is an important theme for this family and for me. I can hear the words, "Not ready to move out on their own." Even though I didn't share my fears openly during our supervision, I was able to reflect on them and relate, with some thoughts from my supervisor, what I was feeling to my work with the family.*

Supervisor: "I wonder if it would be helpful for us to touch base mid-week? Do you have time? This is a difficult case with lots for you to think about. I could meet with you on Thursday in the morning if you are free." *I found myself wondering if I had been distant, not as available to the supervisee, preoccupied, and pulled away when she needed me to be more fully engaged? I hadn't been here for 2 weeks because of the holiday. We had missed a lot. She is fairly new at this work. I have to remember how important it is to be available to her and to everyone for that matter on a very consistent basis.*

• • •

Reflections

This excerpt presents moments in RS that exhibit important attributes for both partners. Notice how the session moves more smoothly, and the two are able to tolerate more uncertainty and ambiguity. Now that the relationship has become better established, the supervisee is more comfortable with thinking out loud and sharing her uncertainty with her supervisor than she was in the first excerpt. Some of the important attributes that were observable in this transcript are listed in the box A Mutually Trusting Relationship Is Under Way.

A Mutually Trusting Relationship Is Under Way

THE SUPERVISOR	THE SUPERVISEE
• Remains curious and tolerates uncertainty	• Explores the relationship of her feelings to the work she is doing.
• Holds the supervisee in mind as she listens to the details of the experience.	• Is aware of the feelings that she has in response to her work and in the presence of infants, toddlers, and parents.
• Invites the supervisee to express herself without criticizing what she said or did.	• When able, shares those feelings with the supervisor.
• Allows the supervisee to have and express feelings about the baby or the parent or the developing relationship.	• Increases attention to "self" and "other" and wonders about the relationship between personal and professional.

SUMMARY

As the months go by, supervisor and supervisee have many opportunities to observe and listen to one another. The time they spend together, regularly and consistently, allows them to enter into many meaningful conversations in which they share thoughts and feelings that are unique to relationship work. The language they use assumes intimacy: babies, mothers, fathers, loving relationships. The words they use evoke deeply felt memories and vivid images. The supervisee's leap of faith, so bravely taken in the beginning of this relationship, may result in new insights and a new awareness of personal responses and reactions when working with infants, very young children, and their families. The supervisor and supervisee are able to explore the emotions vividly aroused. They are comfortable "not knowing" and are willing to share their curiosity and vulnerability with each other.

The end of the first year of this very important relationship signifies the deepening of the RS relationship that the supervisee values as a mechanism to support her work with infants and families and her personal growth within the field. The next chapter outlines the phases of an individual session. Although the content and focus of the sessions change over time, especially in the beginning as the supervisory relationship is developing (as is highlighted in the current chapter), the overall structure of the session remains the same.

REFERENCES

Bertacchi, J., & Gilkerson, L. (2009). How can administrative and reflective supervision be combined? In
S. Scott Heller & L. Gilkerson (Eds.), *A practical guide to reflective supervision* (pp. 121–134). Washington, DC:
ZERO TO THREE.

Boris, N. W., & Grabert, J. C. (2009). How do I reflective supervision to my program? In S. Scott Heller &
L. Gilkerson (Eds.), *A practical guide to reflective supervision* (pp. 41–61). Washington, DC: ZERO TO THREE.

Eggbeer, L., Mann, T., & Siebel, N. (2007). Reflective supervision: Past, present, and future. *Zero to Three, 28*(2),
5–9.

Fenichel, E. (Ed.). (1992). *Learning through supervision and mentorship to support the development of infants, toddlers,
and their families: A source book.* Washington, DC: ZERO TO THREE.

Keyes, A. W., Cavanaugh, A. E., & Scott Heller, S. (2009). How do I, as a reflective supervisor, repair ruptures in
the supervisory relationship? In S. Scott Heller & L. Gilkerson (Eds.), *A practical guide to reflective supervision*
(pp. 99–119). Washington, DC: ZERO TO THREE.

Michigan Association for Infant Mental Health. (2007). *Best practice guidelines for RS/consultation.* Retrieved
April 11, 2009, from www.mi-aimh.org/documents/best_practice_guidelines_for_ reflective_
supervisionconsultationP2009.pdf

Remen, R. N. (1996). *Kitchen table wisdom: Stories that heal.* New York: Penguin.

Shahmoon-Shanok, R. (2009). What is reflective supervision? In S. Scott Heller & L. Gilkerson (Eds.), *A practical
guide to reflective supervision* (pp. 7–23). Washington, DC: ZERO TO THREE.

Weatherston, D. (2001). Infant mental health: A review of relevant literature. *Psychoanalytic Social Work, 8*(1),
39–69.

Winnicott, D. (1965). *The maturational processes and the facilitating environment.* Madison, CT: International
Universities Press.

Reflective Tool 4

Building the Reflective Supervisory Relationship

Reflective Tool 4 helps to clarify important elements of the supervisory relationship. It may be used by both the supervisor and the supervisee to guide them while talking initially about reflective process. It offers ways for each to think about their contributions to the supervisory relationship as they explore the possibilities and power of relationship-based work. It may be referred to throughout their work together, but is not intended to be a checklist or rating instrument. Rather, it is a reminder to each that they have a responsibility to be fully present and emotionally available while meeting with each other and when working with infants, young children, and families.

		SUPERVISOR	SUPERVISEE
ATTRIBUTES OF REFLECTIVE SUPERVISORY RELATIONSHIPS	Building Trust Through Observations	• Enter the relationship in a nonjudgmental way. • Be culturally aware and sensitive. • Ask about beginnings, including previous work and supervision experiences and expectations. • Invite the sharing of details about the infant, each parent, and developing relationships; as appropriate, the thoughts and feelings aroused.	• Enter the relationship with an open mind. • Allow supervisor to support you. • Come prepared to share detailed observations, thoughts, feelings, and concerns; when able, share feelings or worries that arise in the presence of an infant, parent, and relationship. • Share enthusiasm/hesitation/concerns about entering into a reflective supervisory relationship.
	Listening: The Foundation for Relationships	• Remain quiet; follow supervisee's lead. • Acknowledge what it takes to be open and vulnerable to infants, toddlers, and families. • Be accessible, genuine, caring, and emotionally available. • Protect supervisory time from interruption. • Listen for themes that emerge and emotions aroused for supervisee and self.	• Acknowledge importance of consistent supervision meetings for relationship-based, reflective practice. • Listen to your own descriptions of the infant, toddler, and family. • Listen for the feeling words that you choose to use and the emotions awakened. • Listen for connections between the feelings aroused and let them inform your work.
	Reflecting on Shared Vulnerability	• Be open to sharing stories of experiences that would be relevant. • Maintain emotional availability. • Gently encourage supervisee to have and talk about emotions awakened in the presence of an infant or very young child and parents. • Encourage exploration of thoughts and feelings that the supervisee has about the work with very young children and families as well as about one's response to the work. • Wonder how feelings inform supervisee's work and enhance understanding of self.	• Ask questions that allow you to think more deeply about your work with infants, young children, and families as well as about yourself. • Be aware of the feelings you have in response to your work and in the presence of the infants, toddlers, and families. • When you feel safe enough, share those feelings with your supervisor. • Increase attention to "self" and "other" with a deeper level of wondering about emotions and relationships.
	Deepening the Relationship Through Careful Response	• Maintain cultural awareness and sensitivity. • As the supervisee grows more trusting of the supervisory process, encourage greater reflection. • Recognize and understand supervisee's feelings of helplessness, vulnerability, and confusion, as well as strengths. • Wonder about, name, and respond to feelings with appropriate empathy. • Remain curious, open, and content to "not know."	• Allow your feelings to inform the work you are doing. • Explore new insights about emotions and relationships as they relate more personally. • Trust yourself to discuss what you need to discuss and use your growing awareness of self and other to enrich your work with families. • Remain curious, open, and content to "not know."

CHAPTER 5

WHAT ARE THE PHASES OF THE REFLECTIVE SUPERVISION MEETING?

Theresa Atchley, Sonja Hall, Sarah Martinez, and Linda Gilkerson

In our suffering and joy we are connected to one another
with unbreakable and compelling human bonds.
In that knowing, all of us become less vulnerable and alone.

—*Rachel Naomi Remen (1996, p. 140)*

Now you should have a clear sense of the qualities of the supervisory relationship and the nature of the interactions between the people who sustain this relationship—curiosity, shared attention, compassion, and integrating thinking/feeling. In this chapter, we take a closer look at how to structure the process of supervision into predictable routines that contribute to the provision of a safe, trustworthy environment. First articulated by Gilkerson and Shahmoon-Shanok (2000), we describe eight phases of a supervision meeting from preparation to postsupervision reflection and then illustrate the phases in scenarios of individual and group supervision. This model may be particularly helpful for new supervisors who come from backgrounds other than mental health and who most likely have not had an experience of clinical supervision. By the end of this chapter, you will be able to:

1. Picture and describe one approach to the structure of a supervision meeting.

2. Consider how you will structure supervisory sessions.

3. Use Reflective Tool 5 to guide your reflection after supervision meetings.

SUPERVISION PHASES: RITUALS AND ROUTINES OF SUPERVISION

Although reflective supervision (RS) is not a prescribed, linear process, it can be helpful for new supervisors to develop a predictable, trustworthy ritual for the sessions. Over time, these familiar routines will communicate consistency, reliability, and containment. In this chapter, we describe an approach that includes eight phases for the supervisory process:

1. Preparation,

2. Greeting/reconnecting,

3. Opening the dialogue/finding the agenda,

4. Telling the story/focusing on the details,

5. Understanding perspectives/generating hypotheses,

6. Considering next steps,

7. Closing, and

8. Post supervision reflection (Gilkerson & Shahmoon-Shanok, 2000).

As you read about the phases and consider them in action, think about how you would like to structure RS sessions. What will be a comfortable beginning? How will you guide the process along? What would be a helpful way to end the session? How will you take notes after the session? What will you want to remember?

Preparation

The first step is to prepare yourself for the session: take a few minutes to clear your mind, perhaps straighten your desk or get a quick snack if needed, put the phone on forward, and place a Do Not Disturb sign on the door. These simple steps can help you begin to shift attention away from the day's preoccupations and create a protected environment for yourself and the supervisee. Take a few moments to look at the supervision log from the last session and orient yourself to a specific supervisee's needs and strengths, as well as follow-up thoughts. Then, relax, breathe deeply, and begin.

Greeting and Reconnecting

Here you greet the supervisee in a friendly way to make a brief but personal connection. You might ask her about her vacation, or comment on the cast she has on her hand, or just welcome her into your office and say that you are glad to see her. If the supervisee has rushed from another task, the greeting helps her make the transition to the calm space of the supervision session.

Opening the Dialogue and Finding the Agenda

As this can be an awkward moment for beginners, we suggest that you find a few openings that feel both right and productive and use those as you gain comfort in the role. You might ask, "How has this week been for you?" or simply say, "Where would you like to start?" With experience, most supervisors settle on a ritual way to begin. Then your task is to listen carefully and attentively, wondering about what is on the supervisee's mind. What would she like to focus on? When the supervisee experiences, session after session, that you really will begin just where she is, a sense of collaboration and safety is created. Sometimes the supervisee will know just where to start; other times she will need your help. It is better to ask than to guess: "You have shared so much. What would you like us to focus on today?"

Telling the Story and Focusing on the Details

When an issue or concern has been identified, the next step is to hear the story and gather the details: What exactly happened? What was said? What was not said? What was observed? What feelings were expressed? It is tempting to rush in and seek solutions or to normalize, but we encourage you to go slowly at this point. While the supervisee is relating the details, he is also constructing the story of the event and perhaps becoming aware of his own attitudes and reactions for the first time. This detailed recounting also helps the supervisor to see or hear things that the supervisee may have missed.

Understanding Perspectives and Generating Hypotheses

The collaboration continues as you, the supervisee, or both of you begin to share hunches about what is going on. It is very helpful at this point to wonder with the supervisee about each person's perspective: "I wonder how the mother feels about her baby's new ability to walk and climb up on things?", "And what is it like for her toddler to have this new freedom to move on his own?", "And how does this new capacity change the way they see and relate to each other?" As the supervisee develops greater understanding of the key dynamics, hypotheses can be generated in an open, tentative, exploratory way. The supervisee is helped to reflect on her own position and to keep trying on the perspectives of the others. There should be no pressure to rush toward closure or to discuss every case, client, or issue that occurred between reflective sessions.

Considering Next Steps

Practitioners come to supervision with problems to solve, uncertainties to clarify, and issues that are affecting their day-to-day work. After gathering information and formulating hypotheses, you can guide the conversation toward consideration of next steps. This not only gives the practitioner direction, but also helps her contain and organize what she has learned about herself during the session. You might ask, "In the time we have left, given all you have shared and observed, how might you approach your next home visit?" or "What might help you to hear the feelings that you anticipate the family expressing around the new diagnosis?" As with formulating hypotheses, this is a collaborative process. Your greater experience may be a resource at this stage, as the supervisee imagines what might happen in a situation similar to ones you have experienced many times.

Closing

You can end the session with an appreciation of the supervisee's engagement in the work and a confirmation of the next supervision contact.

Post Supervision Reflection

It is crucial to take a few minutes after the session to reflect on and record the key themes and affects expressed, as well as the supervisee's level of engagement and your comfort or discomfort with the session. Taking these few minutes to summarize the session will give you a greater sense of closure and readiness to move ahead to your next tasks at hand.

Now, let's take a look at how these phases can guide supervision meetings. First, we illustrate the phases in an individual supervision with Karen, a home visitor in a prevention home visiting program. Later, we will illustrate the process in group supervision with home visitors in a family support program.

INDIVIDUAL SUPERVISION: A VIGNETTE

Karen is a home visitor, called a "parent educator," working in her community for a large agency's program to assist low-income families in preparing their infants and toddlers for success in preschool and beyond. Her supervisor, Sherlynn, has several years' experience as program manager and in providing RS. Karen is also experienced with RS, having been supervised by Sherlynn for the past year. The program is required to use a parent education curriculum with families.

Preparation

In preparation for her supervision (held twice monthly) with Karen, Sherlynn has set aside other work and has reread her notes from their last meeting. She has noted that Karen is sometimes visibly distressed and frustrated during home visits when a parent has not followed through with a resource referral. Sherlynn had realized that during her last supervision session with Karen she had not been sure how to respond to the intensity of Karen's frustration. Sherlynn had explored with her own supervisor how to help Karen to understand these strong feelings, should the opportunity arise.

Greeting and Reconnecting

Karen arrives and is welcomed in by Sherlynn, who closes the door behind her after telling the receptionist she will be unavailable for calls for an hour.

• • •

Supervisor (Sherlynn): "Hi Karen, how are you?"

Karen: "OK, I think . . . my kids are off school for the summer, so we're all adjusting to new schedules . . . day camp and sports camps."

Supervisor: "Sounds like a challenge."

Karen: "Yes, but my mom came to stay with us for the summer, thank the Lord . . . I don't worry about them with her around."

Supervisor: "That sounds like a relief for you."

Karen: "It sure is! How's your summer?"

Supervisor: "Good . . . I'm really enjoying my garden and the beautiful weather." *The supervisor is using this time to reconnect with Karen and to learn about her readiness to focus on work, by assessing other possible stressors.*

Opening the Dialogue and Finding the Agenda

Supervisor: "So, how have these past 2 weeks of work been for you?"

Karen: "Oh, busy, as usual. But OK, I guess. I have three new families I'm trying to make visits to for intake, but you know how they can be a little hard to pin down for appointments. Two weren't at home, but called me back to reschedule, and one doesn't return phone calls. But I'm used to that. They all came to the parent group last week, and said they were interested in home visits, so we'll see. I'll just keep trying and let you know if any of them really want to be in the program, or if I can even find them."

Supervisor: "Well, you do have a lot going on right now. Is there something you'd like to focus on today?"

Karen: "Well, I've been thinking a lot about Layla and Jamie . . . you remember them? We talked about them about 2 months ago. Layla is young . . . 19, I think, and Jamie is her 18-month-old little girl. They live with Layla's mom, sister, 6-year-old niece, and I think an uncle and aunt. Layla can't read, doesn't work, has no income, and wants to move out! I can't believe it! She's gotta be more realistic. I'm really working hard for them, and starting to feel frustrated, tired, and burned out. I don't even think I'm helping."

Supervisor: "That's not a good feeling when you're working so hard, is it?" *This supervisee, Karen, is clear about her agenda, which is not always the case. Some supervisees are less clear about their feelings; some are less willing to be open about their feelings. The supervisor's own feelings might be stirred up. She may be feeling that she is at risk of losing another staff member. At this moment the supervisor, Sherlynn, is feeling overwhelmed, too, and thinks to herself, "I don't know how to fix this," and then thinks and reminds herself, "Now wait, slow down, I don't have to fix this, I just have to be fully present."*

Telling the Story and Focusing on the Details

Supervisor: "I do remember this, now that you describe the whole family . . . I remember you saying that you read the parent–child activity ideas to Layla before you left, instead of just leaving the sheet like you usually do. Then you told me she couldn't read, and that you were referring her to the literacy program at the high school . . . a good idea, I thought. Tell me what's happened since then . . . and about the hard work you've been doing."

Karen: "Well, she did sign up for the literacy program, which would also help her get her GED [General Educational Development Test] . . . which she needs to get a good enough job, especially if she wants to be out on her own . . . which I can't imagine anyway! But she never went to the classes . . . she had excuses, like Jamie got sick, or nobody would babysit. So we're going to try again next time it's offered with child care. In the meantime, I took her to the Social Security office because she said they'd turned her down for disability benefits . . . she can't get a job because she can't read. They treated her . . . us both, really . . . so rudely. I can understand why people give up, but I didn't . . . I took her to reapply, they told her she wasn't eligible again, so now I'm helping her appeal. And then, I don't know what good it's doing to follow the parenting curriculum during home visits . . . by the time we get to it, we're all tired . . . I'm there at least 2 hours every time I go, and the Social Security visit was more like 3."

Supervisor: *She now notices how stirred up she is feeling in response to Karen's story. She thinks, "Oh, wow, I don't know what to do." Then she realizes she has to understand her own feelings in order to help Karen. "Maybe I'm picking up on Karen's feelings . . . let me calm down, take a deep breath, and explore what Karen is feeling." She recognizes then that Karen needs to understand her own feelings in order to help Layla.* "Wow . . . no wonder you're tired. I'm tired just listening to your story. You are working very hard for her . . . do you feel like she's working as hard as you are?"

Karen: "Not really, I guess. At first she thought the program would help her get stuff she needed, like diapers and formula . . . even a car! That was one of the goals she wanted to make for herself . . . to get a car. See what I mean about unrealistic? She acts sort of helpless herself, but thinks somehow she'll magically get a car and a place of her own . . . without a job or money."

Supervisor: "And how did you handle it when she wanted to make those unrealistic goals . . . how did you help her think about being realistic?"

Karen: "I just tried to explain that her goals in this program need to focus on how to help her to help Jamie to grow and learn, and I always ask her to think about what little step she can do first toward a bigger goal, like moving out. But I don't think she gets it."

Supervisor: "And what do you think about her overall intelligence?"

Karen: "I think her intelligence is fine . . . she seems smart enough when she talks, and she takes care of herself and Jamie."

Supervisor: "I can hear the frustration in your voice, and maybe even some anger?"

Karen: Stops and thinks, and says, "You're not supposed to get angry with parents, but maybe I am, a little."

Supervisor: "But we all get angry, and this is a place where you can talk about it, and understand it, and think about how it might affect your work with Layla. Do you think it does?"

Karen: Again thoughtful, says, "That's a good question. Do you think Layla can tell I'm angry?"

Supervisor: "Well, she might . . . some people are good at reading feelings. Do you think she is sensitive to your feelings?"

Karen: "Well, she sort of changes the subject when I ask what she's done this week. Maybe she does feel my frustration about her never following through."

Supervisor: "I think you're on your way to understanding this more." *Sherlynn is teaching Karen how to use RS, and that feelings happen but they don't have to be acted out with a family. Sherlynn thinks, "I'm doing better than I expected to in this discussion of strong feelings." She briefly wonders if Karen might get to the place where she could even ask Layla about her feelings [when with Karen], much as Sherlynn is doing with Karen [parallel process].*

Supervisor: "And it sounds like you're able to keep a clear idea in your own mind about what you and the program can and can't do for Layla . . . even though her needs seem overwhelming, and you get so frustrated. I'm wondering if there are times with Layla and Jamie that you feel good or hopeful."

Karen: "I feel good when I see Jamie climb on Layla's lap, and they cuddle . . . I think Layla loves Jamie. I felt like Layla appreciated me helping her with Social Security, no matter what happens. She's starting to trust me, I think. Jamie is saying some words and even likes to look at books. I see Jamie's sister and niece playing with her, too. But I don't understand Layla's reading thing . . . she can't read to Jamie she says. But she's smart enough to learn to read . . . so I wonder what happened that she didn't." *Sherlynn has made sure the talk is about both the strengths and the struggles in this session. Karen can talk about the strengths, but the struggles still are predominant. The supervisor needs to be able to hold the positive without minimizing the negative.*

Understanding Perspectives and Generating Hypotheses

Supervisor: "So it's hard to stick with what Layla is doing right, like cuddling and loving and playing with Jamie . . . because the not reading doesn't make sense. Are there questions you could ask Layla to get more understanding of why she doesn't read?"

Karen: "I don't want to open any can of worms . . . I'm not qualified to be a counselor."

Supervisor: "Sometimes questions can help people think for themselves . . . you know, reflect, like we're doing. Can you think of yourself and Layla as exploring together the dilemma of her not reading . . . wondering together rather than counseling? And maybe asking how she feels about going to literacy classes, or getting a job. Are there reasons she's not ready for either of those things?"

Karen: "Maybe she's scared. Maybe she's had bad experiences in school. But if she's not ready, how can I help her? And especially how can I help Jamie if Layla can't use the parenting stuff with her, or read to her even?"

Supervisor: "Can you think of ways to simplify the information and activity sheets you leave, or about ways you might ask Layla about recruiting other family members to help?"

Karen: "Hmmm . . . maybe I can. I'll think about that."

Supervisor: "In the meantime, remember how well Jamie seems to be doing, and that the other family members are there for her too . . . just like you're there for Layla. It's always a pull in this work to feel responsible for our families' successes or failures, instead of trusting them to do the work. Do you think you feel that way sometimes?"

Karen: "I guess I do . . . and then don't feel like I'm helping at all when they can't or won't do something I think they should."

Supervisor: "You just put your finger on it . . . what we can try to do instead is to help them figure out what they think they should do, rather than what we think they should do." *Karen is able to generate her own reflective questions, much as her supervisor, Sherlynn, has asked questions to help her reflect, thus modeling the goal of RS: to continually reconceptualize what one is observing, feeling, and doing, in order to improve the work.*

Considering Next Steps

Supervisor: "So what do you think you'll do next with Layla and Jamie?"

Karen: "Well, I do have lots of questions in my mind about what stops Layla from learning to read, and I think I can ask her about reading in her childhood . . . when we're talking about reading to Jamie. I can just ask who read to her when she was little, did she like books, did she like school, things like that. And see what I learn about her. I'd be less frustrated if I understood her better. And I'd appreciate some help simplifying the parenting stuff for Layla . . . I was afraid I had to do it by the book, and it sure wasn't working that way. Thanks for reminding me that it's OK to be flexible sometimes." *There are ways to offer expertise, such as to offer ideas or to guide. Karen has begun to formulate hypotheses, and was quickly able to wonder about other perspectives. Many supervisees cannot do this so readily, and in such cases, acknowledging feelings and finding ways to continue connecting with the supervisee is the most important task for a supervisor. Because the supervisor has an ongoing relationship with the supervisee, there will be more time to work on reflective skills with the supervisee. Also keep in mind that sometimes insight occurs between or even across reflective sessions.*

Closing

Supervisor: "That seems like a good plan . . . let me know how Layla responds, and we can talk more if you'd like. We can always go back to the drawing board. I'll see you in 2 weeks on the 14th . . . same time, same place."

Post Supervision Reflection

As Sherlynn writes brief notes about this session with Karen, she realizes that she did not pick up on Karen saying that Layla is starting to trust her. Sherlynn feels that this is a big thing in the relationship-building process for Karen, and that she needs to highlight for Karen how important it is, how long it takes sometimes, and that she is succeeding in this (while also helping Karen to not do too much for Layla that she can do for herself). She adds this to her notes for follow-up with Karen. See Reflective Tool 5 at the end of this chapter. It includes a process log for RS with sample notes from this session.

• • •

GROUP RS: A VIGNETTE

This session illustrates the process of small-group supervision (four to six participants) with home visitors in a family support program. The supervisor, Catalina, is also the program director. She is relatively new to this agency and finds group supervision both rewarding and challenging. This group includes six home visitors (Will, Rachel, Elizabeth, Lauren, Tina, and Latoya) and is relatively cohesive. In the first session, Catalina talked with them about confidentiality and discussed with them the role that each group member has in sharing observations and asking questions that promote reflection with one another. As the supervisor, Catalina's role will be to help guide the process through the phases. Together the group decided on a consultation format in which one group member would take the whole session to present his or her work with a family. The group revisited the format after the first three sessions and decided it was working well. See Copa, Lucinski, Olsen, and Willenburg (1999) for another model of group RS.

Preparation

As in individual supervision, preparation for group supervision includes taking some time to prepare the physical and psychological space to be as comfortable as possible and free of distractions.

Supervisor (Catalina): *Catalina cleans off the conference room table, brings in another chair so there is a place ready for each member, puts a pitcher of water on the table, and hangs the sign: Group in Session on the door. She opens up her Supervision Process Log Notebook, takes a few moments to scan the themes from the last meeting, and reminds herself that Elizabeth will be presenting today. She intentionally does not schedule meetings right after supervision group so she will have time to decompress. Group sessions take a lot of energy, and after the sessions, Catalina needs a few moments to refuel.*

Greeting and Reconnecting

Will: "Hi everybody. What a storm! Did you all see the trees down outside?"

Tina: "The wind was awful out our way. How did you all fare?"

Elizabeth: "We were fine, but my kids were up around midnight. The lightning and thunder were so bad, they couldn't sleep."

Rachel: "We just slept through it like a log. How about you, Latoya?"

Latoya: "We've got rain in our basement. What a mess. I hope it dries out by tonight."

Lauren: "Me, too. Our windows leaked and the carpet is soaked."

Supervisor (Catalina): *Listens attentively, but decides this time not to join in. As in this example, when group members arrive, they typically begin talking informally; their conversations may or may not be work-related. Often the conversation will come to a natural conclusion as group members settle in the room and prepare for the reflective time. As a supervisor, it is important for you to think about your role in participating in these pre-group discussions, especially about self-disclosure and its effect on group dynamics. Because the group was very engaged with each other, this time Catalina decided to be an attentive, supportive presence and not share her story. Personal sharing can help build relationships between coworkers. However, when a supervisor joins in too much with personal sharing, this can (a) divert her from the role of holding and facilitating group process, (b) affect the feelings of safety in the group, or (c) prevent group members from fully focusing on their own experience. As a supervisor, it is very important to think about how to gauge self-disclosure so that the focus of the group remains on the supervisees.*

Opening the Dialogue and Finding the Agenda

Supervisor (Catalina): "It's good to see everyone. I'm glad you all made it through the storm last night. I know it wasn't easy. Let's see, today is Elizabeth's turn to present. Elizabeth, do you have someone in mind you'd like to talk about with the group?" *Catalina welcomes everyone to the group and goes right to work. Catalina is warm, open, and comfortable with taking the lead to begin the session.*

Telling the Story and Focusing on the Details

Elizabeth: "So I guess the biggest challenge I am having right now is with Ms. Johnson. She can't pay the rent this month since she is just starting her new job and she may really get kicked out. That would be a huge step backward for them if that happens."

Supervisor (Catalina): "Can you fill us in on the details of the situation?"

Elizabeth: "She got a couple of months behind on the rent when she was laid off from her old job, and the landlord is threatening to evict her and her kids if she doesn't pay the rent in the next couple of weeks."

Supervisor (Catalina): "Can you share some of what you are thinking and feeling about this at this point?"

Elizabeth: "I guess I really want Ms. Johnson to know that I can't fix this for her. Part of me feels kind of guilty about that. I mean, she will eventually have the money; she just doesn't right now. She's really anxious and feels so much pressure from her landlord. I know I'm not supposed to lend her money, but, gosh, I really wish I could!"

Rachel: "That's always so hard. I think we feel that a lot with families who have financial troubles. Sometimes I wonder how they can sleep at night with those kinds of worries."

Supervisor (Catalina): "This, unfortunately, can be a common dilemma—as everyone here knows. Elizabeth, can you think of any more information from Ms. Johnson that could help you understand the anxiety she is feeling?"

Elizabeth: "I guess, I wonder if anything like this has ever happened to her before and how she handled it. And whether she has a plan for what she and the kids will do if she can't stay in the apartment. I'd like to know if she is even thinking about that." *It is common for themes of strong emotion to be expressed during group supervision, especially once trust has been established among group members. It is crucial that, as Catalina does here, the supervisor allow the group member sharing the story the time for it to unfold and to respond to their emotions before moving onto the next phase.*

Elizabeth: "Ms. Johnson says if somebody doesn't help her, she is going to lose her apartment. I feel very pressured to do something every time I go there."

Supervisor (Catalina): "It sounds like you feel she's pushing you to take care of the problem with the landlord." *Catalina pauses, then says,* "Can you tell us more about that?"

Elizabeth: "It's frustrating. I feel like I can't help her at all, and I don't have any answers for her about this huge problem. I don't know what to do."

Supervisor (Catalina): To everyone on the team, "Is there anything that any of you can think of asking Elizabeth that could help her think more about her work with Ms. Johnson?"

Latoya: "Well, this does seem like a tough situation. I am just wondering if there is anything else that the two of you have been working on together?"

Elizabeth: "It seems like this has been our main focus for the past 2 weeks, but there have been lots of things that we have been doing in the past couple of months. After talking about the importance of babyproofing her apartment, she did it all on her own. Also, she found a home day care for her baby after I gave her a list of resources in her area to call. She'll be going back to work soon, and we have been talking a lot about that. I guess that is why it is so hard not to be able to help her with this—so many other things have been good."

Latoya: "It sounds like the two of you have accomplished some good things for the baby's sake."

Supervisor (Catalina): "It is helpful to remember what's been accomplished when you feel stuck. And it sounds like Ms. Johnson has done a lot for herself. Why does it feel to you now that you should be doing more to help her?"

Elizabeth: "I guess because I feel so sad for her. She's worked so hard in the past year, and it seems so unfair for her to have this setback. Plus, what if she ends up on the street? I'll feel awful if that happens."

Rachel: "I think I know how frustrated you feel ... and sad, too. Sometimes it seems like there aren't many ways of really helping families with these kinds of problems. Do you think she is really expecting you to keep her from losing her apartment?" *In group supervision, all members, not just the supervisor, share the responsibility to ask thoughtful questions and to promote reflection. Here the group, with the supervisor's support, acknowledged the experience and validated the feelings of the supervisee. Elizabeth was then able to think more deeply about her feelings and begin to come to her own conclusions about what is happening in her interaction with this parent.*

Elizabeth: "Every time Ms. Johnson brings up the problems with the landlord I feel really pressured to do something. I think she expects me to fix the problems about the apartment, because she keeps bringing it up. What should I do?"

Lauren: "You should try calling legal aid at the community center. They can help her fight her landlord."

Tina: "Wait a minute, Elizabeth, were you asking what you should do about your feelings of being pressured or about what you should do to help the Johnsons?"

Elizabeth: "I guess I really need to understand why I'm feeling so pressured."

Rachel: "Yeah, that has happened to me to. I have a family like that. Every time I go there I feel overwhelmed because there are so many problems."

Supervisor (Catalina): "I think we are all experiencing the pressure Elizabeth is feeling to fix things quickly for the Johnsons. Lauren's suggestion could be helpful for them, but before we move to solutions let's continue to focus on Elizabeth's feelings about the situation and see what we can learn. Elizabeth, can you tell us more about what happens to make you feel so pressured?"

Elizabeth: "It really hits me when she starts to cry. I just feel so helpless. I don't know what to say. I think I really just want her to stop crying." *[Elizabeth pauses, then shares her aha moment.]* "I wonder if she just needs me to listen and be there. Maybe she keeps bringing it up because she's so anxious about it and feels alone. Maybe she just needs to talk about it. The pressure I'm feeling to save her and her family may be coming from me. Maybe Ms. Johnson just wants me to listen." *By taking time to reflect with supportive questioning, Elizabeth is able to process her own thoughts and feelings. She gains new perspective, which can help move the group's discussion to the next phase of the reflective process. Sometimes a group member may jump in and begin to offer solutions. This often happens as a result of uncomfortable feelings evoked in the group members (and supervisor!) as they empathize with their colleague. Your role as the supervisor is to not only contain your own desire to rescue, but also to help the other group members to contain theirs. Jumping in with a solution too early can derail the supervisee's opportunity to work through the feelings she is having and think more clearly about the situation. When this occurs, gentle reminders to the group about giving the presenter more time to fully explore her experiences and feelings can get things back on track.*

Understanding Perspectives and Generating Hypotheses

Supervisor (Catalina): "What an insight, Elizabeth! How does Ms. Johnson respond to you when you just listen to her?"

Elizabeth: "Now that I think about it, the last time we talked about it she was very upset when she began telling the story, but then her tears began to subside. She even smiled a little and said she just needs me to be there."

Supervisor (Catalina): "So you're probably right, she just needs your ear and your caring. Does she have her own ideas about working with her landlord?"

Elizabeth: "She said she is going to try to explain to the landlord that she is starting a new job and will have the money very soon. Now that she is set to start her new job, she's more confident and this may be easier for her to do."

Supervisor (Catalina): "You know I just realized we've left out a big question . . . the welfare of the children, which is our main reason for working with families. It's easy to forget that when families are in crisis, isn't it?" *In this interaction Catalina realizes that she has begun shifting the focus of the group to a "next-steps" discussion without hearing about an important perspective, that of the children. By acknowledging her mistake and redirecting the focus back to this question, she is modeling reflective practice.*

Latoya: "I've been wondering about the kids . . . how all this tension in the home is affecting them."

Elizabeth: "Ms. Johnson has told me she worries about how it affects the kids to see her so anxious and distracted, and upset."

Will: "Doesn't she have a toddler and a baby?"

Elizabeth: "That's right, Michael is 8 months and Marin is 2. The last time I was there and Ms. Johnson was talking on the phone rather heatedly with the landlord, Michael started to cry. Ms. Johnson went to him right away when she hung up and comforted him. She said something about how all this must be hard on a little baby. She also mentioned that Marin has been really clingy lately and that it has been hard for her to deal with. That's probably something we should focus on more the next time."

Tina: "I wonder what the 2-year-old is thinking and feeling. Kids that age can pick up on a lot, but not really understand. It might feel to Marin like her mom's not really available."

Elizabeth: "That is definitely a possibility, and it's good that Ms. Johnson is aware of her children's feelings and wants to be there for them." *The group has worked to come to an empathic understanding of how a major stressor is affecting all members of the family and the visitor, and to clarify both strengths and needs of all. They are then ready to begin considering next steps.*

Considering Next Steps

Rachel: "Maybe you could talk with Ms. Johnson about ways to reassure the kids that she will be there for them."

Elizabeth: "That is a really good idea. Ms. Johnson is a really good mom, and I know she would want to help her kids feel secure even when things are hard."

Will: "How do you think Ms. Johnson would respond to you bringing up this topic?"

Elizabeth: "I think she would be open to it." *This is a time when the group worked together to integrate the different perspectives and consider possible next steps. In some cases a clear course of action or next step will be called for, but many times there is no concrete action to take other than to continue working to increase understanding and build empathic responsiveness. It is important to remember that the reflective process is not always solution driven.*

Closing

Supervisor (Catalina): "Thank you, Elizabeth, for bringing your work with Ms. Johnson to the group. I think we all have learned from thinking about her with you. I'm just wondering how you are feeling about things now, Elizabeth?"

Elizabeth: "I think I've realized today that what I really need to do is just continue to be present for Ms. Johnson, listen, and offer support to her as she figures out what to do, but it's not up to me to fix it. When I get anxious and overwhelmed on the visits, my goal is to stay calm and remember that she has made progress and that she wants to do the best for her kids. Thank you all for your help. I'll keep you posted."

Supervisor (Catalina): "Thanks again, Elizabeth. Who would like to present next time? We meet again in 2 weeks, same time and same place." *At the end of the group's time together it is important to wrap up the session. The supervisor may use this time to do a check in with each member of the group to process their experience or may just ask the group if anyone has any questions or anything to say in closing. The supervisor may ask the person who has discussed a particular situation what he or she is taking away from the RS experience. Ending the RS group by confirming the next meeting time is an ideal way to finish.*

Post Supervision Reflection

Supervisor (Catalina): *Catalina notes that this group, unlike other groups, has achieved a pretty high level of trust, and most members work hard to support the presenter's reflection, rather than to give advice. She notes that she was a little uncomfortable acknowledging her mistake in not bringing the children into the discussion sooner . . . and then decides that this didn't seem to diminish her staff's respect for her leadership. It may, in fact, have illustrated for them the collaborative nature of reflective practice. She suspects that one or two in the group had been thinking about the children but didn't say anything until she did. The group's next session might be a good opportunity to suggest that they can bring things up that she may miss, using this example.*

●   ●   ●

SUMMARY

To maximize the potential to help, it is important to have a framework to rely on in the face of the ever-changing dynamics of interpersonal relationships. The phases of the supervisory process presented here are a tool for your thinking. With this as one framework, you can experiment and tailor the supervisory process to fit your style, your program, and your supervisees. Our most important message is to develop a consistent, reliable, and trustworthy space—both physical and psychological—where your supervisee(s) knows what to expect from you and what you expect from them.

Even with care and attention, supervision is an imperfect process, in which getting back on track is as essential to the method as careful attunement. To provide quality supervision, we recommend that you receive quality supervision. Agencies offering RS must make available an ongoing forum for supervisors to receive consultation and/or supervision around this aspect of their role. Nowhere is the platinum rule more applicable than to the practice of supervision: "Do unto others as you would have them do unto others" (Pawl, 1995, p. 43).

REFERENCES

Copa, A., Lucinski, L., Olsen, E., & Willenburg, K. (1999). Promoting professional and organizational development: A reflective practice model. *Zero to Three, 20*(1), 3–9.

Gilkerson, L., & Shahmoon-Shanok, R. (2000). Relationships for growth: Cultivating reflective practice in infant, toddler, and preschool programs. In J. Osofsky & H. E. Fitzgerald (Eds.), *WAIMH handbook of infant mental health: Early intervention, evaluation, and assessment.* New York: John Wiley & Sons.

Northcutt, T. B. (2000). Constructing a place for religion and spirituality in psychodynamic practice. *Clinical Social Work Journal, 28*(2), 155–169.

Pawl, J. (1995). On supervision. In R. Shahmoon-Shanok, L. Gilkerson, L. Eggbeer, & E. Fenichel (Eds.), *Reflective supervision: A relationship for learning* (pp. 41–49). Washington, DC: ZERO TO THREE.

Remen, R. N. (1996). *Kitchen table wisdom.* New York: Penguin.

Reflective Tool 5

Process Log for Reflective Supervision Session

Reflective Tool 5 is meant to be used as a worksheet for the supervisor following each reflective supervision (RS) session. The goal of the process log is to provide the supervisor with an opportunity to sit back and consider the session, its themes, and affective tone. It also supports the supervisor in considering the session in terms of themes that have occurred in prior sessions and allows the supervisor to consider potential areas or themes to be aware of or to follow up in future sessions. The log is meant to take 5 to 10 minutes to complete and is used to highlight aspects of the session. The second page of this reflective tool includes an example of a completed process log.

Supervisee _____ Date _____

Supervisor _____

			OBSERVATIONS What Happened	REFLECTIONS Feelings, Meanings, and Follow-up
POSTSESSION REFLECTION: PROCESS LOG	Recurring Themes			
	Affect	• How was the supervisee feeling? • How was I feeling?		
	Supervisee's Engagement	• How was the supervisee using supervision?		
	How Was I?	• Was I comfortable? • Was I present? • Was I anxious? • Why or why not?		

	Flow of Session	• Did we use all phases?
		  –Preparation
		  –Greeting/reconnect
		  –Finding the agenda
		  –Focusing on details
		  –Perspectives and hypotheses
		  –Next steps
		  –Closing		

Sample Process Log of an Individual Reflective Supervision Session

Supervisee _____ Karen _____ Date _____ 9/30/08 _____

Supervisor _____ Sherlynn _____

			OBSERVATIONS What Happened	REFLECTIONS Feelings, Meanings, and Follow-up
POSTSESSION REFLECTION: PROCESS LOG	**Recurring Themes**		1. How to use curriculum.	1. New curriculum, little practice. K feeling pressure to do it right. I don't much like curriculum myself, but see why it's needed to guide staff.
	Affect	• How was the supervisee feeling? • How was I feeling?	1. K feeling frustrated, a little angry with parent. 2. Worried about K, at first, then pleased that I could talk about her feelings.	1. K feeling helpless when parents can't do what she thinks they should…does she need to feel "in charge"? I still need practice with understanding negative feelings and how to explore with staff. Good that K thinks parent trusts her more. Next session I should remind K about this success.
	Supervisee's Engagement	• How was the supervisee using supervision?	1. K seems very engaged, is able to look at her own feelings and wonder about them.	1. She's learned to trust the process. Perhaps I should acknowledge more to K how good she has gotten at using supervision for reflection.
	How Was I?	• Was I comfortable? • Was I present? • Was I anxious? • Why or why not?	Not comfortable during anger discussions. Anger scares me, but I relaxed after K was able to consider it.	
	Flow of Session	• Did we use all phases? –Preparation –Greeting/reconnect –Finding the agenda –Focusing on details –Perspectives and hypotheses –Next steps –Closing	Yes.	1. Both K and I have experience enough with reflective work to know the routine. The flow gets to be natural after a while.

How Do I, as a Reflective Supervisor, Repair Ruptures in the Supervisory Relationship?

Angela W. Keyes, Amy E. Cavanaugh, and Sherryl Scott Heller

> *Relationships are all there is. Everything in the universe only exists because it is in relationship to everything else. Nothing exists in isolation. We have to stop pretending we are individuals who can go it alone.*
>
> —Margaret Wheatley (2009, p. 23)

Although reflective supervision (RS) provides many benefits to the organization and the individual, challenges are encountered in the supervisory relationship. These challenges and tensions can be on the part of the reflective supervisor, the supervisee, or a combination of the two. If the issues are not addressed, they can become a fixed part of the relationship and lead to a breakdown in the reflective process. However, if they are addressed sensitively and effectively, these challenges can strengthen the supervisory relationship and provide a unique opportunity for mutual growth.

In this chapter, we provide examples of behaviors that may be indicative of a rupture in the supervisory relationship, attributes that may contribute to tensions or disruptions in the relationship, and strategies to address and repair relationship ruptures. By the end of this chapter, you will be able to:

1. Understand the role that rupture and repair can play in strengthening the supervisory relationship.

2. Increase your comfort in exploring tensions within the relationship.

3. Use Reflective Tool 6 to help you process times when your relationship with a supervisee is out of sync and consider ways to repair the relationship.

RELATIONSHIP RUPTURE

The prior two chapters focused on the development of the RS relationship and the phases of an RS session. All relationships—including supervisory relationships—experience ruptures, periods of disruption, or disharmony. For the supervisory relationship, we define rupture as a breakdown in the collaborative process (Safran & Muran, 2006). The key to a strong and healthy relationship is not to avoid ruptures, but rather to repair ruptures in a healthy manner. As Weatherston and Barron (this volume, p. 63) state, "RS requires the construction of a secure and trusting relationship". Thus, the key to healthy relationships in supervision is the ability to recognize and acknowledge disruptions then work to repair the relationship.

The following sections describe some of the more common kinds of relationship disharmony that we have encountered in our experience as reflective supervisors (and supervisees). Our goal is not to provide an exhaustive list, but rather to present some feelings and behaviors that can impede the reflective process, model ways to think about these issues, and provide some strategies to handle relationship ruptures.

Supervisee Behaviors

An effective and positive relationship between the supervisor and supervisee is critical to the success of RS. Sometimes, issues arise in the relationship that can be attributed to difficulties that the supervisee may be experiencing. It is therefore important that the reflective supervisor be aware of potential challenges and work to overcome them by joining with the supervisee. The following are some examples of problems that may occur in the supervisory relationship.

Supervisee silences. As with most behaviors, supervisee silence in response to questions or comments may be indicative of a variety of things. For example, silence may mean that the supervisee (a) is thinking about what he wants to say or needs time to process something the supervisor has said, (b) disagrees with the supervisor's comment or is uncomfortable with the supervisor's line of questioning, or (c) is uncomfortable with the reflective process (this is more common at the beginning of relationship) or with the supervisor. A quiet participant may not be as obvious in group supervision sessions. For some people, participating in group discussions is frightening, and although they are not actively participating, they are actively absorbing the information. Whatever the reason, whether the RS format is individual or group, it is important for the supervisor to be aware of this individual's behavior and to consider its meaning and impact on the group and the supervisory relationship. As highlighted in chapter 3 (Boris & Grabert, this volume, p. 41), being aware of the supervisee's body language is informative when considering the meaning of his behavior. When RS occurs over the phone, nonverbal behavior is not so easily observed but can still include long pauses, silences, short or rushed answers, or hurried sessions.

When frequent periods of silence occur within and across sessions, the reflective supervisor may respond by jumping in too quickly or overtalking (see the next section on supervisor behaviors for more discussion on this). It is important for the supervisor to be aware not only of the supervisee's behavior but also of her own response to the behavior. Moreover, the supervisor must be careful not to jump to conclusions about the meaning of the behavior but to reflect on it, ideally with the supervisee. One way is to ask, "Is this quietness okay? Does it help you to reflect on your work? If you like, I can be more active." Another way is to process this with your own supervisor and consider various ways to respond to and reflect on the behavior with the supervisee.

Frequent cancellations. Frequent cancellations or no-shows for scheduled sessions indicate that something is not working. The reason could be any number of things, such as: (a) the time and day are bad for the supervisee, yet the supervisee doesn't feel comfortable enough in the relationship to request a change; (b) the supervisee may be hesitant to devote her time and energy to a process that, by definition, encourages her to slow down and dig deep—two tasks that may seem trivial or even threatening to the individual; (c) the supervisee may view RS as optional, especially if management does not appear to value RS (see chapters 2 [Scott Heller, this volume, p. 25] and 7 [Bertacchi & Gilkerson, this volume, p. 121] for more on the importance of management buy-in); or (d) the supervisee may be overwhelmed

How Do I, as A Reflective Supervisor, Repair
Ruptures in the Supervisory Relationship?

101

because of organizational or professional stress (e.g., end of fiscal year, review time, or grant-writing times) or personal stress (e.g., illness in the family, divorce) and is unable to commit time to RS (ironically, this is when RS can be particularly useful).

The bottom line, regardless of the reason, is that cancellations are communications from the supervisee to the supervisor. Your task is to explore these cancellations in a supportive way to learn more about the supervisee and about what is important to him in the present, determine what is hindering his participation, and come to a new agreement about the supervisory commitment. Without consistency in the relationship, building and maintaining rapport become more difficult and can lead to further disruption to the reflective supervisory relationship. It is possible, more often than not, to deepen the relationship through a thoughtful exploration of absences and a mutual recontracting for supervision. It might mean that you understand the supervisee in a new way or that you change the frequency, adjust the format, or regularly ask for feedback. If consistency and active participation cannot be achieved, it may mean that others, such as the administrative supervisor, will need to be involved to address the issue. The agency should have a policy in place for cancellations in RS, and the supervisee should be advised before RS begins of the expectations regarding his participation. If the supervisee's cancellations become a chronic problem, the reflective supervisor should review the supervision contract with the supervisee, and if the issue cannot be resolved, the supervisor should remind the supervisee of the agency policy and the need to speak with the administrative supervisor about the matter. The supervisee should be encouraged to communicate about RS with the administrative supervisor as well, as perhaps the reason for cancellations is an issue that he may feel more comfortable addressing with the director rather than the reflective supervisor. In any event, direct communication between the supervisor and the supervisee about agency policy and the need to address issues with the administrative supervisor is best practice.

Providing just the facts. Sometimes supervisees spend the session focusing more on content and what they have done over the past week rather than processing the meaning or impact of those events. In other words, the supervisee relates facts and details in a relatively concrete manner without reflecting on the underlying meaning of events that have occurred. As a result, the reflective session is used as a time to report the "what" without thinking about the "why" or the supervisee's feelings about the events. There are many possibilities as to the cause of this behavior. Sometimes the supervisee is unfamiliar or uncomfortable with the reflective process itself and is not sure how to move beyond the content (this challenge is discussed in more detail later in this chapter). In other cases, the supervisee sees RS as a time to report what has been done so she can feel accomplished or to ensure that it is clear to her supervisor that she is doing her job. In some cases, it may be how the supervisee processes: In other words, reciting what she has done helps the supervisee to recall her caseload and choose where to start and/or helps her to become comfortable engaging in the deeper reflective process. Or it may be that the supervisee does not yet feel safe enough to trust the relationship with more intimately held thoughts or feelings. You want to understand why the supervisee is taking this approach and then adjust your response accordingly.

One approach to address this challenge is for the supervisor to allow time for the supervisee to both report and reflect on his work. For example, the supervisor could say something like, "Let's take 5 minutes to review, then we'll segue into something you find yourself thinking about a lot." Conversely, the supervisor can simply listen and when a topic arises that seems to elicit emotion, whether positive or negative, slow the supervisee down and ask questions that encourage reflection. For example, the supervisor could say, "Tell me more about that. It seems like this center/client/family really means a lot to you," then pause and allow time for the supervisee to answer. Or when the supervisor senses that the supervisee feels wary and unsure, listening with acceptance and genuine interest to all the details can help increase the supervisee's feelings of safety and build a base for reflection.

Rushing through a session. The supervisee may report that everything is fine or that she is not experiencing any difficulties in the work environment. This scenario seems to be especially common when supervision is conducted over the telephone, without the immediacy of face-to-face contact. As with other challenges, there are multiple possibilities as to why this may be occurring. Perhaps the supervisee (a) is distracted by other demands; (b) believes that RS focuses only on problems or issues and not on celebrations or successes; (c) does not feel connected to the supervisor or the reflective process; or (d) is worried that if she discusses problems, it will reflect negatively on her and be reflected in her work evaluation.

Whatever the reason, it is important that the supervisor neither ignores nor jumps to conclusions about the cause or meaning of a supervisee's behavior, but rather inquires in way that invites collaboration. This inquiry should allow the supervisee to reflect on his behavior and respond in a healthy and non-defensive manner. For example, the supervisor may inquire about any celebrations that the supervisee wants to share or just ask about the current status of a case that the two have discussed in the past (e.g., "We haven't talked about the Smiths in awhile. What is happening with them?" Then as the supervisee responds, the supervisor can gently probe for details). When a more subtle approach ceases to change the behavior, the supervisor may feel comfortable bringing up the behavior and inquiring about it directly as in the following example:

•   •   •

Denise (supervisor) and Gloria (supervisee) lived in different towns and had been conducting RS sessions over the phone for more than a year.

Supervisee (Gloria): *Gloria was the director of a rather large child care center and often had to multitask in order to get everything done.*

Supervisor (Denise): *Gloria and Denise had a long-standing appointment for their RS. However, lately when Denise called, Gloria was not available or was not able to focus her attention on the session. Denise had been frustrated by this behavior and had discussed it with her own supervisor on a number of occasions. Regardless of Denise's patience and gentle probes, she felt that the sessions had gotten stuck. Finally, Denise decided to try a more direct approach and said to Gloria,* "I notice that when I call, even though we have scheduled our time together, you are distracted and it is difficult for you to pay attention to our session."

Supervisee (Gloria): *Gloria apologized and said,* "There is always so much going on, I just don't have the time to do this. I feel so overwhelmed and the more I try, the more I seem to let people down. I know this is supposed to be important and I do value it, but something always seems to come up."

How Do I, as a Reflective Supervisor, Repair
Ruptures in the Supervisory Relationship?

103

Supervisor (Denise): *Denise could hear Gloria's frustration and knew that Gloria had been an active participant of RS in the past. She was also aware that Gloria had just managed a number of staff and client crises and that Gloria's organization was in the midst of an internal evaluation. Denise responded, "Wow, it is hard to have so much on your plate. I can hear how hard you are trying to meet everyone's needs!" [pause] "I certainly don't want to have RS become a burden. Do you think it would help if you and I spent some time coming up with ideas to help you organize things a bit differently?" By responding with empathy and pointing out to Gloria the benefit of reflecting, she showed Gloria that sometimes it is necessary to slow down and step out of the immediate situation in order to get more done. More important, Denise did so in a manner that allowed Gloria to feel safe, nurtured, and heard so that she (Gloria) could hear Denise's message and collaborate with Denise on a solution as opposed to shutting down and becoming defensive.*

• • •

We hope we have demonstrated in this section the importance of being aware of your supervisee's behavior and being open to not knowing; that is, exploring a number of possible causes and modeling how you would want your supervisee to respond to a challenging situation. Often the supervisor may try one strategy unsuccessfully and then need to regroup to try another. In our experience, it is typically best to start with the most subtle approach and then notch it up to a more direct style if needed. Every relationship has at least two partners, thus it is essential to consider your own behaviors and responses and how they may be contributing to difficult interactions. It is important to remember that, as with most of our work in early intervention, there is rarely one right approach but rather many paths leading toward healthy resolution. The key is to select the path that best fits your style (as a supervisor) and your supervisee's needs.

Supervisor Behaviors

Maintaining an awareness of a supervisee's behavior and the impact of the behavior on the RS session and the supervisee's work is important. However, it is equally important for the supervisor to be aware of his own behavior, its meaning, and its impact on the supervisee and the RS session. As in the previous section, the following list is not exhaustive, but rather a list of some common supervisor behaviors that can impede the reflective process.

Overtalking. A supervisor may find that she is overtalking in the session. There can be any one of multiple reasons for this behavior, it may be (a) in response to the supervisee's lack of participation (e.g., supervisee silences or "everything is going fine" statements); that is, when presented with repeated supervisee silences, a reflective supervisor may feel pressured to generate topics for discussion; (b) a way for the supervisor to manage anxiety that may be evoked when encountering a challenge in the reflective relationship; or (c) a means of making herself feel useful to the supervisee. It is important for the reflective supervisor to become comfortable with the silences and to continue to support the supervisee as trust is built in the supervisory relationship (Weatherston & Barron, this volume, p. 63, eloquently describe the power of silence in RS relationship). Often simply being silent allows the supervisee to process her work or her supervisor's comments. It also signals to the supervisee that this is her time and that the supervisor is there to listen and to support her.

When overtalking stems from feelings of anxiety within the supervisor, the supervisor can reflect on this herself or seek consultation from her own reflective supervisor (or colleague) to process these feelings. You might well bring these reflections back into the relationship. For example, "Last time, you were talking about the new caseload requirements. I noticed that I talked a lot more than I usually do—so much that I don't think you had time to share your thoughts about the new model. I thought about this later and realized I was feeling stirred up about these changes, too. I want to make sure you have enough time to talk about this and wonder if you have any more you'd like to share?"

It is also possible that the supervisor's anxiety is a clue to what may be happening for the supervisee or the supervisee's client. In this case, the supervisor might bring his own feelings back into the conversation by saying, "During our last session, I realized that I was feeling a lot of anxiety as you described the mother's interactions about her baby. I'm just wondering if you feel that way at all when you are with them?"

Frequent schedule changes. Just as with supervisees, supervisors may find themselves frequently cancelling or rescheduling. Ideally this would never happen, but in reality there is no way to avoid the occasional need to reschedule a session. Regardless, it is important to keep in mind that changing the time or date of a reflective session can be very disruptive to the supervisee and her schedule. Often the supervisee holds off acting on issues until she can discuss it in RS, so rescheduling may interfere with the supervisee's ability to address a pressing issue. When rescheduling happens repeatedly, it gives the message to the supervisee that she is not important or valued, which is counter to the whole premise of RS.

When a supervisor finds himself cancelling or rescheduling sessions repeatedly, it is important that he reflect on this behavior immediately. As with most behaviors, there can be any one of numerous causes. It may be that (a) the day or time a session is scheduled has become a bad one for the supervisor, and he needs to work with the supervisee to find another time or day that is good for both of them; (b) the supervisor is struggling in his relationship with the supervisee, perhaps because the supervisee has begun to exhibit some of the behaviors discussed in the previous section or something has occurred in the session that is impacting the supervisor emotionally; or (c) there is something going on in the supervisor's personal or professional life that is interfering with his ability to provide RS. In these last two cases, it is essential that the supervisor reflect with his own reflective supervisor about his struggle. Similar to the way in which mental health professionals seek consultation or supervision when their personal or professional challenges influence or impede their work performance, reflective supervisors benefit from having the support and objective perspective provided by their own reflective supervisor. In a confidential setting, the reflective supervisor can process the reasons for his cancellations and work toward a solution. These reflective supervision sessions can occur less frequently than typical RS sessions, such as once or twice per month.

Not taking charge when appropriate. In RS, the supervisor is cautioned against jumping in and providing solutions or taking over the session. However, there are instances when this is a necessary and appropriate part of your commitment to keep the relationship safe. It is a bit of a slippery slope, yet it is

How Do I, as A Reflective Supervisor, Repair
Ruptures in the Supervisory Relationship?

105

one that is important to master. Ideally, the supervisee has thought about the session in advance and comes prepared with topics to discuss, the supervisor can then be a supportive and active listener whose probes allow the supervisee to ponder more deeply and move toward a better understanding of herself and her work, which in the end enables her to respond appropriately to her client. In reality, this is not always the case. There are times when the supervisee is silent or hesitant and the supervisor needs to either explore a bit more directly or sit patiently with the silence. Sometimes the actual processing or aha moment happens between rather than within sessions. This is what we refer to when we guide supervisors and supervisees to "trust the process." However, there are also moments when this does not happen, when the supervisee gets stuck and the probes or silences cause only further frustration. It is in this instance when we, as reflective supervisors, find ourselves slipping into more of a coaching role.

It is important to be aware when you, as a supervisor, are becoming more of a manager than an active listener. Although we do not recommend jumping in and saying, "When I have experienced this I have . . ." or "I think the best solution is for you to . . ." what we are suggesting is that the reflective supervisor may want to present suggestions in the form of a question, "Hmmm, what do you think would happen if . . ." or "I wonder what Ms. Smith would think if you . . . " Sometimes merely making suggestions in the form of a question can jump-start the reflective process. In our experience, individuals new to the field tend to need more of this type of support. However, it is essential that the supervisor is careful not to fall into the habit of repeatedly using this strategy, especially if the supervisee immediately agrees and implements the suggestion without much reflection.

In some instances the supervisee may say, "Ugh! I am stuck, what would you do?!?" or "I am too tired to process, just tell me what to do!" Again your response, as the supervisor, is dependent on the context of the relationship. For example, an individual you have been supervising awhile who is typically reflective may actually be stuck and need a little more support. You can be a bit more comfortable doing this when you are confident that the supervisee understands that this is not the role you will typically play. You can talk about this directly. Whereas if the supervisee is an individual with whom you are also the administrative supervisor, you may want to be more cautious in providing a solution. The supervisee may feel that he has to follow your suggestions as you are his boss (Bertacchi & Gilkerson, this volume, p. 121, discusses the dual role issue in more detail).

POTENTIAL BARRIERS TO RELATIONSHIP BUILDING

In our lists of supervisee and supervisor behaviors that may indicate dysynchrony (or in more common terms, *falling out of sync*), we have suggested some possible causes and responses. In this section, we discuss some of the factors that may contribute to dysynchrony or disharmony in the reflective supervisory relationship. Before dysynchrony or rupture can be addressed, the reflective supervisor should consider possible reasons as to why the supervisee may be feeling or acting in a certain way. Some of the potential factors that we discuss in the following sections are (a) mistrust of the reflective process, the reflective supervisor, or management; (b) limited reflective ability of the supervisee; (c) cultural differences; or (d) inappropriate expectations about RS. As with the prior two sections on supervisee and supervisor challenging behaviors, this list is not meant to be exhaustive, but to present some potential contributors and, more important, model appropriate strategies to address ruptures.

Mistrust

Mistrust can occur in multiple domains; it can be in regard to the reflective process, the actual reflective supervisor, the organization's management, or a combination of the three. For example, a supervisee may be (a) suspicious of the reflective process, which may be attributed to a lack of understanding about RS, particularly about the nature of confidentiality; that is, she may be concerned that the reflective supervisor will report back to the supervisee's administrative supervisor regarding what was said in the RS session, seeing RS as a way of management keeping tabs on the supervisee's performance rather than the organization supporting her professional development and growth; (b) concerned about why she was chosen to participate in RS and suspect that it is because management thinks her work performance requires further monitoring; or (c) confusing supervision with therapy, believing that she is viewed as needing assistance with mental health issues. Even when the staff have attended presentations on RS, participated in interviews or focus groups about it, and participated in planning its implementation (as discussed in Scott Heller, this volume, p. 25), suspicion about RS and its purpose or usefulness may still occur. Even when supervisees are silent or signal that everything is fine, especially at the start of the RS process, it is helpful to remind the supervisee about the purpose of RS.

•   •   •

Ellen (supervisor) and Geneva (supervisee) were at the beginning of a new supervisory relationship. Ellen was new to the organization, and Geneva had just been promoted from lead teacher to center director. Both were a bit apprehensive and uncertain about their new roles. The fact that they had never met prior to beginning RS further complicated the situation. Geneva was especially hesitant to discuss her concerns about the center or to share any personal information.

Ellen: "I'm so happy to have the opportunity to work together. I realize that I'm new here and I don't know everyone just yet. Since this is our first meeting, I wonder how it feels for you."

Geneva: "It feels weird. I don't know what I'm supposed to be saying or what we're supposed to do for this hour every week."

Ellen: "I can understand that you might be a little uncomfortable. It's strange to think about what will happen in RS, but I think once we've had a chance to get to know each other, we'll have a lot to talk about."

Ellen senses Geneva's apprehension about RS and talking openly about her thoughts and feelings with this "stranger."

Geneva: "Well, I really don't talk much about myself. I feel like my personal life is just that—personal—and everybody can see the job that I do here. I know I'm new to the position, but I think I've done a good job so far."

Ellen: "I want to emphasize that my role here is to support you in your job. I assure you that I will never ask you to talk about anything that you're not comfortable sharing. You can dictate the pace and content of our sessions. All I ask is that we both make a commitment to meet regularly so that we can

How Do I, as A Reflective Supervisor, Repair Ruptures in the Supervisory Relationship?

107

develop a relationship that is beneficial to you. I need your feedback to let me know if I'm meeting my goal of being helpful to you, so I'll depend on you to tell me what you need from me."

After a few weeks of regular meetings, Ellen and Geneva built a relationship that allowed Geneva to feel comfortable sharing her thoughts not only about her job, but also about her personal life.

• • •

Limited Experience With Reflective Process

The effectiveness of RS is affected by the supervisee's ability to think reflectively. Reflective function is defined as "the capacity to envision and think about mental states" (Fonagy & Target, 1997, p. 679), in oneself and in others, in the service of building realistic models of why they behave, think, and feel as they do (Bouchard, Target, Lecours, Fonagy, Tremblay, Schachter, & Stein, 2008). The ability to be reflective varies across individuals, with some people being more or less reflective in their daily lives and their relationships. Often supervisees who are more concrete in their thinking wonder about how "to do" RS or what the supervisor is looking for during the session. Fortunately, becoming more reflective is a skill that can be learned with support, often through modeling and the asking of open-ended questions by the reflective supervisor. However, it is a process that may take time and involves the building of trust.

Individuals who have not had exposure to reflective thinking may be uncomfortable with the process. It is challenging and at times frightening to learn a new skill, especially when it is a skill that requires revealing oneself; that is, sharing one's thoughts and feelings about the work. It is not uncommon for those with limited experience in reflective processing to struggle with this new challenge. For some people, simply seeing a situation from another person's perspective means that their own view is incorrect. In other words, for certain supervisees, there is a right answer and a wrong answer; to see a situation from multiple perspectives and use the various perspectives to help determine the best course of action are overwhelming and uncomfortable.

For example, a teacher in an early intervention child care program working with a teen mother who consistently brings her baby into the center with a dirty diaper may see this mom as being lazy and disrespectful. To see the situation from the mother's point of view, that the mother is tired from taking three buses to get to the center, means that the teacher is wrong in her view and that it is okay for the mother to bring in a child with dirty diapers. Helping this teacher to slow down and understand that it is okay for her to feel her own feelings of being disrespected is a first step. Recognizing the mother has a different set of feelings and needs is a second step. Then, learning to accept that both perspectives—the mother's and the teacher's feelings—can be valid and that one does not negate the other is taking yet another step toward accepting the complexity that lives within human interactions. This can be difficult to do when the teacher is already uncomfortable with the reflective process. Yet, repeated experiences of being heard, validated, and respected can fill the supervisee's experience bank with a new way of listening and responding.

Cultural Differences

Cultural factors impact the way we all view and make sense of our world. Cultural factors may include any number of attributes: level of education, professional experiences, race, personal history, job role, ethnicity/culture, gender, life experiences, personality, religious beliefs, or a variety and combination of many other characteristics. These attributes may come into play either consciously or unconsciously by either the supervisor or the supervisee. It is important to recognize that despite a perceived sameness of the supervisor and supervisee (i.e., race, gender, or both), differences may still exist due to the complexity associated with characteristics such as regional differences, personal and family history, and religious beliefs or values (Heffron, Ivins, & Weston, 2005). The reflective supervisor must be mindful of instances when differences arise during the reflective session and be willing to process any negative feelings with the supervisee. Having an awareness of his own beliefs and values and reflecting on the feelings associated with these beliefs assist the reflective supervisor in developing strategies for handling differences in a thoughtful and sensitive manner.

To be effective, the reflective supervisor observes, asks questions, and tolerates differences. For example, a younger mental health professional, who has expertise in counseling, may still feel intimidated or less helpful to an older supervisee who has more years of experience specific to early intervention. Having an opening discussion about the supervisor's and supervisee's professional backgrounds and experiences allows both parties to appreciate where the other is coming from and recognize that RS will likely be a learning experience for both of them. This is demonstrated in the following vignette:

•   •   •

Carol has just begun to supervise India because of staffing changes within the agency where the two of them were employed. India was upset that she had been assigned a new reflective supervisor. India had enjoyed a close, collegial relationship with her former supervisor, with whom she shared many professional and personal similarities. Both were minorities, both had gone back to school to earn their college degree after having children, and were the same age. Carol was new to the organization and the field of early intervention, was a Caucasian, and had just earned a graduate degree in mental health.

Carol recognized that in order for this new relationship to move forward, she first had to acknowledge that India was justified in feeling hurt, perhaps even betrayed by the organization for making the change, that any change (especially sudden change) is difficult, and that feelings of loss for the former supervisor and a reluctance to engage in a new reflective relationship were understandable. The second step was to assure India that no one could replace her former supervisor, but perhaps this new relationship could be given a try, encouraging an open mind but keeping expectations modest.

Carol, after discussions with her own supervisor, realized that there was a lot she could learn from India, who has many years of experience in the field, and that the two of them would need to discuss their different backgrounds and remain open to differences in beliefs and values because of their cultural differences. The third step was for India to process with Carol what India appreciated or found helpful about working with the former supervisor, incorporating those skills or techniques when possible, while also remaining authentic to Carol's own skills and style. She also needed to trust that Carol did indeed respect her experience and was sincere in her acknowledgment that their cultural backgrounds may lead them to draw different conclusions about events (i.e., the change of supervisors without discussing the change with India), and that these issues should be discussed in their sessions rather than avoided. Although India never forgot her former supervisor, the relationship was able to progress and India was able to see the supervisory change as an opportunity rather than a setback.

•   •   •

There are many differences that ultimately exist between individuals by virtue of personal experiences and life history, as well as racial, cultural, or regional differences. Despite interpersonal differences, it is essential that the reflective supervisor presents herself in a real, authentic manner and works with the supervisee to both understand and respect their differences. The supervisor is encouraged to be genuinely who she is and support the supervisee in doing the same. Only then can a true relationship, based on trust and mutuality of effort, be built.

Relationship Pitfalls

Although RS is not therapy, issues that arise in therapeutic relationships can also be present in and affect the RS relationship. Reflective supervisors have to guard against the same pitfalls as mental health practitioners in maintaining effective working relationships with their supervisees. Some common pitfalls include rescue fantasies, overinvestment in the supervisee's performance, overidentification with the supervisee, and transference/countertransference.

Rescue fantasies. Rather than empowering the supervisee to solve his own challenges, a reflective supervisor may wish to "rescue" the supervisee from his problem. A common rescue behavior exhibited by supervisors is to give advice or directly tell the supervisee what to do to solve his problem, rather than allowing the supervisee the time and space to find the solution that works for him. Another rescue behavior is when the supervisor intervenes on the behalf of the supervisee, attempting to handle the problem herself rather than having confidence that the supervisee will be able to do so. A supervisee who is unable or unwilling to implement an action plan or solution discussed in RS may be demonstrating a wish to be rescued because of his own insecurity about the situation and/or his abilities. Supervisors need to be careful not to jump in and attempt to fix or solve the problem for the supervisee. Rather, the supervisor can use this as an opportunity for reflection—to explore with the supervisee the supervisor's inclination to give him advice, intervene on his behalf, or discuss why the supervisee has not implemented an action plan. Through this process, the supervisee may increasingly learn to trust his own abilities, experience, and knowledge.

Overinvestment. A reflective supervisor may also become overly invested in a supervisee's performance, taking it personally when a supervisee succeeds or fails in her professional life. Just as a therapist learns to not take too much credit or too much blame for his client's behavior, so must a reflective supervisor learn to maintain a healthy boundary between himself and his supervisee.

• • •

Susan (supervisor) was responsible for providing RS to five home visitors who worked in her program. Lori (supervisee) and Susan had been working together for over a year and met for RS every other week. Kathy provided RS to Susan once a month; the focus of these sessions was on Susan's provision of RS to her staff.

Supervisor (Susan): *Susan was an experienced social worker who had been with her organization for several years. She enjoyed working with Lori and found that the two had a lot in common.*

Supervisee (Lori): *Lori enjoyed her new job; she found it challenging at times but was glad to have RS to help her keep things in perspective. Lori was expecting her first child in the coming month, and part of RS focused on how best to handle her maternity leave and her clients' needs.*

Supervisor (Susan): *Susan is having her monthly RS session with Kathy. Lori has become the focus of this session.*

Supervisor's Supervisor (Kathy): "So when is Lori's last day of work?"

Supervisor (Susan): "She hasn't given us an official date. The baby is due in 4 weeks. Lori would like to work up to the last day possible so she can have as much time as possible with her baby before returning from maternity leave."

Supervisor's Supervisor (Kathy): "She must be excited about the new baby's arrival."

Supervisor (Susan): "Yes, she is. And she is at that end phase where you're tired all of the time. I am amazed she is still getting around and putting in full days."

Supervisor's Supervisor (Kathy): *[laughs]* "I remember those days."

Supervisor (Susan): "Me, too. I am so excited for her. Spending time with her reminds me of when I was preparing for the arrival of my first child. You think you are ready for it all and then the baby arrives and everything changes."

Supervisor's Supervisor (Kathy): "Can anything really prepare you for that experience?"

Supervisor (Susan): "No. I just remember how in love I fell with my daughter. I knew I was gonna love her, but she was so helpless and amazing at the same time. Boy, it was hard to come back to work. I really struggled with it."

Supervisor's Supervisor (Kathy): "Mmm-mm." *[Kathy acknowledges she hears Susan, but says nothing more in order to allow Susan to process her thoughts.]*

Supervisor (Susan): "I ended up leaving the organization I was working with and moving to another company where I could work part-time. It was just too hard to be a full-time social worker and a mom. I kept bringing the stress home, especially when working with babies who were so needy."

Supervisor's Supervisor (Kathy): "That can be quite a challenge."

How Do I, as A Reflective Supervisor, Repair Ruptures in the Supervisory Relationship?

111

The session continues and the two discuss some of Susan's other supervisees and their cases. The following month when Susan and Kathy meet for RS, the focus returns to Lori and her cases.

Supervisor (Susan): "She is going to terminate with two of her families. They are doing well, and I think the timing works out fine. She plans to touch base with them when she returns just to see how things are going. She just started with another family, but Charles [another social worker] has met them and will pick up that family, as they still need quite a bit of support. As for her other cases, she will keep them. They are willing to wait for her return and know how to reach me if they need anything while she is out."

Supervisor's Supervisor (Kathy): "So how did her final session go with the Smiths and Jacksons?"

Supervisor (Susan): "I don't think she has had it yet. She's been out sick."

Supervisor's Supervisor (Kathy): "Oh?"

Supervisor (Susan): "I think it is more fatigue than anything."

Supervisor's Supervisor (Kathy): *As the session continues, it is clear that a lot of Lori's cases haven't been wrapped up or passed on.* "When is Lori returning from maternity leave?"

Supervisor (Susan): "I am not sure. I know she has 6 weeks' paid leave. Then she said she wanted to take an extra 6 weeks of unpaid leave. She is hoping to wait to put the baby in child care until the baby is 6 months. So the plan is to have her husband take some paternity leave and then her mother come in to help out."

Supervisor's Supervisor (Kathy): "Hmm, I wonder how her families [sick cases] are feeling?"

Supervisor (Susan): "Oh, they seem excited for her. They are asking a lot about the baby and her plans. We have had to work a bit on setting boundaries without hurting the relationship she has with her families."

Supervisor's Supervisor (Kathy): "It must be hard for the families not to know when Lori is going and when she will return."

[Pause]

Supervisor (Susan): "I think they understand. They have all been there themselves. It is so hard to plan around delivery with exact dates. But now that I think about it, perhaps it isn't modeling respect or planning very well for them."

Supervisor's Supervisor (Kathy): *[nods her head]* "Perhaps not."

As the session continues, the conversation turns to the organization's waiting list. There are a number of folks on the waiting list who have not been assigned counselors. As Susan and Kathy discuss this, it becomes clear to Kathy that there are no plans to give some of the cases to Lori upon her return from maternity leave.

Supervisor's Supervisor (Kathy): "What about Lori? Couldn't she pick up some of these cases?"

Supervisor (Susan): "Yes, she can. *[pause]* We just don't have a definite return date from her."

Supervisor's Supervisor (Kathy): "Oh?" *[inquisitive look]*

Supervisor (Susan): "Well, she doesn't have set plans about what to do with the baby once her 12 weeks of leave is up. And she is so excited about this pregnancy. It is her first and all."

Supervisor's Supervisor (Kathy): *[nods]*

Supervisor (Susan): "It is so hard to come back to work, especially after your first child. You just don't realize how in love you are going to be with the baby. And it is even harder to return to work with babies who have such incredible needs. And I don't think Lori needs to work . . . well, not financially."

Supervisor's Supervisor (Kathy): "Have you talked to Lori about this?"

Supervisor (Susan): "No. I mean she hasn't experienced it yet so how can she be expected to understand how she will feel? I don't think it would be fair."

Supervisor's Supervisor (Kathy): *[sits quietly for a moment]* "It sounds like you are really working hard to protect Lori. And I am not sure it is something she is asking for?"

Supervisor (Susan): "Of course she isn't. She doesn't know enough to ask. She doesn't know how much this is going to change her life!"

Supervisor's Supervisor (Kathy): "Yes, first babies really do turn your life upside down, don't they? [pause] But we all have managed to survive it . . . grow from it." *The two continue to talk, and Susan realizes that her investment in Lori as a counselor and a new mother has interfered with her ability to be objective and keep the program and clients' needs in perspective. Susan recognizes that she needs to get more clarity from Lori regarding her maternity leave dates and help Lori recognize that she needs to do the same with her own clients.*

● ● ●

Overidentification. A reflective supervisor may allow the similarities between himself and the supervisee to cloud his reflective judgment. For example, a reflective supervisor who is struggling with a coworker or administrator in his own professional life may be too quick to "side" with a supervisee encountering a similar scenario. This overidentification may lead to too much validating of the supervisee's feelings or behavior, rather than providing the supervisee with the objectivity needed to challenge them to take the other person's perspective and think through a solution. For example:

● ● ●

Supervisee (Renee): *Renee commented to her supervisor, Monica,* "I am really struggling with some of my staff. I know that they have been working in the field for quite awhile and that I am much younger than they are, but still they owe me respect. I am their supervisor!"

Supervisor (Monica): *Monica, an older individual who had been in the mental health field a while but was a new reflective supervisor and was herself being supervised by a much younger professional. She could certainly empathize with Renee's staff as she herself was struggling with the age difference. Thus, she was aware that she needed to respond carefully so as not to alienate Renee by aligning herself with Renee's staff. Monica responded* *with, "Hmm, that must be an awkward situation for all of you. Tell me more about a time when your staff was disrespectful?" As Monica listened to Renee, she became aware that she herself may have been holding back from her own reflective supervisor in supervision because of the age difference and decided that it was a topic she herself needed to discuss openly in her own supervision, especially if she was to be helpful to Renee.*

● ● ●

Transference and countertransference. Finally, a reflective supervisor must be aware of transference, a phenomenon originally discussed in psychotherapy literature. In the context of a therapeutic relationship, transference refers to redirection of a client's feelings from a significant person (e.g., parent, spouse) to a therapist (Racker, 2001). Transference can be manifested as attraction toward a therapist, but can be seen in many other forms such as anger, mistrust, parentification, unhealthy dependence, or even placing the therapist in a godlike or guru status. Similarly, countertransference refers to the therapist's feelings toward the client. Countertransference can be the redirection of the therapist's own emotional history onto the client (Racker, 2001), or it can be a diagnostic clue as to what the client is feeling (Etchegoyen, 2005). A therapist's awareness of his countertransference is just as important as his understanding of the client's transference. When personal transference arises, a reflective supervisor needs to be aware of when a supervisee reminds him of someone else and when the supervisor may be reacting to the supervisee as though he were that person from the past. The concept of transference can also help a supervisee see when she may be responding to a colleague or administrator as though that person were someone from her past or personal life. When a supervisee is struggling to get along with someone, a key question may be, "Who does this person remind you of?" or "Have you ever been in this type of situation before?" Linking the past and present may be a helpful tool for assisting the supervisee to gain new insight on the challenge. For example, a female supervisee was having significant difficulty accepting direction from her male supervisor. When asked the question, "Who does your supervisor remind you of?" the supervisee was able to see how the male supervisor's directive style reminded her of her ex-husband. Having that awareness then allowed her to recognize when that emotional "nerve" was being struck, but to respond to him as a professional, rather than as someone from her past, and to explore these issues in the therapy room, rather than the supervisory session. (See Costa & Sullivan, this volume, p. 149, for a discussion of transference in reflective practice.)

ADDRESSING RELATIONSHIP RUPTURE

Once tension or disruption in the reflective relationship is recognized and the potential causes or contributing factors are identified, the challenge becomes what to do about it. As we have highlighted throughout the chapter, RS works best when reflective supervisors receive supervision. In some instances, tensions can be handled in the moment, but in other cases the supervisor needs time and space to discuss the tension or rupture. It is in this second instance that having access to a reflective supervisor (or colleague) is vital. The following section presents some strategies to use when the reflective supervisory relationship encounters periods of disharmony or rupture.

Facilitate Discussion of Dysynchrony

A supervisor may feel anxious about discussing differences with a supervisee, fearing that talking about disagreement or negative feelings will lead to a breakdown in the RS process and the relationship. However, not addressing tension will also erode the relationship and deprive the supervisee (and the program) of the benefits of RS. One way to bring concerning behaviors into the open for discussion in a nonthreatening way is to wonder about specific patterns or behaviors and to take responsibility for one's own role. For example, a supervisor may observe, "I've noticed that you've cancelled our last three sessions. I'm wondering if we could talk about that. Is there something that is in the way of your coming? Is there anything we can do to make our meetings more consistent or more useful to you?" Or, "I seem to be doing a lot of talking today. I wonder if there's something that you would like to bring up?" The most helpful guide for the supervisor is to hold in mind that the repair of relationship tensions is one of the most powerful opportunities for learning and deepening the relationship. Using care when initiating these discussions and taking a nonjudgmental, genuinely thoughtful approach will help create the safety and openness from which authentic repair can occur. (See Heffron et al., 2005, for an in-depth discussion on the use of self in RS.)

I Messages

It is important to remember that RS is a parallel process, and what is modeled within that relationship is carried into the staff and practitioner–client relationships in the program. Thus, it is important for the supervisor to model effective communication in the RS relationship. A supervisor can model how to take responsibility for one's thoughts and feelings in response to another person's behavior through the use of I messages. Using I messages places the focus on the feelings associated with the behavior, rather than the behavior itself, so that the supervisee can understand how her behavior makes the supervisor feel, and ultimately initiate a discussion of the effect of the behavior on the reflective process. For example, Anne (supervisor) often felt during reflective sessions that Dina (supervisee) wished to be rescued. Anne stated to Dina, "When you ask me to give you advice, I feel uncomfortable, because I think you have more confidence in me than in your own ability to solve this problem. Let's work through a solution together that you can feel positive about."

Rupture and Repair

Once difficulties in the relationship have been identified and discussed, it is important to examine the effect that communication around tensions has had on the supervisory relationship. Rupture or a breakdown in the collaborative process (Safran & Muran, 2006), although difficult, can strengthen the relationship. At these moments, the reflective supervisor has a uniquely powerful opportunity to model parallel process; to give the supervisee a firsthand experience with safe dialogue leading to healthy repair. If tension continues, clearly the supervisory relationship needs additional support. (See box Guidelines When Discussing Difficult Topics and Guiding Principles for a Repair of a Rupture for helpful guidelines.) If the reflective supervisor's attempts to discuss the underlying reasons for the tension directly with the supervisee prove unsuccessful, exploring these issues with his own reflective supervisor may be necessary. It may also be necessary to involve the agency in order to investigate possible changes that can be made to support the relationship or reevaluate the appropriateness of the supervisor–supervisee match. Although ruptures are a normal part of human interaction, it is important that the ruptures are mended before they become a fixed part of the relationship and limit the reflective process.

Anticipating and honoring differences creates an atmosphere that allows disagreements to be openly explored (Johnston & Brinamen, 2006). Discussing different perspectives and resolving conflicts that may arise as a result of these differences assist the supervisee in developing a model for handling similar issues in the work environment. Furthermore, discomfort with the reflective process may worsen when these feelings are not handled supportively within the context of supervision.

Guidelines When Discussing Difficult Topics and Guiding Principles for a Repair of a Rupture

Guidelines When Discussing Difficult Topics

- Ready yourself to be flexible and open—Try not to shut down.
- Accept the challenge to discover, to be open, and to move just beyond your growing edge.
- Be respectful.
- Remember that we are here to understand, not to change, the other.
- Assume good intentions.
- Rally compassion for yourself and other(s).
- Use I statements to express thoughts and feelings.
- Do not name specific people or a person in rebuttal or blame.
- Accept your own realities as well as the realities of others; everyone enters from a different place.
- Use deep listening skills: Truly hear the person and be wholly present.
- Reflect in order to become more aware.
- We are part of a system: Every move touches everyone.
- The *process* is the teacher.

> "A key to discussing difficult topics and repairing ruptures is to remain regulated and calm.

> "As a rock bears witness to rushing waters, allow yourself to observe your emotions as they rise in you."

Note. These guidelines were developed by Candida Brooks-Harrison, LCSW, Director, The Village Enrichment (www.thevillage-ei.com), who has used them in clinical work with parents, couples, and families, in training and supervision, in wide-ranging antiracist work, particularly with The People's Institute for Survival and Beyond, and has generously shared them with Rebecca Shahmoon-Shanok for use in this document and in their work together at the *Relationships for Growth & Learning* project of JBFCS.

Guiding Principles for a Repair of Rupture

- Allow time.
- Be genuine and authentic.
- Reflect and then reflect some more about the rupture or stalemate and its anecdotes or antecedents with others whom you trust. (Let go of control, allow for flow.)
- Respect yourself: Focus on your own feelings and ideas.

- Respect the other: Allow yourself to focus on the ideas and feelings of the other (e.g., exchange places, try role-playing with your trusted colleague).

- Look for positives.

- Discover points of realization about the other.

- Consider acknowledging your part in the stalemate or rupture using I statements.

- Consider apologizing. As you do, begin the steps listed here again.

Imagine the world when every leader follows these steps and says to his enemy,

"Teach me what *you* know."
Now, let each of us begin.
When someone or a situation matters, we mobilize the energy and dedication to repair.
Relationships matter.

(cf. Shahmoon-Shanok, 2000, p. 233)

Rebecca Shahmoon-Shanok prepared these principles in discussions with co-facilitator Candida Brooks-Harrison and Parent Child Center's (PCC) Early Childhood Wellness Program Director, Shelli Appelbaum, and Senior Therapists: Rebecca Matte, Michelle Rusniak, Yvonne Santiago, and Leslie Zucker, and PCC Assistant Clinical Director Christine von Ballmoos, in group supervision sessions from October through November 2008.

When relationship ruptures occur, the reflective supervisor may become frustrated by a lack of connection with the supervisee or struggle with feelings of incompetence and convey uncertainty and discomfort during reflective sessions. The supervisee may sense the supervisor's trepidation and further distance herself from the supervisor as well as the reflective process, creating an additional barrier to overcome. We encourage the supervisor to seek counsel from his own reflective supervisor or a trusted peer for assistance with these feelings of incompetence and uncertainty.

It is important to remember the parallel process that exists in all interactions. The reflective supervisor supports the supervisee in expressing his feelings about the reflective process, the supervisor herself, and the nature of the supervisory relationship. RS creates a ripple effect of positive support and change throughout the organization and the clients served. RS provides a model for open communication, in which supervisees can process thoughts, feelings, conflicts, and ideas in a safe environment. Having engaged in that reflective process, they can address issues with management, colleagues, and clients more thoughtfully and less reactively than they perhaps would otherwise. When an agency invests in RS, it is communicating to its staff that it values the staff's thoughts, feelings, and opinions, and will incorporate those into its mission, making for a healthier and more productive work environment. For RS to have this kind of positive, systemic effect, however, it must begin with support from the top (see Bertacchi & Gilkerson, this volume, p. 121) and continue through the unique relationship between the reflective supervisor and supervisee.

Summary

When problems arise in the supervisory relationship, the reflective supervisor has a unique opportunity to guide the supervisory pair through the process of mending the relationship. The supervisee may be hesitant to express her feelings about the rupture; the supervisor may also be unsure of how to approach the conflict. But with support, the supervisor can convey acceptance and understanding as well as a willingness to share his own feelings and thoughts. Being self-aware and taking time to reflect during the exchange allows the supervisor to hold the supervisee and provide a trustworthy environment for mutual growth. The safe experience of repair in a supervisory relationship provides a model that the supervisee can bring to other important relationships in her work and in her life.

References

Atchley, T., Hall, S., Martinez, S., & Gilkerson, L. (2009). What are the phases of the reflective supervison meeting? In S. Scott Heller & L. Gilkerson (Eds.), *A practical guide to reflective supervision* (pp. 83–98). Washington, DC: ZERO TO THREE.

Bertacchi, J., & Gilkerson, L. (2009). How can administrative and reflective supervision be combined? In S. Scott Heller & L. Gilkerson (Eds.), *A practical guide to reflective supervision* (pp. 121–134). Washington, DC: ZERO TO THREE.

Boris, N. W., & Grabert, J. C. (2009). How do I introduce reflective supervision to my program? In S. Scott Heller & L. Gilkerson (Eds.), *A practical guide to reflective supervision* (pp. 41–61). Washington, DC: ZERO TO THREE.

Bouchard, M., Target, M., Lecours, S., Fonagy, P., Tremblay, L., Schachter, A., & Stein, H. (2008). Mentalization in adult attachment narratives: Reflective functioning, mental states, and affect elaboration compared. *Psychoanalytic Psychology, 25*(1), 47–66.

Costa, G., & Sullivan, L. (2009). What staff development activities can be used to build reflective capacity? In S. Scott Heller & L. Gilkerson (Eds.), *A practical guide to reflective supervision* (pp. 149–181). Washington, DC: ZERO TO THREE.

Etchegoyen, H. (2005). *The fundamentals of psychoanalytical technique*. London: Karnac Books.

Fonagy, P., & Target, M. (1997). Attachment and reflective function: Their role in self-organization. *Development and Psychopathology, 9*, 679–700.

Heffron, M. C., Ivins, B., & Weston, D. R. (2005). Finding an authentic voice: Use of self: Essential learning for processes for relationship-based work. *Infants and Young Children, 18*(4), 323–326.

Johnston, K., & Brinamen, C. (2006). *Mental health consultation in child care: Transforming relationships among directors, staff, and families*. Washington, DC: ZERO TO THREE.

Racker, H. (2001). *Transference and countertransference*. Madison, CT: International Universities Press.

Safran, J. D., & Muran, J. C. (2006). Has the concept of the alliance outlived its usefulness? *Psychotherapy, 43*, 286–291.

Scott Heller, S. (2009). How do I develop an implementation plan to begin reflective supervision in my program? In S. Scott Heller & L. Gilkerson (Eds.), *A practical guide to reflective supervision* (pp. 25–39). Washington, DC: ZERO TO THREE.

Shahmoon-Shanok, R. (2000). Infant mental health perspectives on peer play psychotherapy for symptomatic, at-risk, and disordered young children. In J. Osofsky & H. Fitzgerald (Eds.), *WAIMH handbook of infant mental health* (Vol. 4; pp. 197–253). New York: Wiley.

Weatherston, D. J., & Barron, C. (2009). What does a reflective supervisory relationship look like? In S. Scott Heller & L. Gilkerson (Eds.), *A practical guide to reflective supervision* (pp. 63–82). Washington, DC: ZERO TO THREE.

Wheatley, M. (2009). *Turning to one another.* San Francisco, Berrett-Koehler.

HOW DO I, AS A REFLECTIVE SUPERVISOR, REPAIR
RUPTURES IN THE SUPERVISORY RELATIONSHIP?

119

Reflective Tool 6

Processing Disharmony Within the Reflective Supervisory Relationship

Reflective Tool 6 is to be used when you, as the reflective supervisor, sense that the session or reflective relationship is out of sync. The goal is to help you process what behaviors are contributing to tension or disruption within the reflective relationship, identify potential factors or events contributing to the tension or disruption, and consider responses to support repair. Please note that the items listed in the potential contributors' row are to help you think; it is by no means an exhaustive or exclusive list. This worksheet should not replace a discussion with your own supervisor about the current struggles but rather be used as a tool to enhance that discussion.

Supervisee _____ Date _____

Supervisor _____

		SUPERVISOR	SUPERVISEE
POST SESSION REFLECTION: PROCESSING DISHARMONY	Dysynchronous Behaviors	SUPERVISEE'S BEHAVIOR	• Frequent cancellations • Supervisee silences • Rushing through a session • Providing just the facts
		SUPERVISOR'S BEHAVIOR	• Overtalking • Frequent cancellations • Not taking charge (when appropriate)
	When Exhibited		• Throughout the session • In regard to a specific topic or supervisor/supervisee behavior • Pattern across sessions • New behavior in this session
	Your Affect		• Anxious • Frustrated • Worried • Overwhelmed • Sad
	Your Response		• Probed gently • Overtalked • Tried to fix
	Potential Contributors		• Mistrust • Limited experience with reflective thinking • Cultural differences • Therapeutic pitfalls
	Follow-up Plans		• Wait and see (trust the process) • Revisit event and probe further • Discuss with supervisor • Address directly (use I message)

CHAPTER 7

HOW CAN ADMINISTRATIVE AND
REFLECTIVE SUPERVISION BE COMBINED?

Judith Bertacchi and Linda Gilkerson

The unpleasantness we avoid determines the direction of our life.

—Robert Rosenbaum (1998, p. 65)

As an administrative supervisor, your primary goal is accountability: you hire, orient, guide, monitor, and evaluate. As a reflective supervisor, your primary goal is staff development: you mentor, coach, teach, nurture, and contain. Both of these roles are in the service of providing quality early childhood programs. Both support the workers' self-knowledge and competence—an understanding of their actions and reactions so that they can be an effective change agent with families and children.

In this chapter, we present how these two roles can be effectively combined into an integrated model of supervision, called the "mentoring/monitoring (M/M) approach." We describe the values of the M/M approach, qualities of the M/M supervisor, and some of the advantages and challenges of the dual role. A central thesis is that both administrative tasks and direct service responsibilities benefit from reflection. By the end of this chapter, you will be able to:

1. Describe the M/M model of supervision, its strengths, and its challenges.

2. Contract with a supervisee for supervision using the M/M model.

3. Use Reflective Tools 7a and 7b to build your capacity to use supervision to work through performance issues in an honest, direct way.

THE M/M MODEL OF SUPERVISION

The M/M approach to supervision combines the role of an administrative supervisor with the role of the reflective supervisor. In the administrative role, the M/M supervisor hires staff, communicates job expectations, ensures training in agency policies, monitors productivity, conducts performance appraisals, and makes decisions about the continuation of employment. In the reflective supervisory role, the M/M supervisor collaborates with staff to set professional development goals, supports staff in achieving these goals, and partners with staff to evaluate the degree to which goals have been met. In both of these roles, the M/M supervisor uses process as a primary tool for staff development and program improvement. The M/M supervisor is accountable both for implementing the program's vision and mission and for fostering the individual and collective development of a competent, responsive staff. The M/M supervisor believes that both jobs can be done and receives fulfillment from each aspect of the role as both roles contribute to the quality of the program.

QUALITIES OF AN M/M SUPERVISOR

The M/M supervisor must merge the qualities of an effective, efficient administrative supervisor with the qualities of a thoughtful, responsive reflective supervisor. Some of the capacities necessary for success in the dual M/M role of supervision include the following: (a) use process as the approach to problem solving, (b) understand human development, particularly social–emotional development in children and adults, (c) bring a knowledge of the self and the ability to tolerate, process, and contain conflict, and (d) come to terms with power in supervisory–staff relations.

Use process as the approach for problem solving. M/M supervisors must understand process as the approach to problem solving across domains, direct service work, and governance. Whether problem solving around a staff member's difficulty with completing required paper work on time or working through a staff member's feelings about a mother's discipline strategies with her toddler twins, a staff member can expect that the M/M supervisor will accept and understand the complexity of the situation and the feelings that are evoked. Staff members also know that the M/M supervisor will be available to discuss the situation and/or evoked feelings, process them, and move toward resolution.

Understands human development, particularly social–emotional development in children and adults. It is a great help to understand the supervisee within her life phase in order to better relate to the supervisee's experience of supervision. For example, a young staff member might be in the process of separating and differentiating from her family of origin. Having to ask for help and accept guidance may cause initial resistance within this model. In time, openness about her need for independence coupled with clarification of the purpose of supervision will often go a long way to help a younger staff person negotiate professional and personal development.

Brings knowledge of the self and the ability to tolerate, process, and contain conflict. Rather than be reactive and escalate a situation, the M/M supervisor is able to manage his own emotions in order to stay engaged in difficult situations. He is brave in the face of conflict in order to put an issue honestly on the table. As an M/M supervisor, you cannot leave the tough stuff up to someone else. You must be able to bring concerns about performance into the working supervisory relationship and talk about them in a calm, direct way. The lived experience of discussing differences and conflicts within the supervisory relationship is one of the most valued sources of mutual growth and development for the supervisor and supervisee (Keyes, Cavanaugh, & Scott Heller, this volume, p. 99).

On the other hand, the M/M supervisor learns to know when issues can wait; not every question needs an immediate answer or problem a quick solution. Through communicating that he is going to take time to think over an issue, the supervisor teaches the staff to differentiate levels of need and urgency and to practice containment.

Comes to terms with power in the supervisory–staff relationship. There are times in one's work life when the "power equation" rises predictably in the flow of the governance of a program, agency, or its sponsoring organization. In effective institutions, power issues are not personal issues. Power is based on accountability for implementing the mission and values of the agency or institution. The top leadership has the responsibility to communicate to staff that the supervisors are held accountable by the agency for program quality based on living and sharing the values of the program. The staff members of the program are responsible for performing their job with the aim of best practice. As an M/M supervisor, you are accountable for the quality of the program; the supervisee is responsible for providing quality services.

ADVANTAGES AND CHALLENGES OF THE M/M MODEL

The M/M model has considerable advantages and significant challenges. The advantages emerge from the integration of reflection into all aspects of program implementation. The challenges arise when the M/M role requires the supervisor to expand supervisory capacities beyond the known and practiced domains.

Advantages of the Dual Role

The greatest advantage of the M/M model is the use of reflection for mastery in all aspects of program implementation, from accountability to professional development. This model helps staff members to build the capacity for thoughtful consideration of what they and others are observing, feeling, and doing, and use this capacity in their direct service or management responsibilities. The M/M supervisor continuously models the integration of support and limit setting, providing staff with growth-promoting coaching in areas of need and firm guidance around program requirements and role expectations. The M/M model can help further the relationship of the staff with the institution, as the goals of the larger systems are integrated in supervision with direct service responsibilities. This model provides the director/supervisor with a deeper knowledge of all aspects of the program that furthers the potential for more comprehensive decision making and contributes to the strength of the overall system.

Challenges of the Dual Role

The challenges of the role differ based on the supervisor's personal qualities and previous experiences. Most M/M supervisors will need help with performance appraisals within the dual role. Persons with past experience as administrative supervisors may need more support around the use of reflective process to support staff development; while other new M/M supervisors with experience as practitioners may need support around the demands of accountability. A mismatch between the supervisor's and agency's goals and values is a significant challenge in any model of supervision, including the M/M model, and will exacerbate the personal and interpersonal challenges of the dual role.

Learning to provide an honest performance evaluation. Most supervisors need to expand or enhance their skills to accomplish the combined roles of staff development and staff evaluation. Supervisors who have not had to evaluate staff performance will need to learn to provide an honest performance appraisal, based on the achievement of professional development goals and on job performance. They may need more coaching in setting boundaries and communicating clear expectations. Clearly, staying calm in conflictual situations is a central skill for an M/M supervisor.

Increasing capacity for reflective process. Supervisors who have not had to work with staff to build their practice/clinical skills will most likely need to increase their capacity for reflective process. They will need to learn how to understand the day-to-day pressures of direct service work, understand each person's history as a provider, their own philosophy of practice, and the standards they hold for themselves. They will also need to learn the language of mutuality: learning the words that increase sharing when problem solving, learning to turn an issue into a discussion, learning to support a supervisee's owning his own contribution to an interaction. For example, "You seem upset, you seem to be struggling. Let's try and figure this out together. Let's pull it apart and see what we find. Please share how you are seeing the issue." This is different than the supervisor saying, "You seem upset. This is what I suggest. Try it!"

An M/M supervisor will need to be able to contain her reactivity regarding staff performance. As an administrative supervisor, inadequate staff performance can evoke reactivity and self-protection. If the staff is not performing well, a supervisor cannot succeed in program management. It is all too easy for a supervisor to skip over reflection and think or say, "It's my job on the line. Just do it!" The M/M supervisor encounters the same pressures for accountability but must work to contain her reactivity and invite some degree of dialogue, even when she must require that an unpopular action be taken: "I can hear your struggle here. But this is a requirement of your job. I am happy to talk about your feelings or concerns in more detail, but the reality is there is no wiggle room on this and you just need to do it. We can talk about how this is for you after you have completed the task."

Comfort with demands of accountability. Program accountability rests on the supervisor. At times, accountability means that difficult decisions must be made regarding the match between the supervisee and the expectations of the job. The M/M supervisor has to be able to determine when the match is not acceptable and act. This aspect of the role is a challenge for most supervisors, regardless of their experience, and should not be handled alone. Unlike a family who has the strength to keep the door open so a family member who has failed can return home, if the match between program and staff is not viable, the door must be closed and the staff member will need to move on. If the values or competencies are not a good match and appropriate assessment and feedback have been given, then the M/M supervisor has to make a decision: Should more effort be spent on working with the supervisee or is the evidence such that the disconnect is too great and the best thing is for the staff member to resign or be terminated?

The evidence is gathered in the supervisor's relationship with the supervisee and in the supervisee's relationships with others. The supervisor is in the position of hearing and seeing a great deal, and is obligated to say what has worked well and not worked well. If the supervisee is not aware of the problems and does not have insight into his effect on others, or his general stance, then no matter how hard the supervisor tries, the supervisee may not be able to succeed in his role. It is a tough judgment call, but the bottom line is that if the supervisee has a job and it is not being done, it is the supervisor's responsibility to raise that honestly and to follow through until a decision is made. Helping a staff member to resign or terminating a staff member are challenging supervisory skills that can be learned.

Termination because of an insufficient match is not necessarily a negative reflection on the supervisee. She may be very able to make a contribution in another setting with different values and expectations. The process of termination in larger institutions will include the Human Resources Department. The best interest of the children and families, in line with the values of the agency, always informs the process and timeline of the termination. In time, staff will observe and come to understand that the rare terminations are never based on the whims of the supervisor, but on the values of the program. These supervisory responsibilities will need to be discussed both at hiring and at the point of supervisory contracting and subsequent discussions.

CONTRACTING FOR SUPERVISION IN THE M/M MODEL

Contracting for supervision is the heart-center of the model. Through the contracting process, the model is clearly explained, the roles of the supervisor and supervisee are clarified, and goals are clearly and mutually established. The importance of contracting for mutually determined goals cannot be overstated as these goals provide the benchmarks for staff evaluation and development.

Explaining the Approach

Contracting for supervision involves a clear explanation of the roles of the supervisor and supervisee and the use of the supervisory relationship. It is the supervisor's responsibility to clearly present the model, define roles, and clarify mutual expectations. The box Supervisor Explaining the M/M Model to a New Supervisee is an example of a supervisory conversation introducing the M/M model to a staff member and explaining the contracting process.

Supervisor Explaining the M/M Model to a New Supervisee

I want to talk about our model of supervision here at the [state the name] program. The model we use is called the "mentoring/monitoring" approach. This approach combines administrative supervision and reflective supervision. Administrative supervision supports you in meeting the administrative requirements of your job (e.g., timelines, reporting, record keeping, attendance, meeting job expectations) and in evaluating your performance. Reflective supervision is all about the issues, challenges, and decisions that will come up in your direct practice with children, families, and colleagues. So I will be your supervisor for both your administrative responsibilities and direct service work with children, families, and fellow team members. We will use reflective process as a tool to help you master both aspects of your job—the administrative requirements and direct service responsibilities. Reflection simply means thoughtful consideration of what you are doing, observing, and feeling and modifying your practice based on what you are learning from reflection on your work and from what the job expectations are.

This kind of supervision is different for many people because it is going to combine all aspects of your practice with children and families with the administrative requirements of the job and our agency. In many models, the administrative supervisor provides oversight and evaluation, having contact mostly when there is a problem or an issue. In the model we use here, I will act as your partner in the development of your professional self within the structure of this job in this agency. I will model reflective process and coach you in this essential skill. Just as it has been said that no one needs to take a difficult journey alone, this model of supervision ensures that you are not alone in your work. It does demand work on mutuality and trust, but it's not expected that you feel this way in one day. I believe that trust with each other will grow over time through the discussions and process of our working relationship.

I will not only support you in your direct service work, but I will also do your performance appraisal with you. When it comes to your performance appraisal, which will be in [state the month], it will be based on the achievement of the goals that we mutually set. Some of these I will raise, and some you will raise. I will give you feedback on any concerns that I learn about or have and that you have. Together we will work to address these. That means when it's time to pause and look back, which is a performance appraisal, there should not be any surprises as both of us will have been in communication all along the way. Exploration of strengths will be a part of our discussion as well as the challenges experienced here on the job. Our agency uses these forms for the review *[give copy of forms]*; we can go over the forms in our next meeting. I will also review with you the agency's written policy for performance review. It is the same process as I have just explained.

As we get to know each other and the work, the job expectations and challenges will be formulated into professional goals. I like to use supervision to look at issues of time management; that is, meeting deadlines for assessments, reports, monthly statistics, and so on. There are lots of tricks that can be learned that help with the completion of these sometimes boring and seemingly unimportant tasks. It takes time to realize that macro demands like funding and evaluation are only possible with timely staff reports. And this, of course, is how we all get paid! I also like to use supervision to get to know how each of us approaches conflict and anticipate how we will work through conflicts which will inevitably rise in our work together. Supervision is a process of mutual growth, and I look forward to our working and learning together this year.

Exploring Past History of Supervision

After carefully explaining the model, it can be very helpful to ask the supervisee about her past experiences with supervision. You might begin by asking the supervisee to talk about her first supervisory relationship. Depending upon her work history, the first experience could come anywhere from a summer job while in high school to her first professional role. You want to listen for the positive experiences, negative experiences, and any conflictual messages that the supervisee has internalized. You might also share your experience as a supervisee and any ways that this experience informs your current practice. Exploring supervisory relationships from the past and wondering about how they might impact the present relationship provides a first taste of the reflective process that will continue throughout your supervisor/supervisee relationship.

Importance of Mutually Determined Goals

After carefully explaining the roles, contracting for goals becomes the key to the success of the M/M supervisory partnership. Because the supervision role combines performance evaluation with staff development, it is imperative that the relationship has clear boundaries and expectations. Mutually held goals reduce ambiguity and give shape to the supervisory relationship. The goals evolve directly from the requirements for the work as defined in the job description and as determined by the needs of the program as well as a realistic appraisal of the skill level and professional development of the supervisee. The supervisor maintains the responsibility for upholding the mission and values of the larger agency throughout the contracting process.

Contracting for goals is not a one-time event but a process that can last several weeks. As the contracting process unfolds, within a month or so, the goals need to be written down and both parties should each have a copy. The supervisor profits from keeping a file in his desk of the goals and the themes of all other supervisory meetings (see Atchley, Hall, Martinez, & Gilkerson, this volume, p. 83, for a sample supervisory session recording form). Supervisees are encouraged to do the same as these goals are the basis of many future discussions and will help them chart their progress. The goals also reflect the agency's value of lifelong learning and help with the selection of trainings, classes, or conferences that will support goal achievement. Over time, goals that have been mastered may be celebrated while others continue to be added. Clearly, the goals will become an important part of the performance evaluation. In our field, financial compensation (bonuses/raises) is rarely part of the annual performance evaluation. More likely, the focus will be on the achievement of valued, mutually held goals.

Supervisor Availability

To show the value placed on the supervisory relationship, the supervisor should be available to the supervisee at the beginning of the work relationship. In one program, a new employee was hired and given a start date, even though the supervisor had planned to be on vacation at this time. The rationale was that the program needed the new person to start as soon as possible. The lack of welcome and support in the beginning can become an issue for any supervisee, but especially for one who is uncertain, perhaps nervous, and afraid of making mistakes. It also contradicts the values of this new kind of supervision that were discussed at length during hiring.

Creating the Agenda for Supervisory Sessions

Supervisors and supervisees are responsible for creating the ongoing agenda for the supervisory sessions. Agency business is usually shared first for a few minutes before embarking on the supervisee's agenda items. This differs from the model described in chapter 5 (Atchley et al., this volume, p. 83) in which the supervisee's agenda typically drives the supervisory meetings. The inclusion of administrative issues ensures that information is shared up and down the agency and that expectations are clear. The supervisee is also invited to ask questions or bring concerns about administrative tasks. Over time, the supervisee learns which items or issues are not in need of immediate attention, and can be brought to the supervision meetings, and which are more urgent and need the supervisor's attention between sessions. This approach to the work eventually provides staff with internal guidelines on what is a crisis and what is a concern. When performance issues are a concern, the supervisor addresses these in the context of the supervisory sessions, using a process approach to guide the discussion.

After the administrative business and performance concerns are addressed, the supervisor invites the staff member to talk about her work. It is important that the supervisor develops a transition ritual to move the session from administrative to direct service issues. As described in chapter 5 (Atchley et al., this volume, p. 83), the supervisor might open this part of the session with a statement: "Let's shift our focus from administrative issues to what's on your mind. Where would you like to start?" Here the reflective process is very similar to that described in the previous chapters. In the beginning, it is helpful to have longer sessions to cover all of the administrative requirements and provide the teaching and coaching for the new role.

Checking in on the Supervisory Relationship

Supervisors should become comfortable, periodically asking the supervisee(s) how the process is working for them. This also allows the supervisor to share her thoughts on the process and what changes might enrich the work. Through these discussions the supervisor and supervisee can become more comfortable with differences and disagreements. As staff experience being heard, they will increase their sensitivity to the stated and unstated needs of parents and children. This ability to listen, to contain one's feelings and reactions, to learn to share and talk about meaningful communications with others, including one's team, are directly parallel to the care and service provided in the program.

Supervisor Support

No supervisor is born to the position. The M/M model flourishes when supervisors have an arena to reflect and evaluate their own learning and supervisory practice. Setting realistic goals for themselves and staff will eliminate several predictable obstacles and underscore the developmental trajectories for both supervisor and supervisee. It is always beneficial for supervisors in the same program to meet regularly and discuss their supervisory work. It is also beneficial for directors to have consultation around their supervisory role, either individually or in a director's group (Bertacchi & Stott, 1991). Providing supervision or consultation to directors/supervisors sends a powerful message that supervision is essential to performance at all levels of the agency hierarchy.

Assessing the Supervisor/Agency Match

Because the M/M role is inextricably intertwined with the goals, values, and practices of the agency, it is crucial that supervisors respect the agency and share its overall philosophy and approach. In addition, it is essential that the agency is open to dialogue and change. This is not to say that there is ever a perfect organization. Like families, the hallmark of organizational and program quality is striving. As M/M supervisors strive to achieve greater openness, questioning, and reflective discussions, the agency itself must be flexible and welcoming to staff participation and feedback. The M/M model will only work if there is a good fit between the values of the agency and the supervisor. If the match is not good enough, then the supervisor will want to reassess his commitment to her role in the agency. As with the other match issue discussed in this chapter (that of the match between staff and the agency), a decision to leave or a termination does not mean that the supervisor could not succeed in another setting where the values or working style are more compatible.

WORKING WITH PERFORMANCE ISSUES IN THE M/M MODEL

In this last section, we address one of the most difficult struggles for beginning M/M supervisors: that is, putting a difficult performance issue out on the table for discussion and remediation. Addressing performance issues can be particularly challenging in the M/M model because the supervisor holds both evaluative and support roles. Yet, working through a performance issue can be one of the richest staff development learning experiences. The supervisory relationship is the place for staff to learn new ways of working in this work culture.

In the following example, the M/M supervisor works with a head teacher, Annie, to overcome her avoidance of addressing a performance problem with a new assistant teacher. This example illustrates the parallel process between the supervisor's ability to be constructively direct with her supervisee and the staff member's ability to be constructively direct with her assistant. The key to success is to frame the performance problem in terms of the role expectations and program values. Watch how the supervisor does this repeatedly during the conversations.

Annie (supervisee) is a head teacher in a preschool classroom; she has a new assistant, Emma, who is set on doing things her own way. The head teacher is responsible for training and supervising the new assistant. Part of Annie's job is to teach Emma to complete documentation in a timely manner and so that it can be read by parents and colleagues. Annie finds that Emma is not following the guidelines for writing daily reports to families, and she is not giving them to the head teacher for review before distribution. Annie is increasingly upset at the new assistant, yet is also having difficulty bringing the issues up with her. A parent has come to complain to the director about a note she received from the new assistant. Annie—as the head teacher—has regular M/M supervision from the program director (supervisor). Annie comes to the session and says she wants to discuss the behavior of a child. However, the supervisor needs to bring up the parent's concern. Here's how the conversation might go:

● ● ●

Supervisor: "Annie, I'd like very much for us to talk about (child's name) behavior but I have an issue that I need for us to talk about first. One of the mothers shared with me that your assistant teacher gave her a note about her child's behavior and it upset her terribly. The note said that the child had a bad day, that he was mean to another child, and that is was important for the mother to talk with her child about this unacceptable behavior. Because there is apparent slippage between the assistant's communication and our policy and approach to parent communication, this has to be addressed immediately."

Annie (Supervisee): "I know. You're right. I've got to talk with Emma about parent communication, but I have been so busy I haven't. I will talk with her and go over how our values impact how we communicate with families."

Supervisor: "That's great, Annie. Sounds like Emma needs to build empathy for a parent who gets such a piece of upsetting information out of the blue. How can I be of help to you as you proceed with Emma and your team?"

Annie (Supervisee): "I think I can do this. I'll check in during the week if I need more support."

Supervisor: "Great. You just give me a little notice, and we'll find the time. Bring your notes about how the discussion goes to our next meeting and we can talk about it."

● ● ●

The supervisor provides content and support to Annie, and Annie seems willing to address the issue. Over the next couple of weeks, the most important issue that surfaces in supervision is Annie's dislike of the new employee's insensitivity and her own growing anger with Emma. It seems that her anger is blocking her ability to be straight and honest with Emma, causing her to shut down with the entire team. In parallel fashion, the supervisor is also becoming upset that no change is evident. Now the supervisor has to be brave and use her feelings to open up with Annie; the avoidance has to change.

• • •

Supervisor: "Annie, we need to talk. I know we have been working on a plan so you can discuss the unfortunate lapse in your assistant teacher's work with parents. But the problem persists. What do you really want to tell me about her and your feelings about her?"

Annie (Supervisee) *Her face is flushed, she is visibly upset, and she begins to cry:* "I just don't think it is going to work out, and I have never had this before. Emma has only been here 10 weeks; I can't stand her attitude or the way she talks to parents and, frankly, I don't know what to do."

Supervisor: "What additionally do you need from me to support you in telling her you are concerned? Annie, I will support you in any way I can as you learn how to be more direct. I could even meet with you and your supervisee so you can learn how to do this in the most positive way because you will need to learn how to be able to do this again in the future."

Annie (Supervisee): "I'm scared, but I'd like to try it myself before you would join us. But I'm not sure what to say."

Supervisor: "That's great, let's start by role-playing. Remember you are talking with Emma about our program's approach to parents and policies around communication. It's not a conversation about whether she is a good person or not or whether you like her or not. How about if you think of an opening sentence and then we can role-play from there. Who would you like me to be?" The role-play continues, and as the session ends, the supervisor states, "We're not just dropping this. I want you to contact me about this task before our next session because I want to support you through this so that next time you can do this almost on your own. Annie, I want you to know that this is not an unusual issue for a head teacher, but it is one that has to be mastered, and that's our goal. We're in this together and this is going to be a considerable learning experience for both of us."

• • •

For Annie's professional development, she needs support to come to terms with her own anger and anxiety so she can take action instead of shutting down. The M/M supervisor will continue to help Annie contain her upset so she can act forthrightly in the interest of the program's values.

SUMMARY

The M/M model of supervision combines the staff accountability role of administrative supervision with the staff development role of RS. Although the dual role poses challenges to supervisors, regardless of their prior experience, there are significant benefits to the organization and to the staff involved. Staff grow in their capacity to use reflective process across their areas of responsibility; they understand their daily tasks in the context of the larger organizational mission and values; and communication flows directly from the administration to the staff, and vice versa, in the context of an ongoing collaborative relationship committed to staff's development and program quality. The M/M model provides the supervisor with a deep knowledge of the program—from the boardroom to the classroom—and expands the capacity for comprehensive decision making. The M/M model reduces crises as communication is open and ongoing. To succeed, the model requires a good fit between the values of the supervisor and the agency. Overall, the M/M approach enhances the larger system while strengthening staff competence; the dual approach goes a long way toward ensuring quality for all program participants.

References

Atchley, T., Hall, S., Martinez, S., & Gilkerson, L. (2009). What are the phases of the reflective supervision meeting? In S. Scott Heller & L. Gilkerson (Eds.), *A practical guide to reflective supervision* (pp. 83–98). Washington, DC: ZERO TO THREE.

Bertacchi, J., & Stott, F. M. (1991). A seminar for supervisors in infant/family programs: Growing versus paying more for staying the same. *Zero to Three, 11*(2), 34–39.

Keyes, A. W., Cavanaugh, A. E., & Scott Heller, S. (2009). How do I, as a reflective supervisor, repair ruptures in the supervisory relationship? In S. Scott Heller & L. Gilkerson (Eds.), *A practical guide to reflective supervision* (pp. 99–119). Washington, DC: ZERO TO THREE.

Rosenbaum, R. (1998). *Zen and the heart of psychotherapy.* Levittown, PA: Brunner/Mazel.

Reflective Tool 7a

Being Honest at a Difficult Point in Supervision

Reflective Tool 7a is to be used when you, as the mentoring/monitoring (M/M) supervisor, have a difficult topic to discuss with the supervisee around job performance. The first column contains areas to consider prior to the reflective session, and the second column contains items to reflect on after the session. The goal is to help you frame the discussion in terms of the values of the program and speak directly about the issues that need to be addressed. The purpose of this tool is to help provide the supervisor with an opportunity to sit back and consider the session, its themes, and affective tone both prior to and following the session. It also supports the supervisor in considering potential areas or themes to be aware of or to follow up in future sessions.

		BEFORE	AFTER
PREPARATION AND REFLECTION FOR SUPERVISION ON DIFFICULT TOPICS	**Administrative Aspects**	• Have I framed this conversation in the context of the job requirements?	• Did I succeed in putting the issue on the table with some clarity? • Were there any administrative or programmatic issues that I needed to raise? • Did I ask questions that deepened the discussion?
	Preparation	• Did I give myself a few minutes to prepare for this supervisory session? • Have I made the space comfortable so we can discuss a difficult topic?	• Did I prepare myself to be honest with an issue that is occurring? • Was I prepared to be reflective about not only surface issues but what else might be going on?
	Affect	• Am I aware of the feelings that this issue evokes in me? • What strategies will I use to manage my own affect during this conversation?	• Could I contain my affect and allow the process to unfold? • Was I able to use my own affect to understand what was happening between us? • Did I make sure the supervisee was able to share any issues or questions and feelings with me?
	Conclusion and Follow-up	• How can I best help this person do the difficult thing that needs to be done?	• Did we summarize our meeting? • Did I make sure that next steps for both of us were clarified?

Reflective Tool 7b

Self-Reflection: Supervisory Genogram

The M/M supervisor role requires a clear professional identity and a capacity for self-awareness. Understanding what and who have shaped your perspective on supervision can help you know more about your own tendencies and how others might experience you. We offer this opportunity to develop your supervisory genogram and to play with the ideas and experiences that have shaped you as a supervisor.

A *genogram* is a map of one's heritage which demonstrates the "people, places, ideas and experiences" (Northcutt, 2000, p. 158) that have formed your identity, in this case, your identity as a supervisor. Modeled after the spiritual genogram developed by Northcutt (2000), after completing the Supervisory Genogram, you should be able to:

1. Know who were the most significant persons and significant events in your development as a supervisor

2. Tell how they have affected your growth and development

3. Understand how your views on supervision have changed over time

4. Approach your role with greater self-awareness and readiness to engage.

Establishing a Supervisory Timeline

Draw a horizontal line to represent a timeline of your journey as a professional. Make a vertical line on the timeline to mark when you moved from supervisee to supervisor.

- How long have you been a professional?

- How long were you a professional before you became a supervisor?

- Did you plan to become a supervisor and seek out the role? Did others see you as a supervisor before you did and move you into this role? Did you "fall into the role" without a lot of forethought on anyone's part?

- How many years have you had supervision for yourself?

- How many years have you provided supervision?

- How much training did you have to become a supervisor? Please estimate the amount in days/weeks/years, whichever is most relevant.

- How have your views about supervision changed over time? Mark these changes on the timeline and note the place/setting/context for the changes. Think about important ideas, books, people, or events that have shaped your views about supervision.

Mapping Your Supervisory Relationship History

To your timeline, now add the persons who supervised you at each important time period. You may want to extend your timeline backward to the time before you were a professional to capture persons who supervised you in your first jobs in high school or college.

Supervisor

Use a circle to indicate female supervisors and a square to indicate male supervisors. Within the circle or square, make the outline of a face (eyes, mouth) to express the quality of your relationship. As you do this, think about whether the relationships were close, distant, hostile, or supportive.

- What do you notice about your history with past supervisors?

- How have your first supervisory relationships shaped how you feel about supervision and how you are/might be as a supervisor?

- Which of your supervisors practiced RS? Which supervisors were most likely/least likely to cherish your strengths and partner around vulnerabilities? What were these different experiences like for you?

Supervisees

Now place your supervisees on the map (if there are too many, you can select four that stand out in your mind). If you are just beginning supervision, place several people who you think you will supervise on the map. Use a double circle and double square to show gender and draw faces inside the shapes to show the relationships. Think about the nature of your relationship with your supervisees or supervisees-to-be.

- How, if at all, do these relationships reflect your own supervisory relationships?

- How have you changed as a supervisor over time?

- Do you see any ways that people/events/life cycle transitions have impacted/will impact your supervisory practice, either positively or negatively?

- If you are a beginning supervisor, how would you like your supervisees to describe their relationship with you?

- What personal strengths do you cherish? What vulnerabilities do you feel in your role as supervisor and who will partner with you to build your capacity as a supervisor?

Developed by Linda Gilkerson, adapted from the concept of a Spiritual Genogram (Northcutt, T. B. (2000). Constructing a place for religion and spirituality in psychodynamic practice. *Clinical Social Work Journal*, 28(2), 155–169.)

CHAPTER 8

BEYOND REFLECTIVE SUPERVISION: HOW CAN MY ORGANIZATION SUPPORT STAFF WELL-BEING?

Brenda Jones Harden

Service requires sacrifice . . . perhaps not. One of the fundamental principles of real service
is taught many times a day aboard every airplane . . . when the stewardess says . . .
put your own mask on first before you try to help the person next to you.
*Service is based on the premise that **all** life is worthy of our support and commitment . . .*
[A nurturer often thinks] this is true of every life except his own.

—Rachel Naomi Remen (2000, pp. 20–21)

The major tenet of this guide is that early childhood program staff need support from supervisors and managers to be able to reflect on and thus improve their work with children and families. Although reflective supervision (RS) is arguably the most important vehicle for enhancing staff practice, there are other mechanisms that support staff development and optimize staff interventions with children and families outside of RS. I propose that a staff-oriented infrastructure, in concert with RS, is essential to support early childhood practitioners who often work with highly vulnerable and stressed families, and, too often, without adequate preparation for this psychologically demanding work. In this chapter, you will learn about the structure, resources, guidance, and validation which organizations should provide to early childhood staff to allow them to deliver services in the most effective manner. In addition, you will understand how to foster the staff's sense of physical and emotional well-being while they are working with children and families. By the end of this chapter, you will be able to:

1. Make a case for the importance of a staff-centered organizational structure, in conjunction with RS, to support effective early childhood practice.

2. Describe the elements of a staff-centered organizational structure and the resources needed to support it.

3. Use Reflective Tool 8 to assess staff well-being and select staff-centered strategies to promote safety, nurturance, and competence.

NURTURING THE NURTURER

Stemming from the infant mental health principle of parallel process (Lieberman & Van Horn, 2008; Shahmoon-Shanok, this volume, p. 7), the nurturance of young children is best achieved in a context in which their caregivers (e.g., parents, teachers, home visitors) are nurtured as well. As such, early childhood programs not only represent a holding environment (Winnicott, 1976) for program participants, but also become a holding environment for staff exposed to the challenges of working with the children and families that the programs target.

Building on definitions of occupational well-being (Van Horn, Taris, Schaufeli, & Schreurs, 2004), the holding environment for staff needs to foster their sense of physical and emotional well-being. This entails staff's positive feelings about various dimensions of the workplace, including physical safety, affective comfort, cognitive stimulation, and appropriate behaviors from peers and supervisors. Before ways to foster this sense of well-being are considered, the characteristics of early childhood staff and the challenges they face in their work, particularly in serving families at high psychosocial/environmental risk, are discussed.

Staff Characteristics and Program Quality

Although the evidence is limited, there has been some attention in the early childhood literature to the relation between staff characteristics and program quality. It is interesting to note that there is still considerable controversy about whether level of education is associated with quality of early childhood intervention in the classroom or home (Early et al., 2007; Olds et al., 2002). However, there is a small body of research that suggests more malleable characteristics (e.g., level of knowledge and skill, mental health) of staff may be related to program quality.

Personal Qualities

There are several personal characteristics of staff that are critical for the implementation of quality early childhood programs. For example, in one national survey, program administrators identified the following characteristics as important for their home visitors to possess: (a) positive work behaviors, (b) helper characteristics such as empathy and flexibility, and (c) knowledge of community resources (Wasik & Roberts, 1994). Other research has underscored home visitors' capacity to develop a positive helping relationship with families as key to program engagement (Korfmacher, Green, Spellmann, & Thornburg, 2007). Regarding teacher characteristics, studies show that the mental health of teachers influences their performance in the classroom. Early childhood teachers reporting higher levels of depressive symptoms and lower self-efficacy tend to have more conflictual relationships with students in their classrooms (Hamre, Pianta, Downer, & Mashburn, 2008). Similarly, children who were expelled or suspended from their preschools were more likely to have teachers with higher levels of depressive symptoms (Gilliam & Shahar, in press). In addition, the impact of teacher experience on classroom quality is affected by other teacher characteristics, such as depression (Pianta et al., 2005). Although not focused specifically on early childhood educators, research has suggested that teachers' emotional stability, hardiness, self-efficacy, and coping are critical personality characteristics related to their success in the classroom (Schaufeli & Enzman, 1998). In addition, teachers' capacity for self-regulation (i.e., engagement and resilience) was found to be related to their instructional performance and students' motivation (Klusmann, Kunter, Trautwein, Ludtke, & Baumert, 2008).

Lack of Staff Preparation to Serve Families at High Risk

Unfortunately, although many early childhood programs serve families at high risk (e.g., Early Head Start: Administration for Children and Families, 2006; Healthy Families: Ammerman et al., 2006),

BEYOND REFLECTIVE SUPERVISION: HOW CAN MY
ORGANIZATION SUPPORT STAFF WELL-BEING?

137

program staff are often ill-prepared to address common issues associated with high-risk families. For example, in one study, although more than half of the mothers participating in home visiting programs were in need of mental health, domestic violence, or substance abuse services, only about a quarter of them received those services, which the authors attributed to the lack of staff training and support regarding family risk (Tandon, Parillo, Jenkins, & Duggan, 2005). In addition, emerging research documents the lack of preparation among preservice and practicing teachers for managing children who present social–emotional challenges (Hemmeter, Santos, & Ostrosky, 2008).

Caregiver Fatigue

Beyond the traits that staff bring to a program (e.g., knowledge, experience, psychological characteristics), it is important to consider how working with high-risk populations impacts staff. Increasingly, programs are concerned with caregiver fatigue or secondary traumatic stress (Figley, 1995) in staff working in programs serving high-risk populations. Many families participating in early childhood programs experience a multitude of traumatic stressors, such as interadult violence, child maltreatment, premature death, acute and chronic physical and mental illness, and poverty (Administration for Children and Families, 2006; Lieberman & Van Horn, 2008). Through their intensive work and intimate relationship with trauma-exposed families, early childhood staff may internalize these experiences and consequently evidence trauma symptoms themselves (Figley). Such psychological vulnerability may lead to staff burnout and ultimately staff turnover within an organization.

Staff Burnout

Staff burnout has been defined as having three components: emotional exhaustion, depersonalization, and reduced personal accomplishment (Maslach, Schaufeli, & Leiter, 2001). Although the literature is very limited, there is some attention directed at burnout among early childhood professionals. For example, in a study examining competence, burnout, support, and client engagement in a sample of Early Head Start home visitors, Gill, Greenberg, Moon, and Margraf (2007) found that home visitors had high levels of knowledge about children's development and job satisfaction. However, they reported increasing levels of emotional exhaustion over time, and about one fifth endorsed depressive symptoms above the clinical cutoff (Gill et al., 2007). Several studies examining teacher characteristics have suggested that the chronic stress teachers endure is a strong predictor of their feelings of burnout (Kyriacou, 2001; Rudow, 1999).

Staff-Centered Organizational Infrastructure

Given that staff may not enter the early childhood workforce prepared to work with high-risk children and families, and that the work itself comes at high psychological cost for staff, it is critical that early childhood programs address the well-being of staff. Specifically, early childhood program managers should endeavor to provide a nurturing work environment for staff through the creation of a staff-centered organizational infrastructure, an emphasis on sustained staff development, and staff-specific strategies to enhance a sense of security and psychological well-being. One means of supporting and enhancing staff well-being is through the provision of RS; the prior chapters in this volume address the specifics of providing RS to staff. Although RS in and of itself is critical to supporting and sustaining staff's well-being (Howard, 2008), there are other strategies that should be implemented within an organization to enhance the impact of RS. The rest of this chapter focuses on the components of a staff-oriented infrastructure and how you can begin to implement these components in your program.

ORGANIZATIONAL INFRASTRUCTURE: NURTURANCE IN THE MACRO-LEVEL ENVIRONMENT

The organizational psychology literature is full of references detailing the importance of a stable, flexible organizational system with effective leadership and clear lines of authority for the achievement of organizational goals and objectives (Drafke, 2009). This may be even more essential in human service and early childhood programs, in which the process and the product rest in the functioning of human beings (Gerber, Whitebook, & Weinstein, 2007). Here is what you can do to provide staff with the organizational structure and resources they need to effectively implement their jobs.

Providing Structure

Given the unpredictability of working with families from high-risk backgrounds, it is crucial that your staff experience a predictable organization in which to work. There should be the following:

- Transparency around the organizational mission and policies.
- Clear organizational boundaries regarding staff roles, levels of leadership, and lines of authority should be documented and followed, with current organizational charts accessible to all staff.
- Staff management approaches should be disclosed to staff.
- Managerial staff should continuously address interstaff roles and relationships.
- Staff should be well versed in human resource policies and the reasons the agency has for its specific way of operating. Any opportunity to have the staff contribute to human resource policy development should be seized.
- Well-defined and detailed job descriptions should be devised for each position, with occasional review of these documents to elicit feedback from staff. These should include participation in (and/or provision of) RS.

Providing Resources

Often, programs that serve families devoid of resources are lacking in resources themselves. Early childhood programs are frequently charged to be comprehensive in their approach—to meet the needs of the young children across developmental domains, as well as the needs of their families, often without the fiscal capacity to do so in a quality manner. Nevertheless, it is critical to provide your staff with as many resources as possible, some of which are at low cost, to make their work more doable.

As mentioned in the prior section, an agency handbook that includes the organization's mission and goals, management styles and hierarchies, specific roles and responsibilities of staff, and intervention approaches can be quite helpful to staff as they navigate the complexities of their jobs in an early childhood program. More specifically, resources that can be useful to your staff include the following:

BEYOND REFLECTIVE SUPERVISION: HOW CAN MY
ORGANIZATION SUPPORT STAFF WELL-BEING?

139

- Practice guides that articulate more specifically how to intervene with children and families can provide instruction and support outside of the supervisory process.

- Protocols regarding how to handle certain situations (e.g., child maltreatment, parent suicidality) should be clearly delineated in these guides (see box Vignette 8.1).

- Lists of resources for children and families can also be included so that staff have easy access to referral sources. Ideally, agency management would have formalized these interagency collaborations and devised some system for prioritizing the referrals from early childhood programs.

> **Vignette 8.1**
>
> When changing the diaper of one of the children in the 2-year-old classroom, the teaching assistant noticed fresh bruises on the child's back and buttocks. She became quite alarmed, afraid for him but also concerned for herself because she did not want to have an altercation with the child's parents. Her first thought was to treat the bruises and not involve herself in how the parents disciplined their child. Then, she remembered that she had been told by her supervisor to check her *Practice Handbook* in situations such as these. She consulted it, and was reminded that she was a mandated reporter for any suspicion of child maltreatment. She was relieved to note that she did not have to deal with the parent or call child protective services on her own, but that she was to talk this over with her supervisor and that they together would follow through on the resolution to this problem.

Having said this, your staff must also experience safety in their relationships with the managers and supervisors at all levels. These modest organizational adaptations can go far to help your staff to feel they are standing on firm organizational ground as they implement the program.

SUSTAINED STAFF DEVELOPMENT: NURTURING FOR COMPETENCE

As described at the start of this chapter, many staff personnel lack the preparation for work in programs serving high-risk families. This unmet staff need argues for an emphasis in your program on staff development (Zaslow & Martinez-Beck, 2006). A prime venue for sustained staff development is the RS process, but other mechanisms are beneficial as well.

Providing Guidance Through Experiential Learning

Although training is an essential component of staff development, my experience is that sustained staff development is best achieved through guidance in the context of actual practice. Thus, all staff should receive initial and ongoing training, and multiple opportunities to learn from families, supervisors, and peers in an active, experiential manner.

New staff. Initial staff training should be formalized and offered prior to staff entry into their prescribed roles. This training should move beyond didactic information to more experiential training that involves shadowing other early childhood classroom teachers, family support workers, or home visitors. Shadowing allows your new staff to ask questions that they may not have thought of prior to experiencing the work or may not have been comfortable asking management. Mentoring or coaching helps new staff learn the ropes but also acknowledges the abilities of your staff who are selected to be the coach or mentor. Because of the time commitment required by mentoring and coaching activities, the staff mentors/ coaches should have their workload lightened in other areas so that they can provide appropriate support. Ideally, new staff should be scaffolded through a gradual entry into their roles including that of a reflective supervisee (see Costa & Sullivan, this volume, p. 149, for further discussion of reflective practice activities).

Continuing staff. Ongoing training for staff should also be experiential, addressing issues that emerge from their work with particular children and families, and individualized to their strengths and needs. For example, the staff members who have educational and experiential backgrounds in child development may need more support in their interaction with parents. In contrast, those with education and experience in family support may need more training regarding young child development. Training topics for you to consider include (a) working with children with behavioral problems or other mental health challenges, (b) supporting children with physical and/or cognitive disabilities, (c) interacting with children and families who do not speak English, (d) dealing with mothers who are depressed or otherwise mentally ill, and (e) caring for families affected by violence or substance use.

Experiential staff training can also occur in vivo, in other words, in the immediate context of the work. Periodically, supervisors should observe staff working with children and families and give immediate feedback. In this way, supervisors can help staff apply ideas learned in training sessions to their actual work. Furthermore, the presence of the supervisor in the classroom or in a family's home provides a strong message to staff about the supportiveness and structure provided to them by your organization.

Programs that have mental health providers, or other specialists, on staff or as consultants are in a unique position to provide staff with support and feedback around emotionally complex family or child concerns. For example, a mental health consultant may introduce a teacher or home visitor to specific strategies to engage a child with behavior problems or a depressed parent, and scaffold them to implement such strategies in the context of the classroom or home visit.

Providing validation. Early intervention work is challenging at best. Practitioners struggle to provide the best care possible to the children and families they serve. Not feeling alone in this struggle or inept because they do not always have the answer is validating. (For an example of how the support of a mental health consultant supported a teacher in a Head Start Center, see box Vignette 8.2.) Thus, your staff's competence and skill can be strengthened through less formal interaction with peers and supervisors as well. For example:

- *Case conferences:* Here staff alternate presenting a challenging case. Done skillfully, case conferences provide a mechanism for peer feedback and validation about their approaches, and a forum for helping your staff to internalize particular approaches found to be effective with particular children or families. These sessions can also teach staff about other fundamental issues (e.g., maintaining confidentiality) and enhance other professional skills (e.g., oral presentation). See Copa, Lucinski, Olsen, and Wollenberg (1999) for a description of one organization's approach to and use of case conference presentations.

- *Staff discussion groups:* Staff discussion groups can be devised around child and family issues that the staff members identify as particularly challenging. The group can use the practice or research literature as a foundation for exploring these issues. Mental health and other experts can enrich staff learning around specific issues and cases.

- *Periodic (e.g., quarterly) review:* Regular collaborative review of children and families by the staff and the clinical supervisors or mental health consultants allows for continuous improvement of intervention strategies. All of these approaches help staff intellectualize the issues that they confront on a daily basis so that they are less entrenched in the emotional upheavals characteristic of the work with specific children and families.

Vignette 8.2

During her regular meeting with the program's mental health consultant, the lead teacher in a Head Start Center reported on the increasingly oppositional and aggressive behavior in one of the little boys in her classroom. The mental health consultant came to observe the child and was able, while she was there, to give the teacher strategies for addressing his behavior problems during circle time and center time. They also observed together the child's reunion with his mother at the end of the day, and noted that the parent seemed very tired, anxious, and sad, and quite irritated with her son. With the support of the mental health consultant, the teacher was able to talk to the parent about the child's behavior and refer the parent to the Head Start Center's family support person to get support around parenting and her own well-being.

A SECURE BASE: NURTURANCE THROUGH SUPPORT OF PHYSICAL AND PSYCHOLOGICAL SAFETY

One of the most important social milestones for young children is learning to use the secure base they are provided by caregivers in order to explore and learn about their environment. Applying this principle to early childhood staff, it is critical that your program and organization are perceived as places of security from which the staff receive the resources and support to intervene with children and families. Staff should feel that the organization is invested in their physical and psychological well-being. This sense of being nurtured will translate into the way the staff then responds to and cares for children and families (i.e., parallel process). Thus, your program should focus on "nurturing the nurturer," thereby engaging the staff in sustained self-care activities (Barnett & Cooper, 2009; Rothschild & Rand, 2006).

Ensuring Physical Safety

Early childhood programs are often situated in neighborhoods and communities that may be devoid of resources and affected by violence and other risk factors. For staff to continue to feel invested in coming to work, it is important that they feel that their physical safety is not at risk. Thus, the building that houses your early childhood program must be secure without sacrificing its connection to the community. For example, security guards should simultaneously work to maintain staff safety and engage interpersonally with the children and families who enter the building. Careful planning should be used regarding how children, families, and staff exit the center, ensuring that they are not put at risk (e.g., busy streets, gang warfare). Good lighting and secure parking are also important, especially when program staff arrive early in the morning or depart late in the evening.

More intensive safety strategies should be undertaken for staff whose work is mainly in the community or in families' homes. Technological aids (e.g., cell phones or global positioning systems) should be provided for staff who have to work in dangerous homes or communities. Agency policies should address situations in which staff should not go into homes and communities alone. For example, staff should go in teams to communities with documented high levels of violence and crime. Documents articulating your agency policies and practices should include guidance to staff regarding what to do when they feel their safety is at stake (e.g., a firearm is observed in a home). Rudimentary training regarding self-defense and collaboration with law enforcement may be necessary for some staff members who work in communities or on issues (e.g., child protection) in which there is the potential for danger. Again, transparency is essential in these situations; staff members often feel exploited if they are put in these situations without awareness of the risk. Building in contingencies and supports sends a message to your staff that their well-being is valued by the organizations in which they work.

Ensuring Psychological Safety

The protection of staff physical safety clearly has implications for their psychological well-being. Furthermore, early childhood intervention programs or organizations should invest in ensuring the psychological safety of staff as well. In the main, your staff should feel that they can trust supervisors and managers enough to be vulnerable, to disclose their fallacies and errors in practice, and to support their development in their current roles and in their careers in general. Without this sense of trust in those who are the decision makers for the organization, and the evaluators of staff performance, staff well-being is often in jeopardy. Beyond the specific characteristics of agency managers and supervisors, and what occurs in the RS process, the following strategies may enhance the psychological well-being of early childhood staff.

Strategies to avoid burnout. A major thrust of programs that work with high-risk children and families should be to minimize the potential for staff burnout. As such, there should be constant attention to and recognition of the stress staff may feel working with program participants. They should be instructed in specific strategies to avoid burnout, including using the supervisory process, intellectualizing the participant challenges they face through learning from the literature and peers, and maintaining boundaries in their work (e.g., not working extra hours consistently, not volunteering to take on extra cases, not giving families their home phone numbers).

Strategies for self-care. In addition, staff should be instructed in self-care and other strategies that may reduce the stress they feel. For example, training experiences regarding stress management, time management, and juggling roles and responsibilities may assist them to feel more competent about their performance. Specific de-stressing activities such as meditation, imaging, and self-massage can be taught to staff and actively implemented throughout their workday. There can also be designated mental health or staff well-being events periodically in which staff are not responsible for their typical work and can have more relaxed time to be with coworkers, address burnout, and focus on self-care. These can be small ongoing events such as lunchtime exercise clubs or large events such as an annual wellness day that offers a series of self-care activities for staff.

Mental health consultation and referral for staff. Finally, in some cases, staff may become so overwhelmed with the intensity of the work that their performance is seriously affected. Clearly, the reflective supervisory process is an optimal mechanism through which such situations can be addressed. In

BEYOND REFLECTIVE SUPERVISION: HOW CAN MY
ORGANIZATION SUPPORT STAFF WELL-BEING?

143

addition, programs that have mental health consultants can provide some specific support in these situations. Similar to the employee assistance initiatives that occur in large organizations and corporations, mental health consultants can confidentially direct staff who are experiencing personal challenges as a result of the work or personal experiences to appropriate supports in the community.

Staff validation. The stressful nature of the work of early childhood staff requires that they receive constant and concrete support and validation. Tangible acknowledgment of staff worth may alleviate staff burnout and inappropriate behavior with program participants (e.g., yelling at a child in the classroom, avoiding a home visit). Use of the following strategies sends a clear message to staff that they are valued contributors to the program's service delivery system.

On a regular basis, your staff should be recognized for small and large accomplishments. Having a kudos period at the end of every staff meeting or an annual staff recognition ceremony can both be used to recognize staff for their performance. (For an example of how a program manager recognized the work of home visitors at a staff meeting during an especially challenging, stressful week, see box Vignette 8.3.) Written commentary on staff accomplishments (e.g., *Staff Spotlight*) should appear in participant newsletters, board and funder correspondence, the agency Web site, and public relations materials. Staff should be encouraged to share their work within and external to the organization, such as presenting at agency case conferences or professional conferences. Finally, small tokens or words of appreciation from supervisory and management staff go far to solidify staff's perception of being supported by the agency for which they work, and ultimately their investment in performing well in their roles as early childhood professionals.

Vignette 8.3

Following a very challenging week in which home-based staff achieved a record number of successful home visits and addressed the needs of a particularly high-risk group of families, the program manager opted to change the focus of her weekly staff meeting. When staff arrived, they were greeted with a plate of cookies. The meeting began with the manager identifying an accomplishment of each one of the staff for that week. She also spent some time reviewing the importance of putting parameters around the work they were doing, and not taking it home, asking each staff member to write down how they were going to spend the weekend taking care of themselves. She then proceeded to have them provide anonymous affirmations (e.g., what they appreciated about each other) to each other and spent the balance of the meeting with de-stressing activities, such as self-massage and meditation. Later, she sent an e-mail to staff outlining the administrative matters she had planned to review in the weekly staff meeting.

SUMMARY

A holding environment provides the individual with the resources and supports in which to optimally grow. Early childhood professionals aim to create that environment for young children and their families, but encounter multiple stressors as they attempt to achieve this goal. According to the principle of parallel process, these professionals can create such an environment for program participants only if they are held themselves. To recruit and retain high-quality staff, early childhood programs must become a holding environment for staff, whether they work in the classrooms, homes, or communities of program participants.

Thus, it is critical that early childhood programs provide the organizational infrastructure, sustained staff development, and secure, safe environments that promote the well-being of staff. Many of these efforts can be initiated at relatively low economic cost to programs, but may yield high gains in terms of countering staff burnout and emotional exhaustion. A positive sense of well-being on the part of staff has the potential to benefit staff members themselves, the children and families they encounter, and the organizations for which they work. Programs that engage in staff-nurturing activities, in concert with RS, are making a major contribution to addressing a major challenge in the early childhood field—maintaining and enhancing their workforce.

REFERENCES

Administration for Children and Families. (2006). *Findings from the survey of Early Head Start programs: Communities, programs, and families.* Washington, DC: U.S. Department of Health and Human Services.

Ammerman, R., Stevens, J., Putnam, F., Altaye, M., Hulsmann, J., Lehmkuhl, H., et al. (2006). Predictors of early engagement in home visitation. *Journal of Family Violence, 21*(2), 105–115.

Barnett, J., & Cooper, N. (2009). Creating a culture of self-care. *Clinical Psychology: Science and Practice, 16*(1), 16–20.

Copa, A., Lucinski, L., Olsen, E., & Wollenberg, K. (1999). Promoting professional and organizational development: A reflective practice model. *Zero to Three, 20*(1), 3–9.

Costa, G., & Sullivan, L. (2009). What staff development activities can be used to build reflective capacity? In S. Scott Heller & L. Gilkerson (Eds.), *A practical guide to reflective supervision* (pp. 144–181). Washington, DC: ZERO TO THREE.

Drafke, M. (2009). *The human side of organizations* (10th ed.). Upper Saddle River, NJ: Pearson/Prentice Hall.

Early, D. M., Maxwell, K. L., Burchinal, M., Bender, R. H., Ebanks, C., Henry, G. T., et al. (2007). Teacher's education, classroom quality, and young children's academic skills: Results from seven studies of preschool programs. *Child Development, 78*(2), 558–580.

Figley, C. (1995). *Compassion fatigue: Secondary traumatic stress.* New York: Brunner/Mazel.

Gerber, E., Whitebook, M., & Weinstein, R. (2007). At the heart of child care: Predictors of teacher sensitivity in center-based child care. *Early Childhood Research Quarterly, 22*(3), 327–346.

Gill, S., Greenberg, M. T., Moon, C., & Margraf, P. (2007). Home visitor competence, burnout, support and client engagement. *Journal of Human Behavior in the Social Environment, 15*(1), 23–44.

Gilliam, W., & Shahar, G. (in press). Pre-kindergarten expulsion and suspension: Rates and predictors in one state. *Infants and Young Children.*

Hamre, B., Pianta, R., Downer, J., & Mashburn, A. (2008). Teachers' perception of conflict with young students. *Social Development, 17*(1), 115–136.

Hemmeter, M., Santos, R., & Ostrosky, M. (2008). Preparing early childhood educators to address young children's social–emotional development and challenging behavior. *Journal of Early Intervention, 30*(4), 321–340.

Howard, F. (2008). Managing stress or enhancing wellbeing? Positive psychology's contributions to clinical supervision. *Australian Psychologist, 43*(2), 105–113.

Klusmann, U., Kunter, M., Trautwein, U., Ludtke, O., & Baumert, J. (2008). Teachers' occupational well-being and quality of instruction: The important role of self-regulatory patterns. *Journal of Educational Psychology, 100*(3), 702–715.

Korfmacher, J., Green, B., Spellmann, M., & Thornburg, K. (2007). The helping relationship and program participation in early childhood home visiting. *Infant Mental Health Journal, 28*(5), 459–480.

Kyriacou, C. (2001). Teacher stress: Directions for future research. *Educational Review, 53,* 17–35.

Lieberman, A., & Van Horn, P. (2008). *Psychotherapy with infants and young children.* Washington, DC: ZERO TO THREE.

Maslach, C., Schaufeli, W., & Leiter, M. (2001). Job burnout. *Annual Review of Psychology, 58,* 593–614.

Olds, D. L., Robinson, J., O'Brien, R., Luckey, D. W., Pettitt, L. M., Henderson C. R., Jr., et al. (2002). Home visiting by paraprofessionals and by nurses: A randomized, controlled trial. *Pediatrics, 110,* 486–496.

Pianta, R. C., Howes, C., Burchinal, M., Bryant, D., Clifford, R., Early, D., & Barbarin, O. (2005). Features of pre-kindergarten programs, classrooms, and teachers: Do they predict observed classroom quality and child–teacher interactions? *Applied Developmental Science, 9*(3), 144–159.

Remen, R. N. (2000). *My grandfather's blessings.* New York: Riverhead Books.

Rothschild, B., & Rand, M. (2006). *The psychology of compassion fatigue and vicarious trauma: Help for the helper (Self-care for managing burnout and stress).* New York: W.W. Norton.

Rudow, B. (1999). Stress and burnout in the teaching profession. In R. Vandenberghe & M. Huberman (Eds.), *Understanding and preventing teacher burnout* (pp. 38–58). Cambridge, England: Cambridge University Press.

Schaufeli, W., & Enzman, D. (1998). *The burnout companion to study and practice: A critical analysis.* London: Taylor & Francis.

Shahmoon-Shanok, R. (2009). What is reflective supervision? In S. Scott Heller & L. Gilkerson (Eds.), *A practical guide to reflective supervision* (pp. 7–23). Washington, DC: ZERO TO THREE.

Tandon, S. D., Parillo, K., Jenkins, C., & Duggan, A. (2005). Formative evaluation of home visitors' role in addressing poor mental health, domestic violence, and substance abuse among low-income pregnant and parenting women. *Maternal and Child Health Journal, 9*(3), 273–283.

Van Horn, J., Taris, R., Schaufeli, W., & Schreurs, P. (2004). The structure of occupational well-being: A study among Dutch teachers. *Journal of Occupational and Organizational Psychology, 77,* 365–375.

Wasik, B. H., & Roberts, R. N. (1994). Home visitor characteristics, training, and supervision. *Family Relations, 43*(3), 336–341.

Winnicott, D. (1976). *The maturational process and the facilitating environment.* London: Hogarth Press.

Zaslow, M., & Martinez-Beck, I. (Eds.). (2006). *Critical issues in early childhood professional development.* Baltimore: Brookes.

Reflective Tool 8

Nurturing Staff Well-Being

Reflective Tool 8 can be utilized by supervisors and other personnel in their efforts to support staff well-being. It delineates specific issues that have been linked to staff well-being in early childhood programs. It is recommended that ongoing assessment of staff through formal evaluation and supervisory reflection address whether they continue to exhibit the characteristics listed in column 1, the loss of which has been associated with burnout. At the very least, supervisors should periodically ask staff how they are doing in each of these areas. Next to each desired staff characteristic are listed activities relevant to organizational structure and staff nurturance (beyond reflection) that are useful in sustaining these staff characteristics. The integration of these strategies into ongoing work with staff—in the context of reflective supervision, staff training, or other developmental activities—serves the ultimate goal of promoting staff well-being.

		STAFF CHARACTERISTICS	ORGANIZATIONAL/NURTURING STRATEGIES
AREAS OF NURTURANCE OR SUPPORT	Macro Level (Organizational Infrastructure)	• **Do staff members have the time to complete tasks?**	• Appropriate alignment of staff responsibilities with work hours. • Delegation of tasks to other staff based on abilities and time. • Refraining from using staff for tasks not relevant to job (e.g., using family support workers to staff classrooms). • Training on time management. • Training regarding efficient completion of paperwork.
		• **Do staff members have a full understanding of the program goals and the guidance to meet them?**	• Regular review of agency mission and protocols. • Regular review of external mandates (e.g., Head Start Program Performance Standards). • Attendance at governing and advisory board meetings. • Regular interaction with upper management who provide rationale for program goals and objectives, particularly during times of transition and policy shifts. • Training regarding evidence-based and best practices.
		• **Do staff members have specific training tied to staff/supervisor identified areas for professional development?**	• Training regarding problem solving and decision making. • Training regarding specific issues that characterize participant children and families (e.g., mental health, substance abuse, disabilities). • Observation and monitoring of implementation of best practices.
		• **Do staff members have a sense of pleasure in their work?**	• Administrative/supervisory staff modeling of positive affect/language. • Opportunities to reflect on job with humor. • Welcoming and comfortable workspaces. • Mental health consultation. • Events that allow staff to interact with children and families in different ways (e.g., family holiday party). • Work activities that allow staff to enjoy and learn from each other in the absence of participants (e.g., peer supervisory and support groups).

Continued

BEYOND REFLECTIVE SUPERVISION: HOW CAN MY
ORGANIZATION SUPPORT STAFF WELL-BEING?

147

Reflective Tool 8 (continued)

<table>
<tr><th colspan="2"></th><th>STAFF CHARACTERISTICS</th><th>ORGANIZATIONAL/NURTURING STRATEGIES</th></tr>
<tr>
<td rowspan="5">AREAS OF NURTURANCE OR SUPPORT</td>
<td rowspan="5">Staff Level (Sustaining Competence)</td>
<td>• Do staff members exhibit empathy for the children and families they serve?</td>
<td>• Staff training regarding the stressors children and families experience and subsequent outcomes.
• Case conferences regarding families "overcoming and succumbing to odds."
• Incorporating role-play into staff training and case conferencing.
• Experiential activities in which staff have to view the world from the vantage point of child or family (e.g., observe classroom from eye of infant, consider self-sufficiency goal from perspective of depressed mother).</td>
</tr>
<tr>
<td>• Do staff members have a sense of hope and optimism about their work and its impact?</td>
<td>• Case presentations of children and families who have good outcomes.
• Introduction to effective practices through training and peer sharing.
• Incorporation of positive imagery in staff training and other developmental activities.
• Opportunities to reflect individually and in small and large groups on strengths in children and families, and the small gains program participants have made.</td>
</tr>
<tr>
<td>• Do staff members have a sense of competence about their own abilities and skills?</td>
<td>• Regular positive feedback regarding specific accomplishments.
• Opportunities for sharing accomplishments in staff meetings.
• Highlight staff person in agency publications.
• Staff training, extensive support/guidance, and written agency protocols regarding handling of challenging issues (e.g., mental illness, substance abuse, child maltreatment, suicidality).
• Opportunities to give administration feedback on agency functioning (e.g., anonymous suggestion boxes).</td>
</tr>
<tr>
<td>• Do staff members have the opportunity to interact with colleagues?</td>
<td>• Peer supervision.
• Case presentations.
• Inquiry groups.
• Social experiences with staff (e.g., agency staff picnic, holiday party, mental health day).</td>
</tr>
<tr>
<td>• Do staff members exhibit a willingness to learn/change? And do they have the opportunity to do so?</td>
<td>• Staff experiential training.
• Modeling appropriate practices.
• Identifying specific instances of staff response to training or other learning experience.
• Professional development, planning, and monitoring</td>
</tr>
</table>

Continued

Reflective Tool 8 (continued)

		STAFF CHARACTERISTICS	ORGANIZATIONAL/NURTURING STRATEGIES
AREAS OF NURTURANCE OR SUPPORT	Staff Level (Physical and Psychological Safety)	• **Do staff members have the skills and opportunity to support their own emotional energy/wellness?**	• Incorporation of de-stressing activities in staff meetings and daily work protocols (e.g., self-massage, imagery, meditation, reflection moments). • Training on stress management, problem solving, coping, and avoiding burnout. • Creating balanced classrooms and caseloads (i.e., not overloading particular staff with most difficult children and families). • Providing additional support to staff who have challenging classrooms and caseloads. • Instituting staff "mental health" days. • Mental health consultation. • Administrative/supervisory staff modeling of positive affect/language. • Opportunities to reflect on the job with humor. • Welcoming and comfortable workspaces.
		• **Do staff members have the skills and opportunity to support their physical energy/wellness?**	• Maintaining appropriate classroom ratios and family caseloads. • Instituting physical wellness days. • Creating lunchtime exercise clubs. • Training regarding physical self-care and illness prevention. • Attention to physical workspace (e.g., asbestos, chairs, clutter, dust).
		• **Does the program support the staff's ability to maintain professional boundaries?**	• Separate spaces for staff in which there is no program participant contact. • Participant access to general phone line after hours that is staffed (e.g., alternating staff shifts, answering service). • Staff training and monitoring regarding confidentiality. • Encouragement of staff adherence to assigned work hours (e.g., extended work hours in rare emergencies).
		• **Do staff members feel secure in the workplace?**	• Attention to staff safety in building, parking lots, and in community. • Adherence to confidentiality guidelines around staff personal and professional issues. • Use of technological aids (e.g., phone and emergency button in each classroom, cell phone and GPS system for home visitors). • Linkage with community law enforcement personnel. • Agency protocol regarding how to handle emergency situations.
		• **Do staff members have a sense of higher purpose than just day-to-day job?**	• Participation in professional conferences. • Current events "club" that discusses issues relevant to target population. • Inquiry group that examines issues relevant to target population. • Regular exposure to motivating speakers who remind staff of why they are engaged in the work.

CHAPTER 9

WHAT STAFF DEVELOPMENT ACTIVITIES CAN BE USED TO BUILD REFLECTIVE CAPACITY?

Gerard Costa and Lorri Sullivan

*The world is a looking glass
and gives back to every man the reflection of his own face.*

—*William Makepeace Thackeray (1906, p. 10)*

Staff members differ in their experience with reflective process and their comfort with it. As we view the capacity for reflection as a basic human capacity, we believe that reflection is an ability that can be nurtured and strengthened. As you launch reflective supervision (RS) in your program, we suggest that you consider offering staff learning experiences that promote reflection among all members of the group/team/program. The message you will be conveying is that reflection is a process that staff members all are learning and relearning at every point of their professional lives. Here, we offer you a toolbox of eight reflective activities with specific strategies and activities to build and expand the reflective capacity in both novice and senior staff. We also review central concepts that influence all reflective work, focusing on the importance of paying attention to and using our feelings as part of the helping relationship. By the end of this chapter, you will be able to:

1. Talk with staff about the role of feelings in the helping relationship.

2. Create a safe space for staff to play with and engage in reflective activities.

3. Use Reflective Tool 9 to collect the lessons learned about reflection from the leader and participants.

THE IMPORTANCE OF PAYING ATTENTION TO FEELINGS AND EXPERIENCES

This chapter begins with a brief review of four central concepts in reflective work, all aimed at explaining the critical importance of paying attention to personal feelings and subjective experiences in work with families. These concepts are as follows:

1. The universal experience of transference in human relationships.

2. The power of personal stories in relationship-based interventions.

3. The important distinction between describing feelings and revealing personal lives.

4. The importance of creating a safe environment for reflective activities.

The Universal Experience of Transference in Human Relationships

Transference is ubiquitous—it occurs everywhere and in all persons. Although the clinical meanings of the term deserve special attention, the everyday meaning of the concept is that each new experience is influenced by what has occurred before. Formally, transference refers to the experience a person encounters when the thoughts, feelings, characteristics, and beliefs about people and experiences in the past are associated and confused with ("transferred" to) persons or situations in the present. (See also Keyes, Cavanaugh, & Scott Heller, this volume, p. 99, for a discussion of the potential influence of transference in the reflective supervisory relationship.) It is as if there is a kind of time travel that takes place, when affects and ideas associated with prior relationships are applied to current relationships—where the past and the present merge.

This transference occurs in everyday life and experiences, such as the sudden like or dislike someone may feel for a perfect stranger. In such experiences, the suddenness of the experience of an unknown person suggests that the feelings do not belong to the other person, but are likely triggered by internal memories of others. These can be good or harmful experiences and feelings. We know that babies are powerful transference objects (Fraiberg, Adelson, & Shapiro, 1980; Trout, 1989) to their own parents, meaning that babies are sometimes treated as if they were figures, sometimes harmful ones, from the parental past. Fraiberg and her colleagues referred to this phenomenon as "ghosts in the nursery." We also know that the infants, children, and families professionals work with will elicit thoughts and feelings that may be based on past relationships. A practitioner may meet a family who looks and feels very familiar to her, so she will approach her work with a feeling of comfort. Sometimes the family dynamics may stir up uncomfortable feelings that are based on a practitioner's role in her own family. Many of these feelings will be experienced on an unconscious level so that she may not be aware of the reason why she dreads or looks forward to interactions with certain families. Reflective work is needed not only for the cases in which the practitioner experiences difficulty, but also (perhaps especially) in those cases when she falls in love with the family and is not aware of any difficulties or challenges in the clinical work. In fact, such cases can present a number of blind spots—aspects of herself and the family that she remains unaware of.

The Power of Our Personal Story in Relationship-Based Interventions

As the previous section on transference suggests, each infant, child, and family has the power to activate within a practitioner something about his personal narrative. Many of the tools described in the later section of this chapter (notably Reflective Activity 1) are helpful in making this point clear. Working with families from a relationship-based perspective means that such normal and expected associations between a practitioner's personal life story and the feelings that are activated in his work require that he pays attention to the subjective experiences he has and uses the feelings and beliefs he encounters.

Many interventionists come to their work with histories that may reflect some of the same stressors and injuries being faced by the families with whom they work: child abuse, family violence, parental substance abuse and mental illness, foster care, early loss, and deprivation. Such experiences can be the source of both great empathy, as well as great difficulty in their work. In addition, workers come to care deeply for the infants, children, and families they serve, and when families face adverse experiences or trauma, staff can experience vicarious trauma or caregiver fatigue, even when the worker's own life history may not contain such experiences (see Jones Harden, this volume, p. 135, for more on this topic). In these cases, reflective practices are necessary to ensure that families are being provided with principled, thoughtful help. Costa (2004) examined this issue as a particular threat—and need—for child protective staff who on a daily basis encounter children who are maltreated, most often by those who love them.

In all these cases, attention to the workers' reactions and awareness of their life narratives are critical.

The Important Distinction Between Describing Feelings and Revealing Personal Lives

As was briefly mentioned in chapter 6 (Keyes et al., this volume, p. 99), staff unfamiliar with reflective practices may often confuse the goals and activities of reflective work with psychotherapy. Therefore, it is important that leaders who promote reflective work make clear the distinction between being able to identify and discuss the feelings, experiences, ideas, and reactions to families, and the private, intentional work of engaging in psychotherapy—where one's private, personal life is explored and understood through a specialized relationship with a mental health professional. It is critical that staff feel safe in respectfully and supportively discussing their feelings and reactions to families. Staff must also be helped to anticipate that their own personal experiences, even traumatic events, may be activated through their work with a particular family. Leaders must help staff to be careful not to share too much private information, unless such sharing appears helpful in the understanding of these experiences.

Role of feelings. Relationship-based intervention considers the notion that interventionists form affective, interpersonal connections with families that require attention not only to the workers' actions and tasks, but also to their emotional and subjective experiences. In this perspective, staff should be helped to understand the profound yet often unexamined role their own feelings, reactions, and subjective experiences with infants and families have on their work. (See box How Affect Impacts Experiences for information on how feelings help practitioners.)

How Affect Impacts Experiences

Our feelings help us:

- Organize and interpret information
- Give meaning
- Energize (or deplete)
- Connect
- Divide
- Engage in promoting learning and development

Focusing on reactions. It is important to help a staff member recognize that her reactions or behaviors may be influenced by her own personal narratives. The discussion focuses on how her own personal life history impacts her professional life; that is, how it impacts her interactions with a particular client or coworker (not how it impacts her current life outside of her work). To keep the discussion focused on this, we have found it helpful in approaching work with infants, children, and families to ask the two questions in the box Two Critical Questions for Reflection.

....

Two Critical Questions for Reflection

Questions to help focus on the impact of the helper's personal narratives on his interactions with a client or coworker:

1. Who is this baby to this family?

   This refers to the importance of understanding the nature of the parental relationship. We addressed this briefly in the earlier section on transference and with the concept of "ghosts in the nursery."

2. What is going on inside of you, or what is being stirred up in you, the helper?

   This refers to the essential requirement that all who form helping relationships with families must pay attention to the feelings, personal "narratives," and elements of his own life that naturally get activated by every child and family he works with.

....

In all the exercises provided in this chapter, we have attempted to be mindful of this important distinction. Nonetheless, we must acknowledge that the nature of relationship-based work will activate personal stories and experiences, and workers will often experience—consciously and unconsciously—material from their past that can intrude on the work, but can also inform it. Trout (1988) noted that many in the clinical field of infant mental health will be drawn to a personal psychotherapy, in part related to the nature of their work with families. Trout noted that the famed pediatrician-turned-psychoanalyst Donald Winnicott urged all pediatricians to undergo psychoanalysis. We regard this not as a judgment of pathology but as a recognition that all who work with families, particularly involving the care of infants and toddlers, will necessarily have their personal stories reawakened. Thea Bry, the late supervisor of the first author, once stated during a clinical supervision that "something about this family stirs something up in you but that is between you and your therapist. Our job is to be sure it does not hurt the work." This distinction is an important and critical one, and led another supervisor, David Peters, to remark that "we need supervision to save our patients from ourselves."

We must help individuals and group members to understand that reflecting on their feelings about their work does not require them to share their most personal and private selves. Supervisors will focus discussions on thoughts and feelings within the context of their helping relationships. Although these reflective discussions will be intimate and thoughtful, they are not meant to be a form of therapy. When leading a group, it is important for a supervisor to share some ground rules for reflective discussions. The group rules should set parameters that allow group members to feel safe enough to share their thoughts, fears, and feelings regarding their work; the box Reflective Group Rules provides a list of some rules you may want to include.

WHAT STAFF DEVELOPMENT ACTIVITIES CAN BE USED
TO BUILD REFLECTIVE CAPACITY?

153

Reflective Group Rules

- *Group confidentiality.* All members must agree that the discussions and reflections will be held confidential and not discussed outside of the reflective session.

- *Be open to the thoughts and reactions of others.* It is important to ask for and consider other's responses to the situations and feelings being described during reflective time. It is easy to assume that everyone feels the same way or that they experience the same situation in the exact same way. Listening to the objective opinions of coworkers may help practitioners see the situation in another way or give them another way to look at their experiences with infants, children, and families.

- *Encourage group members to share both the "hits" and "misses" in their work.* It is just as important to spend time thinking about the times things seemed to go well or not so well in their work. They can learn from both types of situations, and participants should be encouraged to think about the lessons they can take from the hits and misses in their work with families.

- *Participants might be asked to share their temperature when describing a situation.* This phrase can be used to elicit more descriptive feedback on what each person might have been thinking, feeling, and experiencing during an interaction. "What was the conversation like for you?" and "How could you tell the mother was upset with you?" are examples of questions that might help identify the temperature of an interaction.

The Importance of Creating a Safe Environment for Reflective Activities

It is now evident that in this context, staff require support to engage in reflective practices, and leaders must establish ways to ensure a safe climate for staff sharing to occur. Such climates are best considered outgrowths of organizational cultures (Bertacchi, 1996) in which staff experience at all levels feelings of trust and safety, and witness models of respectful and reflective sharing about relationship-based work. It is important to understand that as in all meaningful relationships, behavior speaks louder than words, so simply telling staff they are safe to share all they wish does not ensure this will occur. Reflective practices unfold over time and require strong, thoughtful leadership in creating and sustaining the climate to support such discourse. In this regard, parallel process is the key: Administration models and promotes reflection for supervisors, supervisors model and promote the practice in staff, staff members promote this work with families, and families become more reflective with their children.

The importance of reflective practices to the work is also evident when organizations protect time for reflective activities. By so doing, organizations convey that reflective work is considered an essential requirement of working with families, and that it supports both professional development and quality care. Administration's commitment to and support of reflective practice are vital at every stage from the discovery (Boris & Grabert, this volume, p. 41) and implementation phases (Scott Heller, this volume, p. 25) to the RS sessions (Atchley, Hall, Martinez, & Gilkerson, this volume, p. 83; Weatherston & Barron, this volume, p. 63) as well as the reflective environment (Jones Harden, this volume, p. 135, and this chapter). In this way, reflective time is not something that occurs when there is extra time or if some other event is cancelled; instead, it is viewed as an integral component of the program.

Leaders set the tone for group reflective discussions by creating regular opportunities for staff to gather to speak about their work, facilitated by well-trained staff. Often, discussions might begin by asking the participants if anyone has something he or she would like the group to help them think about. This sets a more positive and thoughtful tone than asking if they have any problems or concerns in their work.

The group could be an informal structure in which whoever has something to discuss brings it up to the group. It could also have a more structured format in which for each group one participant is designated to be the discussant or focus of the group session (see Atchley et al., this volume, p. 90, for an example), or groups can have a predetermined case conference-like format (Copa, Lucinski, Olsen, Wollenburg, 1999; Costa, 2006). Regardless of the format, keeping questions and probes open-ended and positive are important to maintaining a supportive group tone. Also remember that it is equally as important to talk about "hits" or cases in which one is in love with a family as it is to discuss those cases in which one is experiencing some challenges or less positive experiences.

The activities in this chapter were designed to activate some personal reactions within the participants so that the material becomes real. It is important to remember that whenever a worker forms a helping or caregiving relationship with a child/family, some personal experiences—often unconscious—from within the helper's own psychological history will necessarily be activated. The box Being Aware of One's Subjective State lists three areas of personal or psychological history that supervisors will find helpful to remind staff to attend to carefully. It is important to help staff remember that attending to their feelings does not necessarily mean disclosing or acting on these feelings. Using their feelings in ways and situations that will benefit the child/family is what is required.

Being Aware of One's Subjective State

Helpers should maintain an awareness of:

- Their own emotional state going into a situation with the child/family.
- Sensitive issues and experiences from their own life/background.
- Any changes in their emotional experiences while with a client.

Managing Strong Feelings in the Moment

As a leader of reflective practice sessions, it is important to keep in mind that each staff member will respond differently to discussions and activities. At times, the intensity of an individual's reaction to a family or an activity may appear out of measure—meaning that the emotional response might be unexpectedly intense or personalized. It is critical that the leader consider his or her role as one of co-regulator—meaning that how the leader responds to the response will convey a sense of manageability of the experience and assist the helper in restoring a sense of calmness and capacity to handle both what is being shared and the nature of the relationship being addressed.

At times, a staff member may express personal *values* (e.g., "I think hitting a child for misbehaving is okay. My parents hit me and I'm okay."), personal *beliefs* (e.g., "I think all mothers should stay home when they have a baby."), personal *judgments* (e.g., "That father is a real lazy guy. I don't know why she stays with him."), or other provocative comments. In group settings, others may react to such statements with agreement or protest. Whether in an individual or group setting, the leader must be able to manage his own reaction in the moment and carefully, tactfully, and sensitively move forward in helping the staff member become self-reflective. The box Facilitator Prompts to Address Provocative Statements lists some prompts or questions that can facilitate this process. These questions were designed to convey an

WHAT STAFF DEVELOPMENT ACTIVITIES CAN BE USED
TO BUILD REFLECTIVE CAPACITY?

155

inquisitive, open posture and to help move the discussion along the way toward deeper insight. What is critical is that the leader monitors his own state and helps co-regulate the others in the group.

Facilitator Prompts to Address Provocative Statements

- "Help me understand more about your experience with this family?"

- "You are so involved with this family because it is clear you feel deeply about your work. Where do you think your feelings come from?"

- "I wonder if we can understand where this family is coming from?"

- "Families are so different from each other. Is there something about this family's culture, history, or experiences that can help you see the world through their eyes?"

- "What would you like to say to this person and what do you imagine they might want to say to you?"

A Toolbox of Reflective Activities

The next section provides eight activities or exercises that can be used to promote reflective practices in individuals and groups. See Table 9.1 for a list and description of purpose of these activities. Each activity is designed to be self-contained, and they can be used in any order (although we have found Reflective Activity 1 to be a very effective beginning into the process of reflective work).

Here are a few general principles to consider in using these tools:

1. Read through each activity and determine whether one or more of the activities lends itself to an issue you want to address. For example, if you are hoping to promote reflection and team building, Activity 6 (Feel Free to Wonder) describes the 2-4-6 Task that can be done as a group and demonstrates the concept of *synergy*—that the whole (team) is greater than the sum of its parts (individuals working alone).

2. Be sure to protect a time and space to engage in the activity:

   a. Select a space that lends itself to privacy and minimizes intrusion.

   b. Ask all participants to turn off cell phones and pagers.

   c. Introduce the activity as both enjoyable and serious to the group's work.

   d. Anticipate the duration of the activity and be sure that all participants are aware of the time expectation so that all can protect time accordingly.

3. It is important to honor the influence of culture and family differences in all discussions.

All tools contained in this chapter were designed to be useful across all cultural and individual differences. It is critical that leaders understand that culture organizes and creates the context for how families and staff approach helping relationships. For example, although staff members may regard a family's limited eye contact or failure to ask questions as indicators of poor engagement, these behaviors may reflect cultural practices that must be understood. Heffron, Grunstein, and Tilmon (2007) described the challenges inherent in addressing issues of diversity in reflective and clinical practice, and offered a series of guidelines for supervisors in respectfully addressing these challenges. It is critical to recognize that differences within cultures can be as great as differences between cultures, and no family, supervisor, or staff member can speak on behalf of a culture or ethic group. Trout and Foley (1989), in writing about a family systems approach to working with families of children with developmental disabilities, offered a

Table 9.1. Description of Eight Activities to Enhance Reflective Capacity

	ACTIVITY	PURPOSE	EXAMPLES OF TIMES TO USE
1	The Earliest Memory Interview	Highlights how present or current experiences can trigger past experiences or feelings	• Good icebreaker • Effective exercise to begin the reflective process
2	The Art of Practicing Conversations	Provides participants with: • A way to acknowledge difficulty or anxiety around certain topics • Opportunities for support • Guidance about appropriate and inappropriate roles staff can serve	• When staff are having problems communicating with families
3	Movies Without Sound: How Do You Really Know the Message That Someone Is Communicating?	Helps participants to: • Pay attention to others' verbal and nonverbal communication • Look outside ourselves and see how others perceive our responses	• When staff are too quick to draw conclusions about families • When staff are unaware of their own nonverbal communication with families
4	Bodies and Feelings: Paying Attention to Our State	Illustrates how the way we feel about a family influences how we: • Engage, • Interact, • Interpret, and • Terminate with clients or families	• Enhance participants' reflective skills regarding their own internal states and responses to others—especially clients
5	A Basket Full of Questions	Provides a format to help participants to: • Talk about their work • Reflect on their work	• Introduction to reflective case discussions
6	Feel Free to Wonder: The 2-4-6 Task and Other Fun Activities	Helps participants to • Think outside the box • Recognize that group processing can enhance problem solving	• When staff are too quick to draw conclusions about families • Good team builder • Promotes group reflection
7	Babywatching: Babies, Others, and Us!	Helps participants to: • Focus on being an observer • Recognize that we often feel with those we observe • Realize it is difficult to observe without interpreting	When staff need to: • Learn how to become objective observers • Become familiar with "wondering" about their observations
8	Becoming an Attuned Observer: Attending to Change	Helps participants to: • Learn to pay close attention to clients' nonverbal cues and emotional states • Become thoughtful and careful observers	• Introduction to reflective case discussions

useful metaphor: practitioners must sit at the feet of families and wonder what it is like for them. This helping posture is one that can help staff become more sensitive to the individual and cultural differences among families. As described in chapter 3 (Boris & Grabert, this volume, p. 41) and chapter 6 (Keyes et al., this volume, p. 99), it is important for organizations to provide training, consultation, and support in helping staff learn about the cultures and groups represented in the community and programs they serve.

The directions for each of the eight exercises are organized in the same format. Each activity or exercise starts with a description of when it is useful to utilize the activity. It is followed by a section that describes the purpose of the activity; that is, what the exercise hopes to teach participants. The final two sections describe the setup of the activity and details the procedures and possible prompts or questions.

THE IMPORTANCE OF SAFETY AND DEBRIEFING

As we noted earlier, safety is a critical element of reflective activities, particularly for those times when others (supervisors and peers) meet a person's comments or reflections with criticism, disagreement, or rebuke. The reflective leader's role is to modulate the discussion so that no participant dominates or sidetracks the intent of the reflective session. It is critical to debrief after an activity as very personal and charged memories and feelings may be stirred up. If the leader notices that a participant appears upset or seems to need more time to process her feelings following the reflective time, an individual follow-up meeting may be scheduled. Reflective Activity 9, at the end of this chapter, provides a framework to conduct a brief post activity inquiry about the "lessons learned."

Transition Strategies

It is essential that the leader provide support to the group to make the transition from the group discussion back to the work with infants, children, and families. Before the reflective time is over, the leader should ask the participants to reflect on and share with the group one or two helpful ideas, suggestions, or comments that they have heard. Once these have been identified, the leader can ask how each participant might put them to use during her next interaction with the family. Group discussions often generate many ideas and suggestions, which could be experienced as overwhelming for the worker. It is more likely that participants will be able to embrace or pay attention to one or two ideas or suggestions if they are asked, "Have you heard anything today that you think is helpful, and how will you use it in your work?"

Another helpful transition strategy is to ask everyone to think about and share with the group one thing they learned from the discussion that they will take back to their work. For example, someone might offer, "It's important to remember that I can't always tell how a family member is feeling based on their body language. Just because she didn't make eye contact with me doesn't mean she wasn't listening to me." Or, "I'm going to try to not ask so many questions the next time I meet with this family. I'll try to let them share more with me when they are ready."

Every member of the reflective discussion has the opportunity to learn and benefit from the experiences of their coworkers. Another good transition strategy might be to ask each member of the group to share something in his personal or professional life that he is looking forward to in the upcoming week. This often adds a sense of humor or lightness as an ending to the more focused reflective discussion. "I'm looking forward to sleeping this weekend" or "I can't wait to hear how Philip's mom made out with the suggestions I gave her about helping him learn to share with his sister" might be examples of the types of responses you can expect from the group. The goal of the transition activity should be to help the group move ahead and end the discussion on a positive and helpful note.

SUMMARY

The concept and process of reflective practices are rooted in the notion that thoughtful, principled help with families requires attention to the subjective experiences of the helper. It is also clear that reflective practices are a critical element of self-care. Staff members who engage in helping relationships form caring relationships that, at times, can feel exhausting, particularly when the caregiver's own needs are often unmet. These experiences deplete practitioners physically, emotionally, and spiritually. By virtue of their responsibility to intervene in crises in which the stakes can feel quite high, caregivers can experience fatigue exhaustion and burnout. Thus, it is essential that staff members are provided with support for reflection and self-care. (See Jones Harden, this volume, p. 135, for more on organizational strategies to support self-care in staff members.)

In this chapter, we have provided strategies and tools to promote reflective practices for those who work with infants, toddlers, children, and families. Our goal has been to provide tools that support thoughtful, principled care for those families with whom we are privileged to work. We hope that you find these exercises as helpful and productive as we have found them.

REFERENCES

Atchley, T., Hall, S., Martinez, S., & Gilkerson, L. (2009). What are the phases of the reflective supervision meeting? In S. Scott Heller & L. Gilkerson (Eds.), A practical guide to reflective supervision (pp. 83–98). Washington, DC: ZERO TO THREE.

Bertacchi, J. (1996). Relationship-based organizations. Zero to Three, 17(2), 1, 2–7.

Balamuth, R. (2000). Re-membering the body: A psychoanalytic study of presence and absence of the lived body. In L. Aron & F. S. Anderson (Eds.), Relational perspectives on the body (pp. 263–285). New York: Routledge.

Boris, N. W., & Grabert, J. C. (2009). How do I introduce reflective supervision to my program? In S. Scott Heller & L. Gilkerson (Eds.), A practical guide to reflective supervision (pp. 41–61). Washington, DC: ZERO TO THREE.

Copa, A., Lucinski, L., Olsen, E., & Wollenberg, K. (1999). Promoting professional and organizational development: A reflective practice model. Zero to Three, 20(1), 3–9.

Costa, G. (2003). Better treatment for Candace: How trained psychotherapists would have approached this case. In J. Mercer, L. Sarner, & L. Rosa (Eds.), Attachment therapy on trial: The torture and death of Candace Newmaker (pp. 135–159). Westport, CT: Praeger.

Costa, G. (2004). *The experience from within: Helping the child protective service caseworker. Best practice/next practice.* Washington, DC: National Child Welfare Resource Center for Family-Centered Practice.

Costa, G. (2006). Mental health principles, practices, strategies and dynamics pertinent to early intervention practitioners. In G. M. Foley & J. D. Hochman (Eds.), *Mental health in early intervention: Achieving unity in principles and practice* (pp. 113–138). Baltimore: Brookes.

Foley, G. M., & Hochman, J. D. (Eds.). (2006). *Mental health in early intervention: Achieving unity in principles and practice.* Baltimore: Brookes.

Fraiberg, S., Adelson, E., & Shapiro, V. (1980). Ghosts in the nursery: A psychoanalytic approach to the problems of impaired infant–mother relationships. In S. Fraiberg (Ed.), *Clinical studies in infant mental health: The first year of life* (pp. 164–196). New York: Basic Books.

Heffron, M. C., Grunstein, S., & Tilmon, S. (2007). Exploring diversity in supervision and practice. *Zero to Three, 28*(2), 34–38.

Jones Harden, B. (2009). Beyond reflective supervision: How can my organization support staff well-being? In S. Scott Heller & L. Gilkerson (Eds.), *A practical guide to reflective supervision* (pp. 135–148). Washington, DC: ZERO TO THREE.

Keyes, A. W., Cavanaugh, A. E., & Scott Heller, S. (2009). How do I, as a reflective supervisor, repair ruptures in the supervisory relationship? In S. Scott Heller & L. Gilkerson (Eds.), *A practical guide to reflective supervision* (pp. 99–119). Washington, DC: ZERO TO THREE.

Mehrabian, A. (1972). *Nonverbal communication.* Chicago: Aldine-Atherton.

Mehrabian, A. (1981). *Silent messages: Implicit communication of emotions and attitudes.* Belmont, CA: Wadsworth. (Currently distributed by Albert Mehrabian: am@kaaj.com)

Scott Heller, S. (2009). How do I develop an implementation plan to begin reflective supervision in my program? In S. Scott Heller & L. Gilkerson (Eds.), *A practical guide to reflective supervision* (pp. 25–39). Washington, DC: ZERO TO THREE.

Stern, D. (1995). *The motherhood constellation.* New York: Basic Books.

Thackeray, W. M. (1906). *Vanity fair: A novel without a hero.* New York: Thomas Nelson and Sons.

Trout, M.D. (1988). Infant mental health: Monitoring our movement into the twenty-first century. *Infant Mental Health Journal, 93*(3), 191–200.

Trout, M. D. (1989). *Working papers on process in infant mental health assessment and intervention.* Champaign, IL: The Infant–Parent Institute.

Trout, M.D. (1992). Infant mental health: A psychotherapeutic model of intervention. Tape six of *The awakening and growth of the human: Studies in Infant Mental Health:* A six-part videotape series. Champaign, IL: The Infant-Parent Institute.

Trout, M. D., & Foley, G. (1989). Working with families of handicapped infants and toddlers. *Topics in Language Disorders, 10*(1), 57–67.

Wason, P. C. (1968). Reasoning about a rule. *Quarterly Journal of Experimental Psychology, 20,* 273–281.

Weatherston, D. J., & Barron, C. (2009). What does a reflective supervisory relationship look like? In S. Scott Heller & L. Gilkerson (Eds.), *A practical guide to reflective supervision* (pp. 63–82). Washington, DC: ZERO TO THREE.

Reflective Tool 9

Wondering: Did the Activity Help Promote Reflection?

Reflective Tool 9 provides a framework to conduct a brief postactivity inquiry about the "lessons learned." The Participants column lists questions for the group participating in the activity. Immediately following each activity, the leader can either distribute a Feedback sheet or, with the group as a whole, ask participants to provide feedback using the following probe questions (or others that the leader develops as ways to wonder about the impact of the activity). If these questions are discussed with the entire group, the leader needs to model the characteristics that promote safety and discussion reviewed early in the chapter. The Leaders column lists questions for the people who led the activity. The activity can be done as a group or individually, as described earlier.

Remember these key points as you gather feedback:

- Be an "active listener," by looking at the speaker, showing in your face and body that you are attentive, and making supportive comments or asking probe questions as needed.

- Restate what the speaker has said if you feel this would be helpful.

- Invite all to share but do not require anyone to speak.

- Be sure to allow all views to be expressed.

- Protect all speakers from feeling personally criticized, by reminding all participants to be respectful of differing views.

- Thank all for participating in the activity and for providing feedback.

		PARTICIPANTS	LEADERS
QUESTIONS	Safety of Environment	• Did you enjoy this activity? Why or why not? • Did you feel "safe"? In other words, you did not feel that your confidentiality was violated, or that you were made to feel anxious or pressured. Why or why not?	• Did you enjoy the activity? Why or why not? • Do you feel that the participants enjoyed the activity? Why or why not? • If you answered no to either of the above questions, what can you do in future trainings to address this?
ACTIVITY FEEDBACK	Experience of Professional Growth	• Did you have any personal insight or an *aha!* moment during or after the activity? Please share. • Do you feel that this activity increased your awareness of ideas and feelings that influence how you are and what you do? Please explain.	• Did you experience any personal insights or increased awareness? • How will this influence your role in leading this or other reflective activities? • How will this influence you in your day-to-day work?
POST REFLECTIVE	Future Behavior	• How do you think this activity might change the way you work with a child and his or her family?	• How do you think this activity will change the way participants will work with a child and his or her family?
	Future Reflective Activities	• Do you have any suggestions about how the activity might be changed or done differently? If yes, please describe.	• Do you have any suggestions about how the activity might be changed or done differently? If yes, please describe.

WHAT STAFF DEVELOPMENT ACTIVITIES CAN BE USED
TO BUILD REFLECTIVE CAPACITY?

161

REFLECTIVE ACTIVITY 1: THE EARLIEST MEMORY INTERVIEW

This is a wonderful group activity that can serve as an icebreaker. It also illustrates the powerful impact of a practitioner's own personal life narrative on her work and relationships with the children and families she serves.

Purpose

This exercise provides an illustration of how present and current experiences can sometimes trigger past experiences and feelings. It is critical that you convey a sense of safety here because often participants will share losses that are painful.

Setup for Group

- Pair off in twos, preferably with someone you do not know well.

- Interview each other and ask two questions:

    1. "Tell me something about yourself. It could be about work or personal, but don't share anything you do not want to share."

    2. "Tell me your earliest memory of an attachment or a loss. It could be a person, place, thing, idea, even feeling."

- Return to the larger group and tell the group about the person *you interviewed* (not yourself)!

Procedures and Prompt Questions

Following the setup directions, have the group pair off and give them about 10 minutes to complete the two-question interview. *Stress that they should reflect on their earliest memory*; not a memory from their teens or later childhood, although these are important, but from as early in life as they can recall.

- When the group reconvenes, ask for volunteers to share the answers of the person they interviewed (for many, it is easier to talk about someone else other than oneself). If the group is too large, explain that you may be able to ask for six or eight responses, and that those not selected should introduce themselves at the end of the exercise.

- Here are some strategies that will help you process or "unpack" the answers of your participants:

    – Allow the participant to talk about the person he interviewed, but you then might go back and forth in asking follow-up gentle-probe questions.

    – Ask each respondent about the sensory aspects of his shared memory. You may be surprised at how a respondent will remember the color or smell of a place (e.g., a visit to a hospital) or may remember the weather on the day of a particular memory.

    – Try to make connections between something the respondent shared and current experiences. Examples like entering a home on a home visit, and suddenly becoming aware that you feel very positively about the home, without realizing that the home is decorated in the same patterns and colors as that of your favorite grandmother whose home you loved to visit as a child.

    – In our experience, one man recalled a very rich memory of his red and yellow crib blanket. He recalled carrying this blanket everywhere, and he could describe the color, smell, and texture. As he did this, he suddenly pointed to his shirt, which was red and yellow, and remarked, "Now I know why I like these colors so much!" We remarked that he "found a way to bring his blankie through life with him!" But we all bring our blankies through life with us, whether they are good blankies or bad ones!

– Emphasize that there are no correct answers here, but that we must remember that we are always engaged in a kind of time travel in which the events and experiences of the present can commingle and get confused with the elements and feelings of the past! (Just like transference issues covered in this and previous chapters.)

– Remind participants that when they encounter certain children or families and certain experiences (e.g., a child who is having a very hard separation from a parent), that these events will always stir up their own personal stories and narratives—and that is why they must always build in reflective time in helping them do the best with regard to their work with families.

Note. This activity is based on one we participated in with Michael Trout, director of the Infant–Parent Institute in Champaign, Illinois. We wish to acknowledge his contribution to our learning.

WHAT STAFF DEVELOPMENT ACTIVITIES CAN BE USED
TO BUILD REFLECTIVE CAPACITY?

163

REFLECTIVE ACTIVITY 2: THE ART OF PRACTICING CONVERSATIONS

Practicing Conversations is an activity that helps staff members (as a collective group) consider ways to begin and accomplish conversations with families that are difficult. In our work as infant mental health consultants, we have used this tool as a way of supporting courageous conversations between a staff member and family. It is important to emphasize that the support of consulting specialists is very important, but the art of practicing conversations can also apply to concerns of a much less serious nature, but ones about which staff might feel awkward (e.g., a preschooler's interest in his or others' private areas).

Practicing Conversations is not quite the same as role-playing, in which one staff might play the role of the parent, another the child, and a third the staff person. It is also not creating a script to use because each person will likely use different language.

Purpose

This exercise provides staff members with ways to acknowledge their anxiety or difficulty around certain topics, indicates opportunities for consultation and support, and ensures that such responsibilities should never be carried alone. It also offers opportunities for staff to discern and receive guidance about appropriate and inappropriate roles they may find themselves serving.

During team meetings, when staff gather together to discuss the children and families they have come to know, team members occasionally identify a concern or difficulty that they wish to address with a particular family. Although certain staff members may have formal roles or positions that involve certain conversations (e.g., the educational coordinator may want to speak with parents about recommending a learning evaluation), we have found that the staff who engage children and families on a daily basis are often the ones with whom families are most comfortable.

For example, in an early intervention program for infants and toddlers with developmental disabilities, the home visitor might express concern about an issue (e.g., use of physical discipline, parental depression), but view him- or herself as inadequately trained to speak with the family about such sensitive issues, deferring for example to the mental health consultant or social worker. This is understandable. One way of addressing this need is the use of mental health and other specialized consultants in infant and early childhood programs. However, this exercise can be a means to support the home visitor (as a nonmental health professional) in having a conversation with the family about parental depression or use of physical discipline. Costa (2006) and Foley and Hochman (2006) presented strategies to support the notion that mental health promotion, prevention, and intervention are the province of all disciplines.

Setup for Group

- During group discussion, when a staff member identifies something she wishes to address with a parent, but feels unprepared or awkward, the leader can suggest that this may be a good time to practice a conversation. Usually, the staff member initiating the discussion is the beneficiary of the activity, in that she will likely feel better prepared on how to proceed.

- Ask the initiating staff person to clearly state the concern she has. For example, suppose a preschool classroom teacher states, "Jimmy is avoiding all contact with the other children, and sometimes he will run around and flap his hands. His language is so delayed, and I just think his parents may have to have him evaluated for autism." (Only certain professional staff are qualified to make diagnoses, but many times staff struggle to know how to talk with a family about the need for an evaluation.)

- The leader would first want to ensure that staff members are aware of professional role limitations, and that certain consultants may be available for work with the staff and as a resource for the family.

Procedures and Prompt Questions

Following the setup:

- The leader might then ask, "How might you begin a conversation with a parent in this situation?"

    - This is an attempt to elicit a first line of dialogue, a way of opening the discussion. We have found this to be an extremely helpful strategy as we have found staff generally able to speak sensitively with families they know, once they get the conversation rolling.

    - This avoids the common pressure in role-playing in which one person has the sole responsibility to create an imaginary starting dialogue, and replaces it with a collective effort. This is based on the concept of synergy, in which the whole is greater than the sum of its parts. Staff as a group tend to be better problem solvers than individuals.

- One staff member may offer an idea. For example: "How about if you begin by saying, 'I've sometimes noticed that Jimmy likes to play alone and is very quiet. Have you noticed the same at home?'"

    - This might lead a second staff person to add, "Yeah. Then maybe you can say something like, 'Do you have any ideas about what that might mean?'"

    - Then a third staff person might say, "You know, it's real important that you talk to the mom when she has time, so maybe you should call the mom and plan a time when she can meet with you."

    - Another might suggest saying something like, "You know, it may be a perfect time to let the mom know that we have staff who are specialists in child development, and that it may be helpful for 'us' to plan a discussion with that person."

- The group, with the initiating staff member as the leader, could then wordsmith the remarks and refine the ideas, perhaps offering language that fits the person involved.

WHAT STAFF DEVELOPMENT ACTIVITIES CAN BE USED
TO BUILD REFLECTIVE CAPACITY?

165

REFLECTIVE ACTIVITY 3: MOVIES WITHOUT SOUND: HOW DO YOU REALLY KNOW THE MESSAGE THAT SOMEONE IS COMMUNICATING?

This activity assists the helper in paying attention to the nonverbal ways in which interpersonal communication occurs. In an often cited analysis of the relative importance of verbal and nonverbal factors when a person is communicating feelings and attitudes, Albert Mehrabian (1972, 1981) reported that 55% of the communicative intent is conveyed by facial expressions, 38% by vocal tone, and only 7% by the words themselves. Thus, when a message is inconsistent, the nonverbal cues win out! You can illustrate this by intentionally mismatching what is said with the facial expression/tone being used. For example, the leader might ask participants (and act out) if they have ever asked a person, "Are you upset with me?" and the other person's words are, "No, I am not upset with you," but the facial expression and tone clearly convey otherwise.

This activity can be done by an individual on his own time, or as a group activity.

Purpose

The purpose of this activity is to help participants pay attention to themselves, as well as the others (e.g., children, family, or colleagues) to whom they are listening. It helps participants to look outside themselves and imagine how others might perceive them when they communicate. This activity can also be a tool in discerning times when what they feel (even when they may be unaware of the feeling) may come through even when they try hard to say or do the right thing. This is a point we also address in Reflective Activity 4: Bodies and Feelings: Paying Attention to Our State.

Setup for Group

- Introduce this activity as one filled with fun that has the power to teach participants about how communication works.

- The task is rather simple: Ask participants if they have ever watched a movie on a plane, on TV, in the theater, and so forth without the sound. Ask them to imagine watching the movie, so they can observe the actors' movements, expressions, pace, interactions, reactions, and so on, but not hear the words spoken or any narration/music.

- Have a brief (no more than 10-minute) clip of a popular movie available so that the group can watch the movie without sound; discuss the prompt questions; then replay the movie with sound to determine the extent to which group members were able to correctly interpret the communicative intent.

Procedures and Prompt Questions

Following the setup, the leader might ask a participant to give an example from a movie she has recently watched. Then show the prepared 10-minute segment, without sound.

- Then ask:

  – "Can you figure out what is going on?"

  – "Can you get a good sense of the plot?"

– "Can you tell who the good guys or bad guys are?"

– "Can you usually tell who is telling the truth and who is not?"

– "Can you describe the overall nature of the scene?"

- Then, show the movie with sound, and discuss and compare the impressions and interpretations between the viewings of the movie with and without sound.

- Caution the participants that although this exercise provides a reminder of the ways in which people convey the meaning of their feelings and attitudes in alternate ways, the participants can sometimes be wrong about their impressions and interpretations. For example:

  – In our clinical trainings we use a segment of an infant mental health training videotape developed by Michael Trout (1992) of a young African American mother named Vanessa who is holding her infant son. Claudio was diagnosed as a "non-organic failure to thrive due to maternal neglect" child. The infant, at 4 months of age, weighs less than he did at 1 month, and he was removed and placed in foster care while his mother was remanded by the Child Protective Service agency to parenting classes. During the episode, the mother is seen as depressed, holding her listless baby and appearing unengaged, even feeding him at one point with a bottle in which the disk was seated in the nipple so that not one drop of formula could be obtained from the infant's frail suck.

  – We play the short segment (about 6 minutes), revealing only the information provided earlier and asking the participants to develop some hypotheses as to what is going on. Invariably, participants are drawn to interpret the problem as related to the mother's youth, and are likely influenced by her minority membership and clear poverty. Some viewers, more familiar with developmental disorders, often note that the infant's listless body suggests some developmental or neurological disorder (e.g., "low tone, no protest to the absence of formula from the bottle), but often remain influenced by what they see as a depressed, poorly educated, inadequate mother and by the diagnosis provided.

  – After playing the clip without sound, and the ensuing discussion, we then play the videotape with sound. It is revealed that the infant had Pompe disease, an almost-always fatal glycogen-storage illness, characterized by failure to gain weight, muscle atrophy, and death. The mother is now understood to be depressed as a reaction to the child's failure to respond or give back to her care, not as a cause of his problems. The child died soon thereafter.

- This powerful lesson cautions all to be careful in making conclusions and prematurely accepting them.

WHAT STAFF DEVELOPMENT ACTIVITIES CAN BE USED
TO BUILD REFLECTIVE CAPACITY?

167

REFLECTIVE ACTIVITY 4: BODIES AND FEELINGS: PAYING ATTENTION TO OUR STATE

This activity is designed to help participants become aware of how their bodies encode their feelings. This notion can be understood by simply noting that when people are happy their bodies—their somatic state—are quite different than when they are anxious, sad, or angry. Daniel Stern (1995), a noted infant researcher, offered the idea that as infants form relationships with people in their lives, they form a schema-of-being with each person. These schemas are actually fused experiences that involve body states (somatic), emotions (affects), ideas (cognitive), and interpersonal components. In our training workshops in infant mental health, we often ask participants to note that "for every emotion you have there is an associated somatic state, and for every somatic state, there is an associated emotion!"

This need for participants to become aware of their own body states helps them be more reflective about what is going on inside of them. This activity offers a simple, but powerful, way to help participants reflect on their relationships with, and their responses to, infants, children, families, and all others.

Purpose

This activity illustrates how the ways participants might feel about a child or family, often without their awareness, can influence the host of ways in which they engage, interact, interpret, and even terminate their work with families.

Setup for Group

- Tell participants that they will be thinking about some of the infants, children, and families in their care.

- Reassure all that this activity is a safe way to acknowledge that it is normal to have different feelings about the families with whom they have working relationships. Some staff or home visitors may have families in which the relationship is experienced as helpful, productive, and mutually satisfying, and which the worker approaches with ease and positive anticipation. Other children and families may stir up more conflicted or difficult feelings in which the worker can acknowledge ambivalence or even a wish, at times, not to see the client.

  – In our trainings, we have often used humor to help staff understand the normalcy of having difficult feelings about their relationship with certain children and families. A home visitor, for example, may approach the front door of the home of a family about whom he feels negatively. As the worker approaches, very loud music is blaring from inside, and the worker gives a soft and hesitant knock on the door, to which no one responds. The worker may repeat the tap with the same outcome. Objectively, all might regard the knock as much too little to be heard, but subjectively, the worker feels satisfied at the effort and returns to his car with relief, happily recording in his notes that no one answered the door! Of course, even if this has never happened, it allows for the disclosure that they sometimes wish this could be the case. They can acknowledge that they feel relieved when they avert contact with certain clients. In the interest of fairness, the leader must also make the point that there may be times that families are relieved that the worker did not show!

  – Participants must also be aware of those feelings about relationships in which the worker falls in love with the infant, child, or family, as these feelings too will show up in their body states as well as their ways of interacting with families. Costa (2006) quoted his supervisor, David Peters, as once remarking,

"When we fall in love with our patients, there are two patients and no doctor." Use this idea as a way of reminding staff that reflective work is required not only for those cases in which they have some difficulty, but also in those cases in which they find ourselves caring deeply. Both types of cases require principled, thoughtful support so the participants ensure that families are being helped in the best possible ways.

- Let participants know that you will be guiding them through an "imaging" exercise about their feelings and body states.

Procedures and Prompt Questions

- Have everyone sit quietly in a comfortable chair (not too comfortable that they might fall asleep), and ask them to close their eyes as the leader guides them in an imaging exercise, using the script below as a guide:

    Think about a client with whom you have a very difficult relationship, one in which you might feel anxious, frustrated, or unsuccessful. You may even feel angry or fearful about the client. Then imagine that you are driving to her home for a home visit, you park the car, and you leave the car and walk up the stairs to her home or apartment and you are about to knock on the door. (Alternately, for those who of you who see clients at a center, imagine that the appointment time is approaching and the receptionist calls to say that the client has arrived).

- The leader should then read aloud the following guided imagery about the body, using very slow and deliberate pacing, so that the listener can focus on each body group and reflect about her state of tension or relaxation.

    Pay attention to your scalp, your forehead, your eyelids, your cheeks, your chin, your mouth and tongue, your neck. [pause]. Okay, now focus on your posture, your shoulders, your chest, your upper arms, your wrists, your hands, your fingers, your stomach, your waist and sides, your breathing. And now pay attention to your thighs, your legs, your calves, your ankles, your feet, your toes.

- Be aware that this exercise, and the act of focusing on one's inner experiences, may stir up memories and feelings from a participant's own history that may make him feel anxious or stressful. Help participants anticipate this and encourage those who find themselves getting anxious or upset to open their eyes and try the activity with their eyes open or stop altogether.

- Wait about 30 seconds after the last statement and ask the group to prepare themselves to share their observations/awareness of what their body states were telling them about their emotions and experiences.

- Repeat this exercise with a child or family member with whom the worker has a positive working relationship.

- The goal of the exercise is not to change the feelings, ideas, or even the relationships participants form with families. This would be an unrealistic goal of this activity. It is aimed at allowing participants to observe and learn about their reactions and become more reflective—more mindful—so that they can use this knowledge to develop a deeper understanding of themselves and those they seek to help. It is good to emphasize that the overall attitude is of acceptance of what comes up so participants do not feel that there is a success/fail factor in this exercise.

It is critical to note and discuss with participants that these states can influence:

- How they greet a person.

- The pacing of their conversation, whether they pause to listen, and how they show with their bodies and faces that they care and are interested.

WHAT STAFF DEVELOPMENT ACTIVITIES CAN BE USED
TO BUILD REFLECTIVE CAPACITY?

169

- The amount of eye contact they use.

- Their tone of voice.

- The posture, gestures, and movements they make associated with what they are saying.

- The overall experience a person has in being with them and how they experience the other.

These nonverbal behaviors can influence how others feel about this client. For example, if a participant rolls his eyes every time a family's name comes up, others will begin to share the bad reputation he is suggesting. It is important for participants to pay attention to what these feelings mean about their work and to share these experiences in RS so that their work with families is not compromised and they can develop strategies to address the underlying meanings for the feelings. These body states can even influence how they say good-bye or terminate their work with a family.

Note. This activity is based on one led by Ron Balamuth, PhD, during a faculty retreat for the Interdisciplinary Council on Developmental and Learning Disorders in 2004. The exercise emerged from his work with Frances S. Anderson (see Balamuth, 2000).

REFLECTIVE ACTIVITY 5: A BASKET FULL OF QUESTIONS

This is a nice introduction to reflection activity for providers who are not familiar with the concept or who may not have experience with case-based discussions. We have found it a good way to get people started sharing some of their thoughts, struggles, and successes in their work with infants, young children, and families.

Purpose

This is an easy activity to get people talking and reflecting on their work, and was a popular one with child care providers. After doing it for several sessions, group members may want to provide their own questions or statements that can be added to the basket. It provides the facilitator with a gentle format for raising some of the emotionally challenging topics that we have found to be commonly experienced but not often examined in work with infants, young children, and their families.

Setup for Group

- Prepare some prompt questions or open-ended statements on index cards or strips of paper and place them in a basket or other container.

- Make sure the questions target both positive and challenging topics. Try to have some that are more fun and lighthearted when the activity is first being introduced. The level and intensity of the questions and topics can be adjusted as the group becomes more comfortable with the process.

Procedures and Prompt Questions

- Have each person select a question from the basket and read it without sharing the question with the group. Allow participants a minute or two to think about their response. If they decide to answer it, ask them to read it aloud to the group and then share their response. Once a person has shared, ask if others would like to respond and allow time for sharing.

- We offer participants the choice to opt out or take a pass on any question they do not want to answer. They are free to choose another question from the basket in that situation.

- Take turns until everyone has had a chance to select and answer a question from the basket. Always remind the participants of the following: (a) they do not have to share anything if they do not want to, (b) the discussions that take place in the groups are confidential, and (c) the group should be a safe place to share our hits and misses in our work.

- The role of the facilitator should be to respond to and help make connections between the experiences of the caregivers and the work that they do with infants, young children, and families.

  – How do their past experiences affect the people they are and who they have become?

  – Why are some children and parents easier to connect with?

  – What is being stirred up in a participant when he reacts to something that happened in his work?

- The facilitator should ensure that all who want to participate have a chance to share their thoughts during the activity and help to maintain a climate of respect for all during the discussions.

WHAT STAFF DEVELOPMENT ACTIVITIES CAN BE USED
TO BUILD REFLECTIVE CAPACITY?

171

- Here is a list of sample questions/open-ended statements that we have used with a group of child care providers in a Head Start program. Feel free to develop your own list or solicit ideas from the group:

  – Talk about a child who reminds you of someone else in your life.

  – I find it easy/hard to work with children who are _____ (fill in the blank).

  – Talk about a parent who you find difficult to get along with.

  – Describe a good day at work. Describe a bad day at work.

  – Talk about yourself as a child—what were you like?

  – What helps you when you feel stressed?

  – Do you remember an adult who was kind to you as a young child? What about one who was mean to you?

REFLECTIVE ACTIVITY 6: FEEL FREE TO WONDER: THE 2-4-6 TASK AND OTHER FUN ACTIVITIES

This activity provides participants with strategies to think "outside of the box" and to see how group processing often enhances problem solving. Three activities are described.

- Activity 1: What's Going on Inside? Task

  This involves helping staff wonder about their "subjective" experiences about an infant, child, or family with whom they have a relationship.

- Activity 2: The 2-4-6 Task

  This involves a classic logic problem. This is a fun, sometimes frustrating, apparently difficult but amazingly simple illustration of how participants can get trapped and fixed in the way they think and problem solve.

- Activity 3: The Nine-Dot Problem

  This is a simple visuospatial problem that can literally be solved only by going outside of the box.

Purpose

All three activities were designed to help staff pay greater attention to the ways in which they can be influenced by feelings and beliefs without their awareness. These are easy-to-administer tasks and generate fun and lively discussion. The three activities represent how feelings, ideas, and perceptions can influence a person's approach to problem solving, often leading to errors of which she can become more aware. The activities can also illustrate how a group tends to do better than someone might individually.

Setup for Group

Prepare the group for each activity by following the guidelines below. Always begin with a gentle prompt to "leave other responsibilities and concerns behind" and ask all to take a moment to "attend to the present" activity.

Activity 1: "What's Going on Inside?"

The leader will recall that we have suggested two key questions as helpful prompts in all case discussions about families that both help participants apply lessons from the field to enhance their understanding and empathy for families and help them become aware of how their subjective experiences about, with, and through a child and family influence their work with them.

- The first question ("Who is this baby to this family?") helps participants wonder about the meaning of the particular baby in the context of the family history and, when there are impaired emotional relationships, wonder about the "ghosts in the nursery" (Fraiberg et al., 1980).

- The second question ("What's going on inside of us?") can provide very useful ways for participants to better understand and empathically respond to families by paying attention to their own feelings and ideas that occur in their work with a particular family. We focus on the second question here.

WHAT STAFF DEVELOPMENT ACTIVITIES CAN BE USED
TO BUILD REFLECTIVE CAPACITY?

173

During a team discussion about an infant, child, or family, a staff member may express some difficulty in working with a family. As an illustration: Suppose a home visitor describes a client in very negative ways, even ways we might regard as judgmental. It is important to note that staff discussions must always be guided by respectfulness for families and should never devolve into gripe sessions or parent bashing as these erode their fundamental obligations for empathy and protection from being regarded with toxic reputations. Nonetheless, staff must feel able—in the safety and confidentiality of supervision and team process sessions—to express genuine feelings and beliefs that, if unexpressed and unchecked, will adversely affect the nature of helping relationships.

- Leaders must maintain their own neutrality at these times in order to help staff members unpack these very powerful moments. The leader might ask the staff member to describe how she feels when she is with the parent or when she reflects on the nature of the work.

  – The staff member might:

    - Express feelings of frustration with a mother who never seems to follow up with suggestions.

    - Express feeling inadequate and the belief that she cannot do enough to help this mother. This, in turn, makes the visitor feel that the mother does not value her efforts, thus making the visitor want to avoid the sessions.

    - Might even admit feeling overwhelmed and depressed when she is on a home visit.

- These are very critical opportunities for leaders to help staff wonder about the nature of these feelings and even wonder about the mother/family and what their experiences have been. For example, the leader might reply with the following observation:

  It sounds like you are upset with yourself for having these feelings and even upset with the mother who makes you feel this way. But I wonder if we can think about where these feelings might be coming from. It is true that the feelings you described—frustration, inadequacy, poor self-value, feelings of being overwhelmed, and even depressed—are your feelings, but maybe one way to think about this experience is that you are feeling what the mother is feeling. Perhaps she somehow induced in you what it feels like to be her. So maybe she is frustrated and feels inadequate and not listened to, or maybe she feels of poor value, overwhelmed, and, at times, depressed. Perhaps what you are feeling is your best way to understand how she feels?

  We sometimes can feel how other people feel, as if we vibrate with (like a tuning fork, we become attuned to) the feelings of others. In psychology, we sometimes use the term *projective identification* to refer to the process whereby others can project onto us how they feel. If this may be happening here, perhaps your feelings are your best way to have empathy for this mother, so that rather than you owning the feeling as your own, you can understand that your feelings are helpful tools in understanding the mother. In this reformulation, perhaps your next visits and conversations can be planned in response to this new idea and you can begin to find ways to talk and feel with the mother about how she is doing and not plan your sessions around activities that are frustrating.

- It is critical to note the obvious caution here that not all subjective experiences staff have originate from families, but in fact are also often reflective of our own experiences and life narratives. It is for this reason we noted earlier that work with every family has the power and potential of stirring up experiences from our own lives. Accordingly, we must find ways to become aware of our own contribution to the relationship and to find ways to address and use these. Reflective practices and supervision are some ways to help us, but other forms of self-reflection are also helpful. Costa (2006) again quoted an early supervisor, David Peters, as stating, "We need supervision to save our patients from ourselves."

- The previous illustration is one of many possible ways in which we can help staff wonder about the nature and origin of their subjective experiences with families.

  – Other examples of the Feel Free to Wonder approach can involve helping staff pay attention to their gut feelings at times. In our clinical and consulting experiences, we have often worked with staff members who have expressed feelings that a family member of their client might be abusing drugs, a mother might be the victim of domestic violence, or a parent might be depressed. Staff members who experience these feelings are often reluctant to speak about these in supervision for fear that they lack evidence for these impressions. This is where our **Reflective Mantra** comes in:

  Feel free to wonder and generate hypotheses, but don't fall in love with your hypotheses. They may be wrong!

  – Nonetheless, once expressed, the supervisor and team can strategize on how they might discern whether the expressed concerns exist and how best to help families.

  – The major point here is to help staff use their feelings in ways to promote empathy and principled, thoughtful interventions.

Activity 2: The 2-4-6 Task

This task is remarkably simple, and we describe how it can be done with individuals and with groups. It was developed by Peter C. Wason (1968) and illustrates very common reasoning strategies and fallacies.

- The leader can use either a handout or a flipchart with the following information as shown in the table below.

NUMBERS	REASON FOR CHOICE	DOES IT FIT THE RULE?	
		Yes	No
2, 4, 6		X	

- Explain to the individual(s) that the handout/flipchart has a three-number series that was generated by a rule, and that their task is to

  – Generate more three-number series (exemplars) that fit the rule, in order to discover what the rule is. The rule is known by the leader (to be revealed shortly).

  – The participant is told to let the leader know when he is certain about the rule.

- If administered to a group, the leader can prepare a handout (with many rows), explain the task, then go around the group, one at a time, to inform each participant if his three-number series fits or does not fit the rule. In this way, each person works individually and does not share his number series, and the leader quietly informs each person about the status of his exemplar.

- The task is remarkably seductive in that almost every person will begin to generate numbers that are even, and separated by 2. For example, here is one person's protocol in the table below:

WHAT STAFF DEVELOPMENT ACTIVITIES CAN BE USED
TO BUILD REFLECTIVE CAPACITY?

175

NUMBERS	REASON FOR CHOICE	DOES IT FIT THE RULE?	
		Yes	No
2, 4, 6		X	
8, 10, 12	Even numbers, separated by 2	X	
14, 16, 18	Even numbers, separated by 2	X	
20, 22, 24	Even numbers, separated by 2	X	

In the above illustration, the participant has generated three sets of numbers that fit the rule. At this point, the participant might confidently inform the leader that she knows the rule: "Even numbers separated by 2." The leader will inform the participant she is not correct.

- Puzzled, many participants will actually persist in generating the same kinds of number series and persist in restating the rule! Some may offer some alterations, such as generating three even numbers separated by 4 (e.g., 12, 16, 20) or 10 (e.g., 20, 30, 40). Again, although all of these exemplars fit the rule, the rule does not involve evenness or separation by a fixed amount.

- Here's why: The actual rule is the following: *Any three ascending numbers.* However, virtually all participants infer that the evenness and fixed distance between the numbers of the exemplar provided are essential to the rule. Only when a participant generates an exemplar that violates his incorrect rule (e.g., 1, 18, 1001) or when he generates a counterexample (e.g., 50, 32, 17; i.e., a descending series) does the true rule get discovered.

- This task is remarkably impervious to solution and in that regard is quite seductive because almost everyone sees it as simple, but almost no one immediately gets it.

- The lesson is simple: Do not be trapped by ideas you bring to the problem. Think outside of the box!

- An alternate way of conducting this activity involves a group administration, in which each member offers a possible three-number series and "rules" to consider.

  – If the group size permits, have one set of participants complete the task individually, as shown earlier, and another set of individuals (same size group) complete the task as a group.

  – Invariably the group determines the solution more quickly because all participants benefit from each person's contribution. This is a wonderful way to illustrate the benefits of group processing and synergy—that the whole is greater than the sum of its parts.

Activity 3: The Nine-Dot Problem

This is a simple, but powerful, illustration of how people often fail to think outside of the box. The task might be regarded as a kind of optical illusion because it reveals how perceptual—and conceptual—approaches to certain problems work.

- The leader draws nine dots (three dots in three rows, evenly distributed) on a flipchart, like the illustration below:

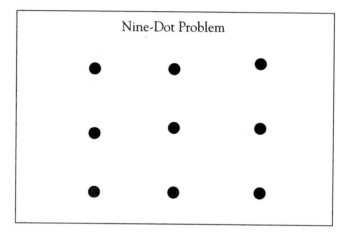

- Provide each participant with a blank sheet of paper, and ask the participants to reproduce the configuration on the paper. The leader says, "In one movement, without lifting your pencil off the paper, draw four straight lines (and only four) that intersect all nine dots."

- Most participants remain in the invisible boundaries of the box created by the nine dots, but the solution requires you to think, and move, outside of the box. Provided below is a correct solution (this is the most common one offered, although all correct answers require you to move outside of the box):

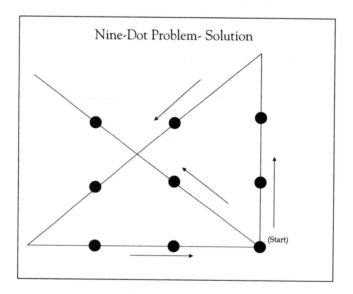

- As with the 2-4-6 Task, the solution appears quite easy once participants become aware of the ways in which they limit their search for solutions.

WHAT STAFF DEVELOPMENT ACTIVITIES CAN BE USED
TO BUILD REFLECTIVE CAPACITY?

177

Procedures and Prompt Questions

- The procedures for administration were described previously for each activity.

- At the end of one (or more) of the activities, ask the group:

  – What lessons can you describe from these activities?

  – How can you decrease the risk of errors in your problem solving?

  – What helped you reach the solutions?

  – How might these activities apply to your work with families?

REFLECTIVE ACTIVITY 7: BABYWATCHING: BABIES, OTHERS, AND US!

This activity helps people focus on their own subjective experiences as observers and begin to identify in objective terms what they are seeing, hearing, and feeling as they focus on infants and adult caregivers. The key phrase that we offer as part of this activity is for participants to "wonder about" what they are seeing. When they wonder they are thinking carefully and thoughtfully about the relationships between infants and their caregivers. Their task is to wonder and ask questions about what they are seeing in order to help them learn more about what the experience might be like for the infant and the caregiver.

Purpose

This exercise is intended to help participants focus on the experience of being an observer and to remind them that they often "feel with" those they are observing. It is often difficult to observe without interpreting, and that is the skill that we are promoting here.

Setup for Group

- The task is to observe unobtrusively the interactions that occur between an infant and a caregiving adult for a brief period (less than 15 minutes).

- The observer is asked to write up a summary of the interactions in an objective manner and present to the rest of the group.

- The observer should then record her own subjective experience while making the observation.

Procedures and Prompt Questions

- Participants should not observe any infants or caregivers they know. They should strive to be anonymous. However, we have had students who felt "the babies were onto them" while they were observing from a distance.

- The observations can take place anywhere infants and caregivers can be found (e.g., the mall, a park, doctor's office, supermarket, riding a bus). In our work with graduate students, we have heard about interactions in a variety of settings ranging from a New York City subway to a mountaintop ski resort.

- The direction given to the observer is to watch and describe the interactions while attempting to avoid interpretation of the events. The emphasis is on what they are seeing and, at the same time, how what they are seeing makes them feel.

- Instruct the participants to observe and wonder about aspects of the infant–caregiver relationship:

    – Describe the content, theme, or purpose of the interaction.

    – Do not assume who the people are to each other. For example, how would you decide if the woman you see is the baby's mother or babysitter? If you decide to try and determine the relationships, give some justification for your decision. What makes you feel this is a mother and baby you are watching? What about what you are seeing helps you determine the roles?

    – What is the extent of infant-initiated/caregiver-initiated interactions?

    – How would you describe the responsiveness/availability of the caregiver to the infant? Is there a match or mismatch between the two?

WHAT STAFF DEVELOPMENT ACTIVITIES CAN BE USED TO BUILD REFLECTIVE CAPACITY?

179

- Do you see a range of emotion/affect displayed by the pair? What does it look like in each of them?

- What is the amount and quality of sensory cues that you observe (visual, vocal, touch, movement) between the pair?

- How would you describe the overall affective (emotional) quality of the relationship?

• Have the observer read the written description to the group and talk about what she saw and what she felt. Allow other group members to comment on the observations and to ask questions.

• Possible questions might include those that address what the observer thought the baby or caregiver was feeling.

- What do you think was going on for the baby?

- Why did you feel the caregiver was enjoying or not enjoying during the interaction?

- How could you tell the infant and caregiver were in sync?

• The box Babywatching Observation Sheet gives a good overview of the direct and objective style of the written record of an actual babywatching.

Babywatching Observation Sheet

Date: Saturday, October 26, 2002

Time: 4:30 p.m.

Location: 1 subway line, NYC

Length of observation: 10 minutes

Observations:

This observer gets on the train at the same time as a young couple with a baby. As they step onto the train, the man helps the woman lift the stroller onto the train. Once on the train, the baby remains in the stroller while the woman and man get settled; they both appear tired, especially the woman, who blows her bangs out of her eyes while she leans back in her seat. The baby is sitting straight up, even though his stroller seat is angled back, alertly looking around at all of the people in the crowded car. His eyes are wide open, and with this broader bird's-eye view, he now looks out at the people in front, to the side, and in back of him, stretching and turning his body to get a better view. While he moves about, the man maintains a gentle but firm hold on him, all the while watching the baby watch his environment, their faces within an inch of one another's. The baby points up to one of the lit signs, babbles at a moderate volume, and then turns to the other side and does the same, once again moving his body this way and that to see what is around him, at one point "scrunching" his body up and down as if he is doing a little dance. After the baby turns, the man whispers something closely in the baby's ear and then gives him a series of "butterfly" kisses on his cheek. The baby smiles but continues to examine what's around him. He then turns back the opposite way; the man once again whispers something and gives him another gentle kiss. The baby then makes eye contact with a man who is standing near him, who smiles at the baby. The baby maintains eye contact for a brief period of about 10 seconds, offers a small smile, and then turns away. Throughout this whole period, the man watches the baby's movements with a look of bemusement; the woman watches from a short distance of about 2 feet. The baby makes eye contact with her once as he surveys the room, and they smile at one another briefly until he breaks eye contact to continue looking around the car.

Subjective Experience of the Observer:

Throughout the babywatching episode, I did not experience any particular overwhelming affective response; however, while watching the baby I experienced a warm feeling of bemusement that I think matched the man's and was fascinated by this baby's gaze to see what he was looking at. I also found the man's combination of firm hold of the baby's body, intense interest, and tender gestures of affection very comforting. I recall thinking how "great" it was that the man did not feel the need to intrude upon the baby's exploration of his environment; he seemed content to simply witness it. Finally, I did also find myself looking at the woman to see what she was doing, as she seemed somehow removed from the man and the baby. As I noted above, she did watch them and make eye contact with the baby at one point, but for most parts of the episode, she remained seated quietly, looking pensively down at the floor.

Note. Thanks to Thea Bry, the late mentor, colleague, and friend to Gerard Costa, for her use of babywatching as an integral part of all formation in the field of infant mental health. Further thanks to Laurie Reider-Lewis for her babywatching completed during her doctoral psychology externship during the 2002–2003 academic year at the YCS Institute for Infant and Preschool Mental Health.

WHAT STAFF DEVELOPMENT ACTIVITIES CAN BE USED
TO BUILD REFLECTIVE CAPACITY?

181

REFLECTIVE ACTIVITY 8: BECOMING AN ATTUNED OBSERVER: ATTENDING TO CHANGE

As in Reflective Activity 5, this activity is another enjoyable way to introduce reflection to those new to the concept. Reflective practices involve self or "internal" observation. Reflective Activity 8 supports growth in this capacity by first engaging the participants in an observation of others in the "external" world. Although the activity involves no discussion of feelings or reactions to families, the leader can help participants understand how all who form relationships with infants, children, and families can see or fail to see aspects of the families and themselves. Participants can discern lessons about why they "saw" or "missed" the changes that occurred and become more attentive to careful observation.

Purpose

The purpose of this exercise is to remind participants of the importance of observation in their work with infants, young children, and families. Participants need to pay close attention to the nonverbal cues and emotional states of those with whom they work. Infants, toddlers, and their families may often show how they are feeling through their behaviors. Participants need to become thoughtful and careful observers as they do their work.

Setup for Group

- Ask people to find a partner for this activity. You might want to suggest they find someone in the group who they do not know very well or do not know at all.

- Tell group members that you are going to ask them to become careful and attuned observers.

- Talk about the fact that being a good observer takes practice and concentration. Sometimes we can see the same event but notice very different aspects or details. Give the example of a group of eyewitnesses to a car accident who give three very different and varied accounts of what happened and what they observed when giving a report to the police.

Procedures and Prompt Questions

- Once the group has paired up, ask the pairs to face each other. Tell them they are to look very carefully at each other without talking for the next 2 minutes. Each participant should focus on noticing details about the other person (e.g., clothing, hairstyle, jewelry).

- Time the 2 minutes out, telling the group when to begin and end.

- Once the 2 minutes haved passed, ask the group to talk about how it felt to be the observer or the person being observed.

  – How was the experience for each of them?

  – Were they comfortable or not comfortable?

  – How did not talking impact the activity?

- Next, tell the pairs to turn facing away from their partners.

Once everyone is facing away from the partners, ask each person to change three things about his or her appearance. Allow a minute or two for people to make the changes.

- Now ask the pairs to turn and face their partners. Ask the partners to see if they can observe and identify the three changes the other person made to his or her appearance. Have them discuss the changes with each other.

- Have some of the pairs share what they observed and describe the three changes that were made. Lead group members in a discussion of how quickly, or not, they were in noticing the changes. Ask them why they think they did or did not notice the changes quickly. See if group members can make any connections from this activity to their work.

- Have there been times when they did or did not notice something that was important?

- What are important changes to be aware of in the behavior of infants, young children, and their families?

ABOUT THE AUTHORS

Theresa Atchley, MEd, is an infant and early childhood mental health consultant. She has been part of the implementation team for several infant and early childhood mental health consultation pilot projects in Illinois including: the early intervention system, community mental health programs, teen parenting agencies, and pre-kindergarten programs. Her role as a consultant has been to support the infusion of relationship-based practices into agencies serving young children and their families.

Carla Barron, LMSW, IMH-E (IV), is an infant mental health mentor endorsed by the Michigan Association for Infant Mental Health. She is currently working as an infant mental health specialist for Macomb County Community Mental Health and is part-time faculty at Wayne State University School of Social Work.

Judith Bertacchi, MEd, LSW, is past director, Virginia Frank Child Development Center and past-Vice President of Direct Services for the Ounce of Prevention Fund. She is a well-known national consultant whose expertise is helping agencies integrate and sustain reflective supervision within their organizational culture. Judy was a founder and past-president of Illinois Association for Infant Mental Health.

Neil W. Boris, MD, professor, Department of Psychiatry and Neurology, Tulane University School of Medicine, is a clinician and researcher whose career focuses on the social and emotional development of children less than 5 years old. He's worked on projects ranging from defining attachment problems in infants and toddlers to testing interventions for HIV orphans in Africa. He's a board member of the World Association for Infant Mental Health.

Amy Cavanaugh, PhD, is a clinical psychologist in private practice and the infant mental health consultant to the Healthy Start Program of the Family Tree in Lafayette, LA. She provides assessment, intervention, and education services for children from birth to 5 years old in the community and for the local family court.

Gerard Costa, PhD, is a licensed developmental psychologist and founding director of the YCS Institute for Infant and Preschool Mental Health, a training/consultation, clinical service and research institute concerned with the optimal development of infants and children from birth to 6 years old and their families, located in East Orange, New Jersey. He is also a former Head Start director. He is a member of the Advisory Board of the Interdisciplinary Council on Developmental and Learning Disorders (ICDL) and serves as a consultant and trainer with ZERO TO THREE.

Linda Gilkerson, PhD, professor, Erikson Institute and director, Irving B. Harris Infant Studies Program, has developed and directed infant/family service programs and infant specialist training programs for over 30 years. A Board Member of ZERO TO THREE, Linda has provided leadership to bring reflective supervision to the early intervention and health care systems.

John C. Grabert, PhD, is a civilian clinical psychologist in Stuttgart, Germany, with the U.S. Army Educational and Developmental Intervention Services (EDIS), Early Intervention Services (EIS), the U.S. Army implementation of IDEA Part C. His work in the last 5 years has focused on training non-mental health early interventionists in early childhood mental health practices.

Sonja Hall, MEd, LCPC, infant mental health consultant, has worked to promote infant mental health programs for 25 years. She has helped design and develop a local infant–family resource program as well as an infant mental health department in a community mental health agency. More recently Sonja has helped start up infant mental health reflective consultation projects for early intervention and schools-based prevention programs in Illinois.

Brenda Jones Harden, PhD, is an associate professor in the Department of Human Development, University of Maryland College Park. For over 30 years, her research, writing, and program development have focused on the developmental and mental health needs of young children at environmental risk, specifically children who have been maltreated, are in the foster care system, or are exposed to multiple family risks.

Angela W. Keyes, PhD, assistant professor of psychiatry at the Tulane University School of Medicine, has assisted in developing a model for mental health consultation to support child care centers in fostering children's social–emotional development as well as teaching techniques to modify children's challenging behaviors in a positive way. Angela provides reflective supervision to the mental health consultants who serve centers working toward improving the quality of care they provide to children from birth to 5 years old.

Sarah Martinez, MA, MEd, LCPC, is a social emotional consultant in early intervention in Illinois where she regularly provides reflective supervision. Sarah has worked in the field of infant mental health for 20 years and is an executive board member of the Illinois Association for Infant Mental Health.

Sherryl Scott Heller, PhD, associate professor of psychiatry at Tulane University Medical Center and Tulane's Institute of Early Childhood and Infant Mental Health, has worked in the field of infant mental health for more than 15 years. For the past 7 years she has developed and led programs that provide reflective supervision to child care providers, child care administrators, and mental health professionals.

Rebecca Shahmoon-Shanok, LCSW, PhD, is founding director, Institute for Infants, Children & Families, Jewish Board of Family and Children's Services, New York City, which reaches underserved children and their families with model services; transdisciplinary post-degree training for leaders and providers of all disciplines; and consultation-training for agencies, systems, and government. A Board Member of ZERO TO THREE for 3 decades, she helped define reflective supervision, teaching and writing about it since its beginnings.

Lorri Sullivan, MEd, is an early childhood educator, teacher of children with disabilities, and serves as the associate director for training and consultation of the YCS Institute for Infant and Preschool Mental Health. She is a member and served on the Board of Directors of the New Jersey Association for Infant Mental Health (NJAIMH). She has developed a model Infant Mental Health Training and Consultation program for child care programs in New Jersey, emphasizing relationship-based intervention and reflective practices.

Deborah J. Weatherston, PhD, executive director, Michigan Association for Infant Mental Health, developed and directed the Graduate Certificate Program in Infant Mental Health at the Merrill-Palmer Institute/Wayne State University from 1988–2004. She is a ZERO TO THREE graduate fellow and a Board Member of the World Association for Infant Mental Health.